Rediscovering the Buddha

Rediscovering the Buddha

Legends of the Buddha and Their Interpretation

HANS H. PENNER

OXFORD
UNIVERSITY PRESS

2009

OXFORD
UNIVERSITY PRESS

Oxford University Press, Inc., publishes works that further
Oxford University's objective of excellence
in research, scholarship, and education.

Oxford   New York
Auckland   Cape Town   Dar es Salaam   Hong Kong   Karachi
Kuala Lumpur   Madrid   Melbourne   Mexico City   Nairobi
New Delhi   Shanghai   Taipei   Toronto

With offices in
Argentina   Austria   Brazil   Chile   Czech Republic   France   Greece
Guatemala   Hungary   Italy   Japan   Poland   Portugal   Singapore
South Korea   Switzerland   Thailand   Turkey   Ukraine   Vietnam

Copyright © 2009 by Oxford University Press

Published by Oxford University Press, Inc.
198 Madison Avenue, New York, New York 10016
www.oup.com

Oxford is a registered trademark of Oxford University Press

Library of Congress Cataloging-in-Publication Data

Penner, Hans H., 1934–
   Rediscovering the Buddha : legends of the Buddha and
   their interpretation / Hans H. Penner.
      p. cm.
   Includes bibliographical references and index.
   ISBN 978-0-19-538582-3
   1. Gotama Buddha. 2.   Religious biography—India. I. Title.
   BQ882.P46 2009
   294.3'63—dc22   [B]2008050913

9 8 7 6 5 4 3 2 1
Printed in the United States of America
on acid-free paper

Acknowledgments

The Mellon Foundation deserves first place on my list of expressions of gratitude for the Emeritus Fellowship that helped ease many of the details and problems that arise in the writing of a book. This is especially the case for someone who has just retired from a long and successful career in teaching and research.

I am also grateful to Cheryl Singleton, who with persistent good cheer and talent became my first editor, transforming several formats and drafts into what eventually became a manuscript. Marianne Alverson, Elizabeth Lawrence, and Ellen Mittleman were especially helpful in their comments on an early version of part I. Last but not least, Anna's enduring patience, loyalty, and solid support throughout the work of this project richly deserve praise and thanks.

Preface

Books on the Buddha are becoming shorter. As a result, we do not read about his previous lives hundreds of millions of years ago. We remain ignorant of the conditions of his birth, his boyhood, or his contest with Mara at the time of his awakening. We remain uninformed about his former lives, his travels to the abode of the gods, and his conferences with them. His trials and tribulations during his life as a teacher, his dinner with a courtesan, the miracles he performs, and the grand episode of his birth and funeral also remain unknown to us. What we find is a short "outline" of the life of the Buddha. Such abridgments are often presented as if his story is fully preserved without sacrifice of sense, and in some cases we are led to believe that a shortened version, an outline, shorn of myth, is a more genuine representation, a more rational picture, of the actual historical facts; after all, the Buddha was "just a man." I believe it is time to correct this situation.

The history of Buddhist scholarship teaches us that the legends of the Buddha are the result of a slow degeneration from an authentic, elitist, rational, otherworldly ascetic movement into a nonrational, popular religion, an evolution from history into myth. The stress in scholarship on Buddhism, therefore, is on discovering what might be the oldest, "authentic," and thus the "original" material in the stories that reflect actual episodes in the life of a historical person and a doctrine that is rational as well as ethical. An example of the influence of this prevailing approach to understanding Buddhism can be found on the first page of a popular book on Buddhism written by a Buddhist monk:

> Among the founders of religions the Buddha (if we are permitted to call him the founder of a religion in the popular sense of the term) was the only teacher who did not claim to be other than a human being, pure and simple.... We can call the Buddha a man *par excellence*. He was so perfect in his 'human-ness' that he came to be regarded later in popular religion almost as "super-human."

I believe it is time to correct this well-crafted introductory paragraph on Buddhism and to make an attempt at rediscovering just what the legends say. We should resist accepting outlines of the Buddha's life as a substitute for the legends, and reintroduce ourselves to the language of myth once again without assuming that myths are nonrational or that they represent historical events or contain hidden messages, codes, and symbols that require years of philological, psychological, anthropological, sociological, or theological training that will allow one to decipher the proper "authentic" or "original" meaning of the legends. The basic theoretical assumptions regarding language, history, religion, and myth that remain fundamental to the history and authority of Buddhist studies in the Western world will not make this rediscovery an easy task.

This book consists of two parts. Part I is a construction of the "life" of the Buddha. It is the construction of a "biography" just as any biography is a construction or interpretation. My construction of the Buddha's life in part I follows a specific framework that is not found in other books on this subject. It begins with a cosmology and ends with the Buddha's royal funeral and the forecast of Metteyya, the Buddha to come. My basic thesis in composing part I is that if we want to understand Buddhism and the "life of the Buddha," we must place them back into the complex mythical/cosmological structure in which we find all of the legends. As you read the story you will discover what scholars have always known, that the fundamental framework of the legends is mythological, not historical. The mythological framework in turn is embedded in a cosmology that not only is made explicit in the legends but is also well known in South and Southeast Asia. The mythical/cosmological framework is the basic "grammar" or "syntax" of the legends. It is important to remember that I did not say that this structure is the basic "semantics" or meaning of the myths. Nevertheless, the "semantics" (meaning) of the myths of the Buddha presuppose the specific cosmological grammar that can be found throughout the legends. To put this another way, the grammar of the myths is a necessary condition for understanding the semantics, the meaning of the myth; it is one of the constraints from within which the episodes and discourse of the

Buddha's life are told. This is the primary reason for the format of part I. The more we know about the story, the better off we will be in our interpretation of this most remarkable, if not incredible, religion that appeared in India, swept an emperor, named Ashoka, off his feet, and then spread across both North and Southeast Asia only to disappear, for all practical purposes, in the land of its birth.

Part II is an analysis and an interpretation of the legends in the context of modern scholarship on the subject. Part II includes a critique of three major areas in the study of Buddhism. The first involves the long Western quest for the historical Buddha, a quest that is intricately connected to the question, what do superhuman agents mean? or what is myth? The second is a focus on the mistaken and now popular notion, made famous by the great German sociologist Max Weber, that Buddhism is "otherworldly asceticism," that Buddhism is a religion for monks, for ascetics. We can correct this mistake by a rediscovery of the householder as fundamental to an adequate understanding of Buddhism. We will take a careful look at the Buddhist notions of giving, the gift, and merit not only as conceptual explanations of action (karma) but also as the mediation of the oppositional relations between the renouncer and the householder. The analysis will show that it is this basic opposition (renouncer/householder) mediated by the gift that is a defining characteristic of Buddhism.

The third area involves an analysis of the Buddhist notion of "the Great Being," or "the superhuman agent," who becomes either a Buddha or a Universal Monarch of the four cardinal quarters of the cosmos. Part II will demonstrate that the legends have a coherent structure, a logic that is a necessary part of their signification, and that the meaning of the myths depends upon a framework consisting of three necessary elements: the cosmology, the existence of superhuman agents (of which the Buddha is one among many), and the Buddhist doctrine of karma.

My hope is that part I will surprise and delight you, and that its content may tempt you to go to the Buddhist sources for more. You may not agree with some or all of my explanations in part II. That is as it should be. Critical analysis and argument lead to disagreement; they are what often provide the stimulus for further progress in our knowledge of the world we live in, including Buddhism, religion, and myth.

Finally, you will notice that I have not included footnote markers where you usually expect them at the end of sentences and quotation. Notes are very important, but they often interrupt the tempo and continuity of reading, which is especially important for part I. I have also translated all words of Buddhist texts into English. I have done this because I firmly believe that the appearance of Pali and Sanskrit words, including diacritical markings, in the text does not add anything of linguistic or semantic significance for those who do not know the language and are not specialists in the study of South Asian Buddhism. I also find it false to think that certain words cannot be translated. Language, by definition, is effable, not ineffable. Certain words may be technical, very complex, or used in a variety of ways, but this can be made known to the reader. I have done that throughout the book by using endnotes easily located by the page number in the left margin of the notes section at the end of the book.

Contents

Part I

1. Cosmology and the Great Declaration, 5

2. The Perfection of Giving, 11

3. The Birth and Early Life of Gotama, 21

4. Flight from the Palace, 27

5. Enlightenment and Liberation, 33

6. The Buddha Begins to Teach, 39

7. The Buddha Becomes a Wonder-Worker, 49

8. The Buddha Meets a King and Two Brilliant Ascetics, 55

9. Rules, Rules, and More Rules, 59

10. The Buddha Goes Home, 65

11. The Buddha Receives a Gift and Befriends a King, 69

12. Meeting a Murderer, a Visit Home, and a Quick Trip to Heaven, 77

13. Devadatta Attempts to Kill the Buddha, 85

14. The Buddha's Last Days, 91

15. Once the Buddha Was a Universal Monarch, 101

16. The Last Watch and the Funeral, 107

Part II

17. The Quest for the Historical Buddha, 123

18. The Cosmological Structure, 143

19. The Legends as Rites of Passage, 161

20. The Great Agent: Universal Monarchs and Buddhas, 177

21. The Gift, the Renouncer, and the Householder, 201

Notes, 221

Bibliography, 235

Index, 239

PART I

According to the Buddhist scriptures, after the Buddha's funeral the
monks gathered together and selected a few of the very best experts
among them to repeat what the Buddha had said during their lifetime together. Each of the chosen monks began by stating where
the discourse had occurred. When you open one of the volumes
of the English translation of the canonical scripture of Theravada
Buddhism, you find something like the following introduction to
each section or chapter: "Thus I have heard. Once the Buddha was
staying at Savatthi, in Anathapindika's park at the Jeta Grove. The
monks had gathered together after their alms-round and a serious
discussion arose about former lives. The Buddha, having powers
surpassing those of human beings, heard what they were saying.
Getting up from his seat, he went to them, sat down on the prepared
seat, and said, 'Monks, what conversation did I interrupt?'" The
monks then repeat what they had been discussing, and the remainder of the chapter is the Buddha's response.

The main source for these dialogues and part I of this book
is the canon of Theravada Buddhism, the Buddhism of South and
Southeast Asia. Called the *Tipitaka* (*The Three Baskets*), it is written
in Pali, a language related to Sanskrit, and is divided into three large
sections. It does not contain a complete biography of the Buddha.
This omission is not due to the fact that the monks were not interested in his life. On the contrary, the *Three Baskets* contains vivid
descriptions of his many lives in past aeons and also his life in the

present aeon and the people he met. We are informed, for example, that he had backaches, ate gourmet meals, and did not suffer fools. A "biography" of the Buddha of our era did appear in the second century A.D. Written by Ashvaghosha and entitled *Buddhacarita* (*Acts of the Buddha*), it became and remains one of the most popular among the known biographies of the Buddha. It seems obvious that Ashvaghosha, as well as other later biographers, did not make up the story but relied on important oral traditions.

These oral traditions about the Buddha are confirmed for us at Sanci, the site of a great memorial mound now dated no later than second century B.C. The architraves of the four gates portray many of the important events in the Buddha's life. We may thus safely conjecture that these legendary episodes in stone were the product of a communal system of narratives that must have been known to Buddhists for quite some time before they were carved into those beautiful gateways at this famous memorial shrine in North India.

The reason we do not have a canonical biography of the Buddha seems to remain a problem for many scholars. It remains a problem because most scholars think of the story as anchored in history, so that "biography" is obviously defined by a person's birth and death. The problem is solved when we realize that it is impossible to write a complete biography of the Buddha simply because it cannot be done. Why? Because his life spans aeons and aeons of time. The *Three Baskets* does its best to cover these chapters in his life by including the *Jataka*, legends of his former births, 547 of them! The memorial at Sanci portrays many of them, as does Borobudur at Java, another great memorial and one of the wonders of the world. In many of the episodes that the monks recount, the Buddha identifies himself as being a particular person or agent in a former life. These episodes presuppose a very important doctrine in Buddhism, the doctrine of life as an indefinite series of births, deaths, and rebirths, the doctrine of karma. It is a doctrine that Buddhism has in common with Hinduism, with a radical twist: the Buddhist doctrine of karma rejects transmigration, since it rejects the notion that there is such a thing as a self or immortal soul. We will probe the subject of "biography" in Buddhism a little more deeply in part II.

Many scholars point out that in Southeast Asian countries Vessantara is as popular as the Buddha himself, as if this should come as a surprise. If you already know the story of Vessantara, you also know that the Buddha ended his narrative with "The followers of the Buddha were Vessantara's attendants, and I myself was King Vessantara." Vessantara simply disappears from most books that include his name in a chapter on "the life of the Buddha." But, then, most chapters on "the life of the Buddha" also omit many of his miracles, his birth, his funeral, his conversations with Sakka, the chief of the thirty-three gods, or the problem he had allowing his stepmother to join his community as a renouncer. These episodes and many more are all included in part I of this work.

Because the Buddha remains the central figure in Western scholarship about this religious tradition, it seems odd that many of the key events in his life are simply omitted in introductions to Buddhism. Why is this so? One of the truly outstanding scholars of Indian Buddhism, Étienne Lamotte, has answered this question as follows: "The above historical sketch is not exactly identical with the mythical life of the Buddha as it is conceived by Buddhists . . . . The wonders and prodigies which, according to tradition, marked the events of his life from conception to cremation have been passed over in silence in order to present the biography in a more rational light." This assertion tells us more about Lamotte than it does about the life of the Buddha. Moreover, it does not seem to concern him that his "historical sketch" may be more fiction than fact. We shall take a hard look at all of this in part II.

Part I is a compilation. Its main source is the Pali Text Society's English translation of the *Tipitaka*, an immense piece of translation work that you should be able to find in most academic libraries. At times I have used other authoritative sources that I believe fill out an event or episode that is reflected in the canonical texts. I have abridged many of the repetitions and given my own translations where I believe the Pali Text Society's translation needs clarification, revision, or correction. You will find complete references to translations and other primary sources used in parts I and II in the notes and the bibliography. I have also used the endnotes of the book to indicate my translation of complex or troublesome Pali terms, as well as words that seem to have a technical definition or sense in Buddhism.

Before his great awakening, the Buddha is known by several names in the various legends. He is known, for example, as Gotama, Sakyamuni, and also Sidhattha. I have used Gotama throughout part I as the name of the Buddha before his awakening. I use the word "renouncer" throughout the book; this may strike some as strange. It is my translation of *pabbajja*, the Pali word for "renunciation." More specifically, it is the technical term for someone ordained into the Buddhist monastic order. The renouncer rejects the life of the householder and *all* its modes of life. The renouncer owns nothing, produces nothing, values nothing; the renouncer is alone. Nevertheless, he is always related to the householder. It is important to remember that Buddhist ascetics, whether they are Buddhas or "sons of the Buddha," are always defined by their relation to the householder. The relation "householder <———> renouncer" is the basic definition of Buddhism; although they are in opposition to each other, they are also bound to each other, and it is their relation to each other that defines them. Although this relation of opposition will be discussed in the last chapter of the book, it is important that you keep it in mind throughout your reading of part I.

Finally, a bit of advice as you turn to chapter 1 and begin the adventure of reading this "biography." First, resist the temptation to look for hidden or symbolic meanings; take the myths just as they are, that is, take them literally. The monks did, and so do most Buddhists. If you do so, assuming the translations are reasonably accurate, you will know precisely what the myths mean, for they mean exactly what they say. Furthermore, by the end of part I you will discover that there is no end to further interpretation. It is this process that has produced Buddhist history and is also the reason this book has a part II.

Second, do no forget what the Buddha told the monk in the Jeta Grove about the length of an "aeon" on the next page of this book. It provides the framework for all of part I and will provide you with an important guideline and perspective for understanding the meaning of time, history, and biography in Buddhism. It may even help provide the framework or context for what the Buddha discovered during the night and called "perfect happiness."

I

Cosmology and the Great Declaration

Why is there something rather than nothing? Because nothing at all is impossible. There is no beginning. There is no end. The universe is a pulsating evolution and devolution, an everlasting expansion and contraction in which countless galactic systems are created and destroyed throughout vast cosmic aeons in which countless Buddhas have appeared and will appear in the future. Some say that an aeons is 10,000,000,000,000,000,000,000,000,000 years long; others say that although it is not infinite, it is not calculable.

Once at Savatthi in the Jeta Grove a monk asked the Buddha, "How long, lord, is an aeon?" The Buddha told him, "It is not possible to count how long using years, centuries, or even many thousands of centuries." The monk then asked whether a parable could be used to illustrate, and the Buddha said: "Suppose there was a great rock mountain about five miles wide, five miles long, and five miles high without any cracks but one solid mass. Suppose also at the end of every one hundred years a man were to stroke it just once with an expensive piece of cloth from Kashi (Varanasi). Well, that mountain in this way would sooner be done away with and ended than would an aeons. So long, monk, is an aeon, it is incalculable."

The architecture of cosmic space in this pulsating universe consists of three spheres. The highest sphere is without form or sensation. The middle sphere is form only, without sensation. The lowest sphere consists of both form and sensation; it includes our world, with Mount Meru as its axis and many hells below and six heavens above, with Tushita as the fourth.

Our world is ruled by Sakka (Indra), the king of all deities, who rules from his abode in the second heaven, Tavatimsha, at the summit of Mount Meru. Sakka presides over the first heaven just below the summit that contains the palaces of the four guardians of the four classes of beings in the world. In the North is the palace of Kuvera, who rules over human beings. Viruha rules the South, the domain of the ancestors. In the East, Dhataratha rules the gods, and Virupaka rules the antigods from his palace in the West.

After many aeon this world contracts, and most of the various beings are reborn in the middle sphere of form only. Mind-born they dwell there, feeding on delight; they are self-luminous, traversing the air, dwelling there for many aeons. But the world begins to evolve once again. At that time there was only water, all was darkness. No sun or moon nor stars appear, there is neither day nor night, no months, fortnights, years, or seasons. And at that time there is neither male nor female; beings are simply identified as beings.

After a long period, savory earth began to spread over the waters; it looked just like the skin that forms on hot milk as it cools. It was the color of fine clarified butter, very sweet, like wild honey. Conditioned by previous births, some greedy being said, "What is this?" and tasted some of the savory earth. It desired more, and craving arose in it. Other beings also tasted the savory stuff, and as a result their self-luminance faded away. As this happened the moon, sun, and stars appeared together with the year and its seasons. The world began to evolve and expand once again.

The beings continued to feast and be nourished on the savory earth for a very long time. In the course of time their bodies became more solid, and differences in their appearance became apparent; some became good-looking, others became ugly. The good-looking ones began to despise the others, saying, "We are better looking and better off than they are." Because of their arrogance and conceit the savory earth disappeared. When the savory earth disappeared, something like mushrooms appeared, which also had the color of clarified butter and was as sweet as wild honey. The beings feasted on these outgrowths for a very long time, finding them to be good food and nourishment. As they continued to feast, their bodies became even more solid and coarse. The difference in their looks increased, as did arrogance and conceit. As a result, the sweet outgrowths disappeared.

Then creepers appeared, growing like bamboo with a savory flavor, and the beings feasted and were nourished by the creepers for a very long time. As they feasted their bodies became even more solid and the differences in their appearance increased, as did conceit and arrogance. As a result, the creepers also disappeared.

When the creepers vanished, rice appeared in open spaces outside the jungle; it was free from mildew, had no husk, and was pure, fragrant, and clean-grained. What rice the beings took in the evening for supper stood ripe the next morning for breakfast, and what they had taken for breakfast was again ripe and ready, without reaping, for eating at dinner. They did so for a long time and as a result grew more solid still, the differences in their looks even more pronounced. Females and males developed sexual organs and became preoccupied with each other. Passions were aroused, and lust entered their bodies, resulting in sexual activity.

One day the following thought occurred to a being with a lazy disposition: "Well now, why should I be bothered to get rice in the evening for dinner and in the morning for breakfast? Why don't I just gather it all at once for both meals?" And he did so.

Another being came to him and said, "Let's go get some rice."

"Never mind," said the lazy one, "I've gathered enough for both meals."

Following his example, the other fellow gathered rice for two days at a time, saying, "That should be enough." It did not take long before others gathered rice for four days, and then eight days. These beings then began feasting and living on hoarded rice. The rice mildewed and husks began to envelop the grain, it had to be reaped, and where it was reaped it did not grow again, only clumps of stubble remained.

This degeneration from the mind-made, self-luminous life of delight led those beings to come together and lament the increasingly wicked ways that had become rife among them. Some of them said, "Let us divide up the rice into fields with boundaries." And so they did. But then one day a greedy-natured being, while guarding his own plot, took another plot that was not his and feasted on its produce. The others seized him and rebuked him for stealing, telling him never to do such an evil thing again. "I won't," he replied. But he did it again a second and third time. Again he was seized, admonished, and punished by being hit with the fist, stones, and sticks. This was the origin of theft, censure, lying, and punishment.

Then those beings came together and lamented the arising of these evil things. They thought: "Suppose we appointed a certain being who would show anger when anger was due, censure those who deserved it, and banish those who required banishment. In return we would grant him a share of our rice." They agreed and went out looking for one among them who was the best looking, most pleasant, and capable, to ask him to do this for them in return for a share of their rice. They found such a person, and he agreed. Then all the beings elected him and gave him a share of their rice.

He was given three titles. The first, Mahasammata, means "People's Choice." (King Mahasammata, the first king, is the ancestor of the Sakyan kings and thus of Gotama himself.) "Lord of the Land" was the second title to be introduced, and king was the third title because he "delighted others in his use of the law." This, then, is the origin of the caste of nobles, often called the "warrior caste." Their origin was from those very same beings, just like us, and not others, taking their place according to their fitness for the duties of the universal Norm.

At that time other beings agreed that they should put an end to stealing, lying, and punishment, and did so. They became known as Brahmins. Some of them made leaf huts in the forest and meditated, gathering alms for their evening and morning meals, then returning to their huts to meditate. Others, however, could not meditate, so they settled in towns and villages compiling books and teaching. This is the origin of the caste of ritual specialists and teachers known as Brahmins.

Other beings adopted various trades, which became the origin of the caste known as merchants or Vaishyas. Those that remained were hunters and became the caste known as Shudra, that is, polluter or servant. (Note that in this account the nobles are first, then the ritual specialists, followed by merchants and servants. In Hinduism the hierarchy of the caste system places the Brahmin first, then the noble or warrior, followed by merchants and polluter/servants.) At a later time a nobleman became dissatisfied with his own caste rules and left the life of the householder to become an ascetic. A Brahmin, merchant, and servant did likewise, and from these four castes the class of ascetics came into existence.

Those among all four castes who have led a bad life in body, speech, and thought, and who have held wrong views will, as a consequence of such wrong views and deeds, be reborn in a state of loss, an ill fate, a life in hell. Likewise, those who have led a good life in body, speech, and thought, who have the right view, in consequence of such a view and deeds will at death be reborn in a good destiny, a life in heaven. Those who performed both good and bad in body, speech, and thought will, as a consequence, experience both pleasure and pain at death.

Whoever of these four castes becomes a monk and destroys the corruptions, has done what had to be done, laid down the burden, attained the highest goal, destroyed the chain of becoming, and became liberated by the highest insight—he is declared to be chief among all in accordance with the universal Doctrine.

Over a hundred thousand aeons ago there was a city in the sphere of the gods called Amara. It was beautiful, resounding with the sounds of elephants, horses, drums, and chariots. Amara was a prosperous city, a dwelling place for doers of merit. In that city of the gods dwelled a very rich Brahmin named Sumedha. He knew the Sacred Words (the Vedas) and rituals and served as a model for all in the performance of his duties as a Brahmin.

One day while sitting in seclusion, he began to think about life as a process of becoming, subject to birth, aging, sickness, death, and rebirth. "There must be a way," he thought, "a complete release from this continual round of existence that leads to anguish. After all, as heat exists so does coolness, where there is evil there is loveliness too." And, moreover, he thought, "When a man who is sick does not go to a physician, who can cure him? The defect is not in the physician. So, when someone is not satisfied with life but does not seek the teacher, that is not a defect in the teacher or the way."

After all this, Sumedha gave away his immense wealth to rich and poor and went up to Mount Dhammaka, near Mount Himavant, where Vissakamma, the master architect, built him a hermitage after receiving an order from Sakka. Sumedha soon gave up the hermitage, chose a tree for his dwelling place, and clothed himself in a bark garment. He also gave up his regular diet of grains and ate wild fruits. Within a week he had attained the highest knowledge. While he was meditating, becoming a master in the teaching of ascetics, the Conqueror named Dipankara arose in the world.

Hearing the multitude of people, Sumedha went through the air. Upon seeing the delighted populace, he descended from the heavens and asked them, "Why are you so elated, so joyous? For whom are you preparing this road?" They told him that an incomparable Buddha had arisen in the world, the Conqueror named Dipankara, and it was for him that they were preparing the way. When Sumedha heard this he asked them to give him a section so that he could clear the road himself.

Both deities and people from all directions followed the Buddha Dipankara, and flowers from heaven and earth rained down upon him. As Dipankara approached, Sumedha laid down on the muddy road, thinking, "While lying on this earth I could realize perfect happiness here and now, I could become an Enlightened One. But what would be the use of crossing over alone? I will cause the world together with all the gods to cross over, and by my act of merit I will cut through the stream of endless rebirths, shatter the three spheres, embark on the Eightfold Path, and cause the world with the gods to cross over."

Dipankara, who knew the arising and cessation of the three spheres, then spoke the following declaration: "Do you see this ascetic lying on the path?

Innumerable aeons from now he will be a Buddha in the world. His mother will be named Maya, his father Suddhodana, and he will be called Gotama."

Upon hearing this declaration, all the deities and the people rejoiced, fear vanished, people felt content, and flowers on land and in the water blossomed and rained down from the heavens. All the gods and people proclaimed, "Great is your aspiration, may you obtain your wish, may you, great hero, fulfill the ten perfections and flower with a Buddha's knowledge." Praised and lauded, Sumedha entered the forest.

Dipankara, who lived a hundred thousand years teaching the Way, caused many people to cross over before he himself attained final happiness, and a Conqueror's memorial was built for him in Nanda.

2

The Perfection of Giving

After several world evolutions, a king named Sivi lived in a city called Jetuttara. He had a son named Sanjaya. When Sanjaya came of age the king introduced him to a princess named Phusati, the daughter of King Madda, and handed the kingdom over to him, thereby making Phusati his consort queen.

Now Phusati, after many aeons of rebirths, would become the mother of Gotama. Before that time, however, and after passing to and fro between the worlds of the gods and humans, she became the chief queen of Sakka, king of the gods. One day, Sakka realized that her time was exhausted and took her to one of the glorious pleasure gardens called Nandana. There, sitting together on a fabulous couch, he told her to choose whatever on earth she wanted. Not knowing the circumstances of her rebirth, Phusati felt slightly faint and asked Sakka what she had done to be sent to the world of humans from such a lovely place? Sakka replied that she remained dear to him and that she had done nothing wrong, but that all of her merit had been used up, was gone, and her departure was near. She should make ten wishes before she died. Phusati agreed. When she made her wishes she left that sphere and was conceived in the womb of King Madda's queen. She grew up in royal splendor, surpassing all in beauty. When she became sixteen she married Prince Sanjaya.

Sakka remembered that only nine of the ten wishes had been fulfilled, and he resolved that her tenth wish, "a goodly son," would now be brought to pass. Now at that time the Buddha-to-be was in

Sakka's heavenly sphere, called the heaven of the thirty-three gods, and the merit for his life there had come to an end. Knowing this, Sakka approached the Buddha-to-be and said, "Venerable sir, you must enter the world of human beings; without delay you must be conceived in the womb of Phusati, queen consort of the king of Sivi."

Phusati, finding herself pregnant, desired to build six houses of charity, one at each of the cardinal gates of the city, one in the middle of the city, and one at her own door; each day she distributed six hundred thousand pieces of money.

The queen lived with a large retinue of attendants until the ten months were fulfilled—this is the term of birth for all Buddhas. One day she told the king that she wished to visit the city. When they reached the section of the city for merchants, she began to have labor pains and gave birth to Vessantara.

By the time Vessantara was sixteen, he attained mastery of all the sciences, and his father decided that it would soon be time to make him king. Sanjaya and his wife agreed that Vessantara should marry Maddi, his first cousin from the family of King Madda. Princess Maddi soon gave birth to a son who they named Prince Jali, and by the time he began to walk the princess gave birth to another child, a daughter, who they named Kanhajina.

At about this same time there occurred a severe drought in the neighboring kingdom of Kalinga. The king tried everything in his power, including a seven-day fast, to bring rain to the parched kingdom. Nothing worked. The people then suggested that the king send Brahmins to Vessantara and ask him to give them his glorious rain-making white elephant. The king agreed and chose eight Brahmins for the mission, giving them provisions for the trip to Jetuttara.

When they arrived they went early in the morning to the charity hall at the eastern gate on the day of the full moon to await Prince Vessantara's monthly visit. Because of the vast crowds, they had no opportunity to catch his attention and decided to head for the charity hall at the southern gate as a better place to meet him. They headed for a mound of earth and shouted, "Hail, victory to the noble Vessantara" as he arrived from the eastern gate. They caught his eye, and he drove his great elephant over to the hill on which they stood. "What is it you want?" he said. And the Brahmins replied, "We desire a very precious thing, your noble rain-making elephant." King Vessantara immediately fulfilled their wish, dismounted from its back, and gave the Brahmins what they desired, along with all of the priceless ornaments on its feet and back, nets of jewels on its belly and ears, the jewels on its head and trunk and the priceless rug and blankets together with the canopy. All this he gave to the Brahmins besides five hundred grooms and stablemen. And when he did this the earth began to quake.

As the Brahmins rode the great elephant out of the city the people shouted, "Who are you? What are you doing? Where are you taking our noble elephant?" Looking down at them, the Brahmins said, "And who do you think you are?" giving them rude gestures as they rode through the city and out of the northern gate.

The people were outraged and began to shout, saying, "This country is ruined!" A representation of all the people was sent to King Sanjaya, telling him what had just happened and about the anger of the people. They admitted that it was quite right to give Brahmins food, drink, and clothes, but what possessed Vessantara, his son, to give them the people's precious and saving elephant? They told the king that if something were not done the people might well act against both king and prince.

Hearing all this, King Sanjaya suspected that they wanted to kill Vessantara. He told them very clearly that he would dissolve the kingdom before obeying the people's will. Vessantara was without fault, noble in what he had done, and thus it would be out of the question that he should kill him. The representatives of the people quickly replied that they agreed, Vessantara did not deserve to be killed, imprisoned, or physically punished. He should be banished, sent into exile. The king agreed but requested that Vessantara be allowed to spend one happy night at home before his banishment. This was agreed upon, and King Sanjaya sent this sad verdict to his son Vessantara.

Vessantara was dumbfounded when he heard the news. He could not see any offense in what he had done and simply could not understand why the people were so upset with him. "Why," he asked, "do they want to banish me? Is giving gifts a crime?"

The agent simply replied, "Because it is the will of the Sivi people; they told me to tell you so."

Vessantara agreed, making it clear that it was not because of an offense but because of a gift of an elephant that he was banished. This being so, he asked that he be given one day's delay to give the gift of seven hundred (that is, seven hundred elephants, horses, chariots, cows, slaves, food, drink, seven hundred of everything that can be given). The agent agreed and returned to report it to the people.

Vessantara then went alone to Maddi's living quarters, where he sat on the royal bed and told her everything that had happened. He also said that once he had gone she should choose a husband herself if a man would not choose her. Maddi at first did not understand what he was saying. "Why," she asked, "do you say such things to me?" The Buddha-to-be replied, "The people are angry with me for the gift of the elephant; tomorrow I make the gift of seven hundred and depart the next day from the city for the wilderness. The forest is beset with wild animals. Who knows whether I can survive it."

Midi would have none of this, telling Vessantara that it was not right for him to go alone, and that wherever he went she would be with him. She told him that she would rather die, choose death, unless she could live with him wherever he went. "So with the children too, we will follow you wherever you lead us, you will not find us a burden," she said, and then praised and described the wilderness as a paradise of beauty and peace.

All through the night the royal family talked about life in the wilderness. And as they conversed the dawn came, and after dawn up rose the sun. Vessantara, Maddi, and the two children bid their parents farewell and took their places in a carriage with a team of four Sindh horses. Vessantara wanted to look at the city just one more time. The earth quaked, splitting the earth around the carriage, and it turned so he could view the city. "Oh, look!" he exclaimed to Maddi. "See the lovely place from where we have come, our house and our ancestral home!" He then turned the carriage and headed for the wilderness.

Four Brahmins had missed the event of the seven hundred gifts and had followed the carriage out of the city. Vessantara asked them what they wanted, and they begged him to give them the four mighty horses. He agreed, and the family dismounted from the carriage. But then another Brahmin appeared and asked for the carriage. The Buddha-to-be gave it to him. Vessantara told Maddi, "You take Kanhajina, she is light, and I'll take Jali for he is a heavy boy." They swung them up on their hips, and the family began the long journey to the wilderness on foot.

Having left the city of Jetuttara after breakfast, they reached the kingdom of Ceta by evening. The trip was about one hundred miles, but the gods shortened it to a day's journey. They refused to enter their uncle's city and the kingship that was proffered to the Buddha-to-be. Staying overnight in a quickly made but richly adorned and secure bedroom, they were given a fine breakfast early the following morning.

They left Ceta accompanied by sixty thousand warriors who traveled with them for about forty-five miles to reach the edge of the wilderness. They were told that about forty-five more miles remained in their journey, and that they should travel in a straight northward direction to reach their hermitage.

After traveling northward through the forest for two days, they reached the hermitage that Vissakamma under orders from Sakka had built for them. They settled into their cells, putting on the dress of ascetics. With staff in hand, Vessantara walked up and down the covered walk and then went to his wife and children as one who by himself had found enlightenment. He then asked Maddi a favor, "From now on we are ascetics and contact with a woman is a spreading sore for a renouncer. Therefore, please do not approach me at improper times." Maddi consented, and they lived on the wild fruits that Maddi gathered for them. They did so for seven months. By the power of the Great Agent's compassion, even the wild animals of the wilderness within twenty miles of their hermitage lived in harmony with one another.

At that time an old Brahmin named Jujaka lived in the kingdom of Kalinga. Jujaka had deposited all his money with a local Brahmin family, who in the course of time had spent it all and ended up bankrupt. Since they could not return his funds to him, they offered their young daughter to him as repayment. He accepted the offer and took the young woman with him. The young daughter served him well, and many a husband pointed her out as a model for their own wives, telling them, "Look how she carefully tends to that old man, while you ignore the needs of your younger husband!" She soon became the object of jokes and mockery at places where the women would meet during their daily trips to the riverside or local shops. She would often come home in tears, describing the day's events to her old husband. One day she told him that she would leave if he did not find someone to do this work for her. The old Brahmin told her that this was simply out of the question, since they did not have the money to hire such a person. His wife then told him that she had often heard the women talk about a person named Vessantara, who lived in the Vamka hills and gave anyone whatever they desired. She was sure that if he found Vessantara he would give him a servant. Fearing that she would leave, he agreed to look for Vessantara.

After a difficult journey he seemed to enter a paradise, and found Vessantara alone at the hermitage. He told Vessantara that he had come to beg from him. He wanted his two children for servants, and he wanted them immediately before Maddi returned from the forest.

When he heard why the Brahmin had come, Vessantara was filled with happiness and invited Jujaka to meet his wife when she returned and then stay overnight. Jujaka refused, stating, "Women are not very generous, always causing trouble and blocking plans. Do it now and the merit you gain by giving a gift with resolve will be increased."

Vessantara agreed and then told the Brahmin that if he took the children to their grandfather he would without doubt give Jujaka a great deal of money. Jujaka also refused this idea and told Vessantara that he would take them to his wife as her servants. Vessantara then went looking for the children. He called for them, "Come, Kanhajina, come here my dear girl, fulfill my perfection and consecrate my heart. Do what I say and become the boat for my crossing the sea of becoming to the further shore." He finally did find the two children hiding under lily pads in the lake to which they had fled, and brought them to the Brahmin.

Both Jali and Kanhajina were absolutely heartbroken and wept as they hugged their father's feet. He tried to comfort them and told them that he had given them away because this gift would contribute to his goal of achieving the perfection of giving, which would eventually lead to the perfection of wisdom and enlightenment. And then, like someone appraising oxen, he put a price on his children as they stood there. He told his son how much money the Brahmin should get for each of them when they wanted to be set free.

So having set a price on each child, Vessantara took his water pot, called the Brahmin to come near, and with a strong desire for attaining omniscience, said, "Omniscience is a hundred times, a thousand times, a hundred thousand times more precious to me than my son!" While pouring the water out, he made a gift of his children to the Brahmin.

Jujaka tightly tied Jali's right hand to Kanhajina left hand with the vine of a creeper and beat them as he led them away. The Great Agent, full of grief, entered his leaf-hut and wept bitterly. He knew, however, that you do not attempt to redeem a gift once it is offered; you do not regret giving a gift once it is given.

Maddi had spent the whole day gathering fruits and roots; by the time she arrived at the hermitage it was quite late. In fact, a full moon soon became the light that led the way home. When she arrived she immediately noticed that the children did not come to meet her; she then saw the future Buddha sitting in silence without the children. A sharp and painful thought crossed her mind, "The children must be dead." "Why are you silent?" she cried. All he said was, "Why are you so late?" Maddi, thinking she must have done some wrong, searched a wide area three times by the light of the moon. Then the night gave way to dawn and as the sun began to rise she returned home. Convinced the children were dead, she returned to where Vessantara was sitting. Overcome by fatigue and the pain of loss, she fainted in front of him.

"She's dead," he thought. Not having touched her for the past seven months, he broke his ascetic vows and felt her beating heart. He took her in his arms and stroked her cheeks and breasts; little by little Maddi regained consciousness, and when she was once again fully awake she said, "Where have the children gone?"

"I have given them away to an old Brahmin," he replied.

"Then why did you remain silent while I, weeping, searched the hermitage?" she asked. He told her that at that moment he did not want to cause her pain, and she should not grieve at the loss of the children because there is no greater gift, and they would get them back. Maddi agreed that the gift was noble, that no greater gift existed, and they rejoiced together with the thirty-three gods as the earth and the heavens trembled.

As they sat talking together, Sakka thought: "Yesterday Vessantara gave his children to Jujaka and the earth quaked as a witness. What if a vile person asked Vessantara for his wife, leaving him alone and destitute? I will take the form of a Brahmin and beg for Maddi. This will allow Vessantara to attain the supreme height of the perfection of giving." So at dawn, Sakka in the form of a Brahmin visited the hermitage.

Vessantara met him and offered him food and cool water from the cave up above the compound. After a pleasant talk, Vessantara asked what he was doing in the forest.

Sakka, in the form of a decrepit old Brahmin, replied, "Your majesty, I am very old, I have come here to beg for your wife Maddi."

The future Buddha remained silent. Now one might think that what was going through his mind was the thought that "yesterday I gave away my children, how can I now give away Maddi, my precious and virtuous wife and be left alone in the forest!" Not so! Vessantara, indifferent, unattached, thought, "I am indeed weary and won't hide that, but I will not shrink from the delight of making gifts." With this thought he quickly drew water into a pitcher and poured it over his right hand as a sign of a donation, and gave Maddi to the Brahmin as the earth trembled.

Maddi felt no resentment or sorrow and remained silent, thinking, "He knows what is best." Sakka praised Maddi's courage and resolution to do as Vessantara wished and thought, "Now I must not delay, but give her back and go." He said, "Sir, I give Maddi back to you. Live in peace so that you may do works of merit again and again." Then as he spoke, he rose into the air and revealed himself: "I am Sakka, king of the Gods, and I grant to you eight favors." Vessantara then chose the following eight: (1) Let my father call me back home soon and give me my royal seat. (2) May I condemn no man to death. (3) May all people look to me for help. (4) May I not seek my neighbor's wife. (5) Grant long life, Sakka, to my beloved son and may he conquer the world with justice. (6) May there be plentiful food at every dawn. (7) May the means of giving never fail and may I always give with gladness. (8) May I no more be born upon the earth but advance to heaven.

When Sakka heard Vessantara's requests, he announced, "Before long, the father you love will wish to see you back again," and then the Mighty One, the king of the gods, went back to his own sphere, and Vessantara and Maddi lived happily together in the hermitage Sakka had built for them.

Jujaka and the children finally completed the long journey to the city of Jetuttara. King Sanjaya immediately recognized his grandchildren, and Jali and Kanhajna told him what had happened. The king asked them to come to him, but they refused, saying, "We are slaves to this Brahmin, and that is why we stand so far away." King Sanjaya then paid the old Brahmin the price that would free them. Living a pompous life, the Brahmin soon died of gluttony and the king arranged for his funeral. The proclamation of his death was made, but no relative could be found, and thus all the goods and money were returned to King Sanjaya.

The king then ordered that the road be leveled from Jetuttara to Mount Vamka and expanded to a width 128 feet, and that it should be decorated with flowers, supplied with wine and cakes along the way, and accompanied by cooks and confectioners, dancers, musicians, and tumblers. Once the fourteen thousand chariots were ready, the army commenced its march to the hermitage with Prince Jali as their guide. When they reached the shores of Lake Mucalinda, Jali ordered them to form a camp.

The roar of the army could be heard as far as the hermitage. Vessantara and Maddi heard the noise and climbed up a hill and peered down on the troops. Vessantara was certain that they were an enemy force come to do them harm. Taking a closer look, Maddi saw the banners and flags fluttering in the wind and knew that they were their own people.

At that moment Sanjaya sent for his queen and told her, "Phusati, I think it is best if I go alone to meet them because too great a crowd may shock them. When you think we have been up there long enough to reassure them, do come up with friends." Sanjaya mounted his caparisoned elephant together with Jali and Kanhajina and headed for the hermitage.

The king, at first in sorrow, told Vessantara that all was well with them, the kingdom, and the children; the conversation was somewhat strained and tense. Then Queen Phusati thought that surely by now they must have overcome any anxiety and left the camp with a large company for the hermitage. The earth once again quaked when they were all joined together at last.

Vessantara entered his cell and took off his bark cloth, came out once again, and said, "This is the place where I have spent over nine months practicing asceticism, the place where I have achieved the perfection of giving." Then they tended to his hair and beard, poured the water of consecration over him, and he became as magnificent as the king of gods. The earth quaked and the oceans roared a mighty roar as he mounted the richly caparisoned elephant, girding himself with a sword of great price, surrounded by sixty thousand of his birth dates.

So they all, bathed, consecrated, and richly clothed in robes and ornaments, proceeded to the camp below and amused themselves in the hills and woodlands with sports for a whole month.

After a month of merrymaking, Sanjaya asked his commander in chief whether the road was ready for a return to the city. He was told that it was, and together with Vessantara, the army, and a host of others he left Mount Vamka for the city of Jetuttara.

It took them two months to make the trip. The city was made ready and the company was received with great joy, song, dances, and plenty of food and drink. On that day Vessantara set all creatures free and thought, "What shall I give to them who come tomorrow after hearing of my return?" Sakka, hearing this, sent down a shower of seven kinds of jewels like a thundershower, filling the back of the palace waist-high and knee-deep throughout all of the city streets.

The future Buddha, after countless aeons, had now mastered all the required perfections and was reborn in Tushita heaven, from where in due course he would descend into his mother's womb and become known as Gotama.

3

The Birth and Early Life
of Gotama

At the beginning of our aeon the future Buddha continued to live in the heavenly domain known as Tushita, and because of the results of past karma he had the ability to know that his last rebirth was about to take place. He knew the time was right because the age of human life in our aeon was neither too long nor too short; in fact, it was the age in which human beings lived to about a hundred years. Observing the four great island-continents that encircled Mount Meru, he chose Jambudipa, that is, India and Kapilavatthu, for the place of his birth. He also chose the warrior caste, the caste that gave birth to the great universal ruler, as his proper rank and announced that his father would be King Suddhodana, king of the Sakyas and a descendant of the solar race; Queen Maya would become his mother.

At that time in Kapilavatthu the festival of the full moon day in the month of Asala (June/July) was about to be celebrated. Queen Maya, participating in the preliminary rituals of the festival, pre-pared herself for the night and then entered her bedchamber. As she slept she had the following dream: Four great kings came and raised her together with her bed to the Himalayas. Their queens came and bathed, anointed, and bedecked her with fragrant flow-ers. They prepared a heavenly bed for her with its head to the east and laid her upon it. Then the future Buddha in the form of a white elephant approached from the north, circled the bed three times, and appeared to enter her side. Feeling no pain, she received the fruit of the womb, just as knowledge united with mental concentration bears fruit. Thus the future Buddha, mindful and fully aware, passed from heavenly Tushita and descended into his mother's womb, and a great immeasurable light surpassing the splendor of all the gods appeared throughout the cosmos. And when he had descended into his mother's womb, four young gods, protectors of the Four Great Kings, took position at the four quarters of the world so that nothing could harm him or his mother.

The next day the queen told the king about her dream, and he immediately summoned sixty Brahmins to discover what would happen. After greeting them and feeding them according to proper ritual rules, the king told them her dream. The Brahmin said, "Be not anxious, O King, the queen has conceived and you will have a son. If he dwells in a house he will become a king, a Universal Monarch; if, however, he leaves his house and renounces the world, he will become a Buddha, a remover of ignorance in the world."

During her pregnancy Queen Maya remained pure, blissful, feeling no fatigue or sorrow. In her tenth month she longed for the lonely forest where she could practice meditation and set her heart on traveling to Lumbina, a delightful grove with trees of every kind, just like the grove in Indra's paradise. She asked the king to go with her, and so they left the city for that glorious forest. While in the grove Queen Maya perceived that the time of her delivery had come, and while among a host of courtiers she went to the foot of a great tree and grasped the tip of a supple branch which had bent down to the reach of her hand; the constellation Pushy shone brightly, it was the full-moon day of Visakha (April/May). As she seized the branch while standing, the future Buddha was delivered from her side without her suffering any pain or illness. His birth was miraculous like that of many heroes in the past. He did not enter the world in the usual manner but was purified through many galactic ages, remembering his previous lives; he was born fully aware and not thoughtless as people are.

Brilliant as the morning sun, he lit up the space all around him and instantly took seven firm and straight steps. Surveying the four quarters with the bearing of a lion, he uttered this proclamation: "I am born for enlightenment for the well-being of the world; I am the first in the world, I am the best in the world. This is my last rebirth in the world of becoming."

At that time the great sage Asita, chief among all ascetics in both discipline and knowledge, and dwelling in Tushita, saw the thirty-three gods celebrating. "Why are they so happy?" he wondered. "They never seemed as joyful before, even when they defeated the anti-gods in battle. What could they possibly have seen to make them so happy?" He traveled by means of intense mental concentration and asked them. They told him that "the Buddha-to-be, incomparable among all humans, has been born for the benefit and happiness of all peoples in the country of the Sakyans at the Lumbina tree; therefore, we are exceedingly happy." Having heard this, Asita quickly descended from heaven and went to Suddhodana's palace. Sitting down among the Sakyans, he said, "Where is this young prince? I too wish to see him." The Sakyans then showed the child, glowing like the sun, to Asita, and Asita was filled with rapture. The child had the characteristic thirty-two marks of a "superhuman agent." "He is indeed unsurpassed, supreme, among all humans," Asita said.

Viewing the child, Asita suddenly remembered his own impending departure, grew unhappy, and began to shed tears. The Sakyans, watching him sob, became disturbed and asked him whether there would be any obstacle or anything negative in the life of the young prince. Asita said: "I do not recall anything destined to be harmful to the prince. Nor will there be any obstacle for him. Do not be concerned. This young prince will reach enlightenment. Purified, having compassion for the benefit of all, he will turn the wheel of the Doctrine. His holy life will be famous. Not much of my life, however, remains, and I will certainly die before then. I shall not hear the Doctrine and I am therefore afflicted and miserable."

As is usual in the birth of all Buddhas, Gotama's mother, Queen Maya, died when he was seven days old. She ascended to Tushita heaven as her dwelling place. Mahaprajapati, the queen's sister and Gotama's aunt, became his stepmother. On the fifth day after his birth 108 Brahmins were invited to attend the ritual of name giving at the palace.

Day by day as Gotama grew, the kingdom became mighty and rich; soon enemies of the kingdom did not exist. It rained in due time, grain grew according to the season without the labor of tilling, and herbs grew abundantly in juice and substance. Women were delivered in due time safely and easily. A husband did not transgress against wife nor wife against husband, and poverty disappeared. It was as in the primal days of Manu, righteousness and virtue were practiced, joy was experienced, and the people were as happy as if they lived in paradise. And when the appropriate year arrived for those who were in the warrior caste, Gotama, together with his family and Brahmins who were ritual specialists, performed the rite of initiation that marked his passage into adulthood as a prince and a student of his proper royal status. His grasp of the tradition, the sciences of his profession, and skills in archery astonished those dwelling in the domains of both earth and the heavens.

Fearing that Gotama would turn toward asceticism, his father arranged that he marry Yashodhara, the daughter of a family possessed of long-standing good conduct, a maiden as lovely as the goddess of fortune in beauty, modesty, and gentle bearing. The king vowed that he would do all in his power to make certain that the prince would see nothing that would turn his mind from his life as a prince and husband, a householder. He therefore built three palaces for the prince when he was sixteen years old, one each for the rainy, hot, and cold seasons. Soft music came from the rooms, and women versed in the subject of sensuous enjoyment and sexual pleasures danced as beautifully as the choicest heavenly nymphs. They entertained him day and night with soft words, wanton swayings, laughter and kisses, and seductive glances.

Recall that all future Buddhas must first of all know the taste of sensuous pleasure; only then after a son is born do they renounce the life of the householder and depart to the forest. The accumulated good merit of past deeds possessed by every future Buddha is the cause of enlightenment, yet it is reached only after enjoying the pleasures of the senses.

One day when he was twenty-nine, tired of the confines of the palace, Gotama decided to take a tour of the parks outside the city. The king heard about his son's plans for an excursion to the parks and gave orders that anyone with any kind of affliction should be kept off the royal highway leading out of the city. Thus all those who were aged, ailing, crippled, and the like were driven off the highway, and it became supremely magnificent, bestrewn with flowers, hanging wreaths, and fluttering banners, filled with crowds waiting to see the king's son in all his glory and majesty. The prince mounted a golden chariot with the horses' gear gilded in gold and headed for the highway and the park for the first time.

But the gods watching this joyful procession as beautiful as paradise itself created an illusion of an old man in order to incite the king's son to leave his palace. Seeing the man, the king's son asked the charioteer, "Who is this man with the white hair, supporting himself on a staff, eyes veiled by brows, limbs relaxed and bent? Is this some transformation in him, or his original state, or is it mere chance?" The charioteer, confounded by the gods, told the prince what he should have withheld, saying, "Old age it is called, that which has broken him down; the murderer of beauty, the ruin of vigor, the birthplace of sorrow, the grave of pleasure, the destroyer of memory, the enemy of the senses. He too sucked milk in his infancy and became a handsome youth, and in the same natural order he has now reached old age." Gotama stared at the old man and shook his head. Looking at the crowd he said, "Thus old age indiscriminately strikes down memory, beauty, and valor, and yet such a sight does not seem to perturb the world. Turn the horses back, I want to go home quickly, for how can I take pleasure in the park when the fear of old age takes over my mind?" They returned to the palace, and Gotama was so lost in his anxiety that the place seemed completely empty.

Time passed, and once more Gotama thought it would be good to take a tour of the park. As they traveled down the royal highway the gods once again created a man with a body afflicted by disease; the son of Suddhodana saw him and said, "Who is this man with such a swollen belly and a body that heaves with his panting? His shoulders and arms are fallen in, his limbs are emaciated and pale. He calls out piteously for his mother, leaning on another for support." Gazing down on the sick man, he said, "Is this evil peculiar to him, or is the danger of disease common to all people?" The chariot driver said, "Prince, this evil is shared by all, for although we feast yet we are oppressed by disease and racked by pain." Hearing the truth, Gotama's mind was truly perturbed, and he began to tremble like the reflection of the moon on rippling water. In his pity he murmured to himself, "This is indeed the calamity of disease for humanity, and yet the world sees it and feels no alarm at all. Vast, alas, is the ignorance of all who sport under the very shadow of sickness." He ordered the chariot back to the palace once again, all feeling of joy having vanished.

Seeing him return a second time, Suddhodana made an inquiry into his sadness and felt that the prediction might well come true. Sensing this and noting that his son took no pleasure in the objects of sense, sounds, and the like in the women's apartments, he made plans for a third excursion to the park, hoping that it might cause a change of mood. He ordered the royal highway decorated and sent courtesans skilled in the arts to the road; guards were posted with special care, and the king changed the charioteer and chariot.

As Gotama traveled along the highway, those same gods fashioned a lifeless man so that only the charioteer and the prince, and none other, saw the corpse being borne along. The prince asked, "Who is being carried along over there by four men and followed by such a dejected company? He has gorgeous clothes yet they bewail him." The driver's mind at that moment was taken over by the gods, and he said, "This is someone bereft of intellect, senses, breath; he is like a mere log or bundle of grass. He was at one time brought up and cherished most lovingly with every care, and now he is being abandoned." Gotama was startled and said, "Is this law of existence peculiar to this man, or is it the law for all creatures?" The driver replied, "This is the last act of all creatures. Destruction is inevitable for all in the world, be they of low or middle or high status." The prince, known for his courage and strength, suddenly felt faint and leaned against the chariot railing. "This is the end that is declared for all creatures, and yet look at the crowd along the road, they are in good cheer; the world throws off the fear and pays no heed whatever," he said. "Turn back!" he ordered. "We cannot continue, this is not the time for pleasure, for how could a person of intelligence be heedless here in the hour of calamity, when he knows of impending destruction?"

But the charioteer did not follow the prince's order. Instead of turning back, he continued to the park, obeying the king's command given at the palace;

the park had been prepared as if for a wedding, with trees in full bloom, and pavilions and tanks beautiful with lotuses. As the sun began to set, Gotama remained miserable, for he simply could not understand how everyone around him remained confident and happy, ignoring the fact of inevitable destruction, that life was subject to sickness, old age, and death. He could not find happiness in this inevitable law.

On the return trip to the palace, a messenger stopped the chariot to inform Gotama that his wife had given birth to a son. The prince decided to name the newborn son Rahula.

4

Flight from the Palace

Life in the palace became ugly and gloomy. One day an inhabitant
of the heavens appeared before the prince in the form of an ascetic.
Startled, Gotama asked who he was. The recluse told him that his
knowledge that life was nothing more than an endless cycle of birth,
death, and rebirth had led him to adopt the homeless life. Relatives
and strangers had become the same for him; greed and hate had
ceased to be. He told Gotama that wherever he found himself, at the
root of a tree, a deserted sanctuary, a hill, or a wood, that became his
home. He had no possessions, no expectations; intent on gaining
freedom from rebirth, he accepted whatever was given to him. And
then before Gotama's very eyes he flew off into the sky. Gotama now
knew very clearly what had to be done, and he made plans to leave
the palace for the homeless life.

   One night he found mother and son fast asleep. He wished to
hold them both in his arms, but he knew that they would be disturbed and awakened from their warm and comfortable sleep. He
therefore passed them by and descended to the lower part of the palace and into the stables in the outer courtyard. He awoke his groom,
Chandaka, and said, "Quickly, bring my horse Kanthaka, for I want
to depart from here to gain freedom from rebirth." As the east gate of
the city opened quietly, they left Kapilavatthu without aid from anyone, crossed the river, and headed for the forest. He was twenty-nine
years old.

When the world's eye rose in the west, the prince saw the hermitage of the ancestral Bhagus. Gotama noticed the deer sleeping in perfect trust and the birds sitting at peace. He felt content, rested, as if his goal had been attained. Alighting from Kanthaka, he told Chandaka that it was rare to find a person who was as loyal and competent as he. "Why speak many words, you have done me a great kindness. Return with the horse, I have arrived at the desired place." And as he spoke the great prince unloosed his ornaments and gave them to Chandaka. "You must return to the king and with full confidence give him this message from me," he said. "Tell him that I have entered the forest to put an end to birth, death, and rebirth, not because of some yearning for paradise or out of a lack of affection or anger. Tell him he should not grieve for me, since union, however long it lasts in time, will cease to be."

On hearing these words, Chandaka was overcome with anguish at the thought of returning to Kapilavatthu without the prince. "Separation is inevitable, you must overcome this affliction," Gotama told the groom, "for if affection should lead to my return, still death would part us from one another against our wills. Since such is the case, my good friend, be not conflicted; go your way." Gotama then drew his sword and cut off his hair together with its headdress and also his beard, put on the clothes of a mendicant, and became a homeless wanderer, a renouncer.

He traveled eastward about 250 miles, crossing the countries of the Sakyas and Koliyas until he reached the region of the Mallas, where he met Alara Kalama, a sage well known for his doctrine and technique for meditation. Alara accepted him as a student, and Gotama mastered both doctrine and practice very quickly. Alara soon recognized that Gotama was his equal both in the knowledge of doctrine and in the practice of meditation. But Gotama concluded that Alara's teaching did not lead to disenchantment, to enlightenment, to perfect happiness but only to the cosmological sphere of nothingness, a domain above the heavens, from which there is rebirth into the lower spheres. Not being satisfied with this teaching, he left Alara's hermitage.

In his continued quest for enlightenment and supreme peace, he met Uddaka Ramaputta, who invited him to become his student. Gotama accepted the invitation and quickly mastered both doctrine and practice, only to discover once again that Uddaka's teaching and the meditation that led to the sphere of neither sensation nor nonsensation did not lead to enlightenment and supreme peace but only to rebirth. Not satisfied, he left the hermitage.

Now Gotama's quest for enlightenment took him on a southward journey through Magadhan country until he reached Uruvela. He found a delightful grove with a clear flowing river, the Neranjara, and nearby a village for alms. Gotama thought, "This is an agreeable place; it will serve for striving." While settling down in the grove, the future Buddha met five mendicants who had come there before him; they had taken vows and were practicing the disciplined life of ascetics. They requested that they be allowed to join him as his students, and he agreed.

Since nothing he had learned or put to actual practice had led him to enlightenment and freedom from rebirth, Gotama began to practice an extraordinarily difficult method of yoga. At first with teeth clenched and tongue pressed against his mouth he beat down and crushed thoughts that came to mind. He discovered that although this aroused tireless energy and steadfast mindfulness, his body became exhausted and overwrought by such painful striving. He abandoned this method and began practicing the breathingless meditation, a technique that came close to stopping breathing altogether. The results of such striving produced violent winds through his head, and he felt as if someone were tightening a tough leather strap around his head. He looked as if he were dead or dying.

He soon realized that this technique did not lead to enlightenment and thought that perhaps a strict diet might be the right path. He decided to take in very little food; lentil or bean soup, a piece of fruit, or perhaps a few sesame seeds. He soon became emaciated, his spine appeared as a string of corded beads, his backside looked like a camel's hoof, and his ribs appeared as the rafters of an old roofless barn. The radical diet made his belly adhere to his backbone, and if he touched the skin of his stomach he also felt the skin of his back. The future Buddha now knew that even the most radical and austere of all ascetic practices did not lead to enlightenment and freedom from rebirth. Gotama thought to himself, "There must be another path to supreme happiness and wisdom."

Reflecting on the various methods he had tried, he suddenly remembered an event that took place when he was a young child. It took place on the day that his father, the king, participated in the annual ritual of plowing. While the ritual was taking place, Gotama sat at the edge of the field in the cool shade of a rose-apple tree and suddenly found himself in a state of peace and calm that was beyond the unwholesome and unsettled states of mind; he found himself absorbed in thought that was delightful and happy. And as the shadow of the trees moved throughout the afternoon, his nurses noted that the shade of the rose-apple tree stood still over the little prince.

"Could it be," he thought, "that this is the path I am searching for?" One thing seemed certain: his emaciated body and the path of radical asceticism did not prepare a person for enlightenment. The future Buddha was now thirty-five years old; six years had passed since he renounced the royal life of a prince, and he seemed to be just as far from enlightenment as the day he left the palace and cut off his hair. He decided then and there to take a new path toward the accomplishment of his goal. He headed for the river and a bath.

Now at that time a girl named Sujata lived in Uruvela, near the river where Gotama was taking a bath. When she became eligible for marriage, she made a promise to a spirit that dwelled in a banyan tree that if she married a man equal in rank and if her firstborn was a son she would make a yearly offering to the sacred spirit equal to a hundred thousand pieces of money. She was now prepared to fulfill her part of the promise.

Sujata wanted to make her offering on the auspicious full-moon day of Visakha (April/May), which as it happens also marked six full years from the date that Gotama became an ascetic. When that day arrived, she resolved to make an offering and rose early in the morning just when night turned into day, and ordered the servants to milk the cows. They gave up their milk freely without being milked. Upon seeing this Sujata took the milk, placed it in a new vessel, prepared a fire, and began to cook it. While she watched the milk-rice cooking, Sujata noticed that immense bubbles arose and turned to the right together, and that no smoke went up from the fireplace. She also saw the four guards of the cardinal points of the cosmos standing guard over the fireplace, Maharaja tending the canopy and Sake stoking the fire, making it blaze brightly. The gods of the four great continents suffused the milk-rice with the sap vital to superhuman agents. When Sujata saw all this, she said to her servant girl Punna, "Run quickly and get everything ready at the sacred place of the banyan tree." Punna, of course, did as she was told and ran in great haste to the foot of the tree.

Now the future Buddha had retired for the night after his bath and had five great dreams. On reflecting upon them he reached the following conclusion: "Without doubt this is the very day that I shall become a Buddha." When the night was over and he had cared for his person, he came early in the morning to the sacred banyan tree to await the hour to go begging. When he sat down he illuminated the whole tree with his radiance.

Then came Punna, and saw the future Buddha sitting at the foot of the tree contemplating the eastern quarter of the world. And when she beheld the radiance from his body lighting up the whole tree with a golden color, she became very excited and said to herself, "Our spirit has come down from the tree today and has seated himself, ready to receive our offering in person." And she ran in haste and told Sujata of the matter. When Sujata heard the news she was overjoyed and said to Punna, "From this day you will be my eldest daughter." She brought out a golden dish worth a hundred thousand pieces of money and put the milk-rice in the golden bowl. Then she covered the bowl with another, also made of gold, wrapping it in a cloth; she adorned herself in all of her ornaments, and with the dish on her head proceeded to the foot of the banyan tree.

As soon as she sighted the future Buddha she was overjoyed, supposing him to be the tree spirit; she kept bowing as she came closer to him. Taking the bowl from her head, she uncovered it, drew near, and took a position close to the future Buddha. Sujata placed the dish of milk-rice in his hand and saw that in fact he was a holy man; she did obeisance and said, "Sir, accept my donation, and go wherever it seems good to you." The future Buddha replied, "For this you will receive great merit." Her offering marked the most fruitful moment in her life, and the meal gave him the strength to win enlightenment.

After consuming the milk-rice he took the golden dish, saying, "If I am to succeed in becoming a Buddha today, let this dish go upstream; but if not, let it go downstream," and he threw it into the river. The bowl swam until it came into the middle of the river and then, like a fleet horse it ran upstream for a distance of about 130 feet, keeping to the middle of the stream all the way. It then dived into a whirlpool and hit against the bowls that had been used by the last three Buddhas and took its place at the end of the row. The future Buddha then took his noonday rest on the banks of the river in a grove of trees in full bloom.

Seeing what had just taken place at the banyan tree, the five mendicants who had become his students left in disgust, thinking that Gotama has given up the life of an ascetic for the comforts of food and leisure.

5

Enlightenment and Liberation

It was the time of the full-moon night of April/May. No longer afflicted with the pangs of hunger, the future Buddha went toward the tree of enlightenment along a road the gods had prepared with celestial perfumes and flowers; celestial choruses poured forth heavenly music and shouts of acclaim. As he headed down the road there came from the opposite direction a grass cutter named Sotthiya who was carrying grass, and when he approached and saw that it was a holy man he gave him eight handfuls of grass. Gotama took the grass and headed for the tree of enlightenment.

The future Buddha approached the tree and stood on the southern side facing the north. Instantly the southern half of the world sank until it seemed to touch the Avici hell, while the northern half rose to the highest heavens. This was obviously not the right place for meditation. Walking around the tree with his right side toward it, he came to the western side and faced east. The western side of the world then sank until it seemed to touch the Avici hell, while the eastern half rose to the highest heavens, as if a huge cart wheel was lying on its side and someone was stepping on the rim. This clearly was not a place for meditation. And so he walked around the tree and came to its northern side and faced south, and the earth pitched once again as before.

He then came to the eastern side and faced west; it is the side that all Buddhas have sat cross-legged, the side that neither sinks nor raises. He then said, "This is the place, the immovable spot on which all Buddhas have placed themselves! This is the place for destroying the net of desire." Gotama then took the handful of grass and shook it out there, and the grass fell in such symmetry of shape that not even the most skillful painter or sculptor could design. Then the future Buddha turned his back to the trunk of the tree and faced east and made his great resolution: "Let my skin and bones, my flesh and blood dry up! But never from this seat will I stir until I have attained the highest wisdom of liberation and enlightenment." He then sat down cross-legged, in the position from which nothing could move him.

It was at that moment that Mara, the tempter, exclaimed, "Prince Gotama is desirous of passing beyond my control; I will never allow it." He then shouted his war cry to his army that extended in front of him for several miles. Mara mounted his great elephant, causing several arms to appear on his body, each with a different weapon, and commanded the army to march forward. He overran all of the armies of the gods, including Sakka's, the chief of all the gods. As Mara and his army marched forward, not a single deity was able to stand his ground, and the future Buddha was left sitting completely alone.

Mara, of course, was delighted with this overwhelming victory and said to his soldiers: "My friends, Gotama, the son of Suddhodana, is far greater than any other man; we shall never be able to fight him head-on. We shall, therefore, attack him from behind." Gotama, realizing he was now all alone, looked to the north and saw Mara and his army coming like a great flood. He said, "Here is this great army exerting its strength and power against me. My mother and father are not here, or any other relatives; I am all alone. But I have mastered the Ten Perfections which will serve me as my shield and sword."

Viewing the scene, Mara caused a whirlwind, thinking, "By this force I will drive Gotama away." In an instant all the winds began to blow. Although these winds would have flattened mountains that were miles high, uprooted huge trees, and reduced villages and towns to rubble, when they reached the future Buddha they lost all their power and were not able to cause so much as a fluttering of the edge of his robe.

Then Mara caused a rainstorm, saying, "With this water I will overwhelm and drown him." Although the rain came down in torrents and had risen over the tops of trees, this mighty inundation did not wet the robes of Gotama.

He then caused a shower of rocks, in which immense mountain peaks flew smoking and flaming through the sky. But on reaching the future Buddha they became celestial bouquets of flowers.

Frustrated, Mara then caused showers of live coals, hot ashes, sand, and mud, but all fell at the feet of the Buddha-to-be. He then shouted at his army, "Attention! Why are you all just standing there? Seize him, drive this prince away!" Mara, seated upon the shoulders of his mighty elephant, drew close to the future Buddha and said, "Gotama, arise from your seat! It does not belong to you, but to me." The future Buddha said, "Mara, you have not fulfilled the Ten Perfections, nor have you devoted serious effort for knowledge, the welfare of the world, nor liberation. This seat does not belong to you, but to me."

Unable to restrain his fury, the enraged Mara hurled his discus. The future Buddha continued to reflect on the Perfections, and the discus changed into a canopy of flowers, and all of the weapons hurled by the army became wreaths of flowers and fell to the ground before him.

Then the Great Agent said to Mara, "Mara, who is a witness to your giving gifts?"

Mara replied, "All these, as many as you see here are my witnesses," and he stretched out his hand in the direction of his vast army that responded in a mighty roar of approval.

Mara then said to the Great Agent: "Gotama, who is witness to your having given gifts?"

"Your witnesses," replied Gotama, "are living beings and I have no living being present. However, not to mention all the gifts I gave in my past existences, let me mention only the great gifts I gave in my Vessantara existence, which shall now be testified to by the solid earth, inanimate as she may be." Gotama then took out his right hand from beneath his robe and stretched it toward the mighty earth and said, "Are you witness, or are you not, to my having given a great gift in my Vessantara existence?"

The mighty earth thundered back, "I bear you witness!" in a roar as if to overwhelm the army of Mara. This great response caused Mara's extraordinary elephant to fall on its knees before the future Buddha, and the followers of Mara fled in every direction, leaving their head ornaments, weapons, and cloaks behind them. Seeing all this, the multitude of gods cried out, "Mara is defeated!" "Prince Gotama has conquered!" "Let us go celebrate the victory!" And as the great celebration began, the sun slowly settled behind the western horizon.

Gotama seated himself cross-legged at the east side of the tree of enlightement, known as "the Bodhi tree," facing the east. The future Buddha had mastered the strict isolation from sensual pleasures and unwholesome states of living for six years. Given this form of life, he began the fourfold set of meditations that he learned from Alara, with the belief that they would become the foundation for gaining wisdom concerning sickness, old age, and death as well as liberation from rebirth.

He quickly entered into the first meditation, which involved strict mental isolation involving applied and sustained thought, and produced a feeling of rapture and pleasure. He then entered the second meditation, in which concentration produced the cessation of thinking and evaluating; it produced a feeling of well-being. He then directed his concentration in the third stage of meditation to the cessation of delight and balance of mind, producing a feeling that was dispassionate. He then entered the fourth stage, which produced the cessation of pleasure and pain and the feeling of pure equanimity. In his discussion of this fourfold meditation as the prelude to enlightenment, the Buddha often stressed that the feelings that arose in each of these four stages did not invade or remain in his mind as thoughts do in an unenlightened life. He stressed that the point of this preparation for enlightenment was the purification of the mind; it produced a mind that was bright, unblemished, malleable, steady, imperturbable, calm, and cool. He was now ready to begin a meditation that lasted through the three watches of the night.

In the first watch of the night (that is, between dusk and 10:00 P.M.), he perfected the beginning of wisdom. With his mind concentrated, purified, steady, he directed it to the knowledge of recollecting his past lives: one birth, two births, five, fifty, a hundred, a thousand, a hundred thousand, through many aeons of contractions and expansions of the cosmos. He knew that such and such were his name in each particular life span, that he had belonged to a certain clan. He knew the specific food he ate there, and the pleasures and pains and end of each life. He remembered the passing away from that state and the arising in another until the arising of his current life. It was the realization of perfect knowledge of his previous lives, their modes and details. Ignorance was destroyed, knowledge arose, darkness was abolished, and light appeared. It was this knowledge that he attained in the first watch of the night. He came to the definite conclusion that all existence, the whole world, is as unsubstantial as a plantain tree.

During the second watch of the night (between 10:00 P.M. and 2:00 A.M.), the future Buddha acquired the second knowledge with which he surveyed the death and rebirth of all living beings everywhere. He saw the entire cosmos as reflected in a mirror, the good karma that leads to a happy rebirth and the bad karma that causes a miserable one. The Buddha-to-be directed his mind to the knowledge of the passing away and reappearance of beings, by means of a vision that was purified and surpassed that of ordinary human beings. He discerned how beings were inferior and superior in accordance with their karma; those with bad conduct of deed, speech, and thought, who revile the noble ones, who hold wrong views and acquire karma under the influence of wrong views, appeared after death in the domain of deprivation, the bad destiny of the lower realms. But those beings who live good lives in deed, speech, and thought, who hold right views and acquire good karma according to right views, after death are reborn in the good destinies of the upper heavens. It became clear to him that no security can be found in this unsubstantial world, that the threat of death was ever present. There simply is no resting place in any of the domains for rebirth. He found nothing substantial in the world of becoming, just as there is no core to be found in an onion when its layers are peeled off one by one. This was the second knowledge he attained in the second watch of the night. Ignorance was destroyed; knowledge arose as happens in one who is resolute and pure.

During the third watch (from 2:00 A.M. to dawn), he directed his power of meditation at the knowledge and the extinction of the four forces that hinder a person from reaching liberation: sensual desire, the desire for existence, ignorance, and wrong views that arise because of ignorance. As the master of meditation directed his meditation to the real nature of the cosmos, he realized that all creatures are born over and over again; they age, die, pass on to a new life, and are then reborn again. Greed and delusion blind them.

The Buddha-to-be then surveyed the twelvefold links of dependent origination and realized that beginning with ignorance (the first link), they lead to old age and death and rebirth, and that beginning with the cessation of ignorance they lead to the cessation of birth, old age, death, and rebirth. Having reached the summit of knowledge, comprehending that where there is no ignorance there is then the cessation of karma formations, he realized that he had achieved the correct knowledge of all that there is to be known and he stood out in the world as a Buddha. From the very summit of the cosmos downward he could detect no self anywhere. Like a fire when its fuel is burned up, he became tranquil. He had reached the perfection of knowledge and thought to himself, "This is the path that many great sages of the past have traveled. Now I have attained it. Rebirth is destroyed, ignorance dispelled. I have run through a course of many births looking for the maker of this dwelling and found him not; painful is birth again and again. But now I see you, builder of the house, and you will not build this house again. All your rafters are broken, your ridge-pole is destroyed, the mind set on destruction of all attachments has attained the extinction of all desires." As he reflected upon his liberation, the sun rose brightly over the eastern horizon.

6

The Buddha Begins to Teach

The Buddha realized that his discovery through the watches of the night was not only profound but that it would be difficult to explain, to make clear for the comprehension of others, especially to those who lived the life of householders. Could he teach others what he had just discovered through his own efforts?

Seated cross-legged at the foot of the tree of enlightenment at Bodh-Gaya near the town of Uruvela, the Buddha experienced the peace of liberation and rehearsed the causal law of the interdependent origination of all conditioned things that explained both the cause of unhappiness and the cycles of rebirth. The Buddha realized that the cessation, the rooting out of ignorance, was the key to the cessation of the conditioned factors and forces and thus the entire wheel of this unhappy existence. He then concentrated on the significance of the twelvefold causal law of the dependent origination of suffering, grief, and unhappiness for seven days. At the end of the seventh day he left the tree of awakening to meditate under the banyan tree of the goatherd and experienced the peace of freedom and happiness for a week. He then settled under the Mucalinda tree for the third week. During that time a great storm with cold winds arose out of season, and the king of serpents, Mucalinda, encircled the Buddha with his coils seven times and spread his hood over his head to protect him. At the end of the seven days the sky cleared, and Mucalinda gave up his form as the great serpent and appeared in front of the Buddha in the form of a young boy honoring him with joined hands.

The Buddha then approached the Rajayatana tree from the foot of the Mucalinda and continued to enjoy his release from the causes of ignorance, suffering, and rebirth. At the end of the fourth week two merchants, Tapussa and Bhallika, were traveling along the district road, and a god who happened to be a relation of theirs in a former life spoke to them, saying, "My good fellows, a recent enlightened one is staying at the foot of the Rajayatana tree, go and serve him the Lord with rice and honey cakes." The merchants approached the Buddha and, standing at a respectful distance, said, "Lord, do receive our rice and honey cakes that this may be great merit for us for a long time." It occurred to the Buddha that an enlightened being does not receive food with his hands, and he wondered what he should use to receive it. At that moment the four great kings of the four quarters of the world presented the Buddha with four bowls made of rock crystal, which were immediately formed into one from which he received his food.

After the Buddha finished eating, the merchants spoke to him, saying, "We have come for refuge and the teaching; please accept us as lay disciples, householders who have gone from refuge for life from this day forward." Thus they became the first laypersons in the world to be followers of the Buddha. And yet, as the awakened one sat at the foot of the tree, he continued to hesitate. Once again he thought about how difficult it would be to understand the Doctrine that he had discovered and to follow the path that he himself had taken that leads to liberation. He knew that the Doctrine went against the worldly stream of living. He knew that this world delights in the pleasures of the senses, and that his teaching demanded the renunciation of all attachments and desires. He thought, "If I were to teach the Doctrine that goes against the stream of life and people did not understand me, it would be a profound weariness and disappointment to me."

Brahma, highest of the gods, knew what the Buddha was thinking. He knew that the world would be lost, would perish if the Perfected One inclined to inaction rather than teaching the Doctrine. At that very moment, just as a strong man might extend or flex his arm, Brahma vanished from the Brahma world and appeared before the Buddha, and after a respectful salutation ended his speech by saying, "Venerable sir, the world will perish if the Awakened One does not decide to teach his Doctrine. Therefore, teach it! Those with little dust in their eyes will be lost if they do not hear the Doctrine. However, if they hear it they will attain liberation." Brahma's arguments aroused the Buddha's compassion for those who are lost and said, "Let liberation be opened to all who are able to hear!" Brahma bowed to the Buddha, circled round him on the right side as is the rule, and vanished.

Now that he had decided to teach the Doctrine, he began to consider who should be the first to hear it. Who would best understand it quickly? He decided that he would approach his first teachers, Alara and Uddaka, but was informed by a god that both had recently died. He then thought of the five ascetics who had lived with him; with purified vision he saw that they were now staying at the Deer Park near Varanasi. He thus set off for Varanasi determined to find them.

Taking the main road that led to Varanasi, he met a naked ascetic, Upaka, who stopped and spoke to him: "Lord, you appear quite pure, very bright. Who has sent you on your mission? Who is your teacher? What is the teaching that you profess?" The Buddha replied, "I am victorious over all, omniscient, unde-filed, freed from all craving, gaining liberation and wisdom by myself alone. Who then should I follow? For me there is no teacher, I have no equal in the world or among the gods. I alone am a Fully Enlightened One." On hearing this, Upaka, shaking his head in disbelief said, "If you say so," and walked off taking a different road. The Buddha headed for Varanasi, a journey that would take about a fortnight.

The five mendicants, Konkani, Bhatia, Kappa, Maharaja, and Assai, became quite displeased when they spotted the Buddha in the distance head-ing toward the Deer Park. They quickly agreed that since he had left the life of radical asceticism they would not greet him, nor stand up when he arrived. As the Buddha arrived, however, they quickly stood up and went to greet him. One of them brought water to wash his feet, another took his outer robe, and a third brought him a seat and greeted him as "brother Gotama."

The Buddha immediately rejected this familiarity and said: "Monks, do not address the Awakened One by name and as brother. The Perfected One is an Accomplished One, fully enlightened. Listen, the end of rebirth has been attained, and I shall teach you the Doctrine. If you practice the Doctrine as instructed, realizing it for yourselves, you will reach the supreme goal of this sacred life for the sake of which young men renounce the life of the householder."

The five monks simply could not believe him. "How can this be, brother Gotama?" they replied. "After all, isn't it true that you abandoned the ascetic life for a life of plenty? How could you achieve the supreme knowledge of lib-eration when living a life of luxury?" The Buddha told them that he had never abandoned the life of homelessness for a life of abundance, and asked them whether they had ever heard him speak like this before. They finally agreed to listen to him.

The Buddha then delivered his first discourse on the Doctrine, known as "The Turning of the Wheel of Doctrine." This is what he told them: There are two extremes, monks, that should not be practiced by those who have renounced the life of the householder. What are they? The first is conjoined with the passions, the indulgence of sensual pleasure. It is base, vulgar, ignoble, and useless. The other extreme is conjoined with self-torture and pain, and it is also useless, unprofitable, and vulgar. By avoiding both of these extremes, monks, the Perfected One has gained knowledge of the Middle Way that produces insight and knowledge, leading to peace, to knowledge, to enlightenment, and liberation and happiness.

What, monks, is the Middle Way that gives insight and knowledge that leads to peace and liberation?

This, monks, is the noble truth of suffering. Birth is suffering, old age is suffering, sickness is suffering, death is suffering; being joined to what one does not like is suffering, being separated from what one likes is suffering; not getting what one desires is suffering; in brief, the five kinds of objects of attachment are suffering.

This, monks, is the noble truth of the cause, the origin, of suffering. It is a desire that leads from birth to rebirth, accompanied by pleasure, greed, and passion that finds its pleasure now here, now there; in brief, it is the desire for pleasure, desire for existence, the desire for impermanence.

This, monks, is the noble truth of the extinction of suffering: it is the complete annihilation without remainder of this desire, giving it up, renouncing it, by being delivered from it, by leaving it no place.

This, monks, is the noble truth of the path that leads to the cessation of suffering. It is the noble Eightfold Path, namely, Right Belief, Right Intention, Right Speech, Right Action, Right Livelihood, Right Effort, Right Mindfulness, and Right Concentration.

And what is Right Belief? It is the knowledge of suffering, the knowledge of the origin of suffering, the knowledge of the cessation of suffering, and the knowledge of the way of practice leading to the cessation of suffering.

And what is Right Intention? Renunciation, the abolition of ill will and harmfulness, is Right Intention.

And what is Right Speech? To refrain from lying, slander, harsh and frivolous speech is Right Speech.

And what is Right Action? To refrain from taking life, from taking what is not given, and from sexual misconduct, that is Right Action.

And what is Right Livelihood? The Ariyan path of discipleship, the life of the renouncer, is right livelihood.

And what is Right Effort? Arousing the will and energy of mind to prevent the arising of evil mental states, to overcome evil mental states that have already arisen, and to produce wholesome states that have not yet arisen, and then to let them fade away, to bring them to greater growth, to the full perfection of development. That is called Right Effort.

And what is Right Mindfulness? Here a monk abides contemplating, clearly, mindful, putting aside yearning and fretting for the world. He contemplates feeling as feeling, mind as mind, and objects as objects without becoming attached to feeling, mind, or objects with yearning and fretting.

And what is Right Concentration? Here a monk, detached from sense, desires and unwholesome mental states, enters the four levels of meditative cognition. The first is with thinking and pondering, born of detachment yet filled with joy and delight. The second level gains inner tranquillity and oneness of mind that is without thinking and pondering, filled with delight and joy. With the fading away of delight he enters the third level, filled with serenity and evenness of mind. Having given up pleasure and pain, gladness and sadness, he finally enters the fourth level that is beyond pleasure and pain, purified by peace and mindfulness.

The Buddha told the monks that when these four truths in their complete significance became known to him through the purification of his body, mind, and speech, he became thoroughly enlightened with complete and full awakening, with the knowledge that the freedom of his mind was unshakable, that this was indeed his last rebirth.

He told them that a Perfected One is free from obsessions, does what has to be done, lays down the burden, attains the ideal; his fetters of becoming are destroyed; freed by the highest knowledge, he knows liberation and happiness. However, a Perfected One does not think of himself as liberated or happy, he does not think of himself in liberation or happiness, neither does he think "liberation and happiness are mine," nor does he rejoice in them. Why? It is because it is thoroughly understood by him.

The Buddha then told the monks to listen very closely to what he had to say about the Doctrine. The Doctrine, the Buddha said, is similar to a raft. Suppose a man on a journey came across a great span of water and discovered that the shore he stood on was dangerous and fearful but that the shore on the other side was safe. Looking around, he also discovered that there was no ferry or bridge for crossing to the other side. Then he thought, "Suppose I collect twigs and branches and grass and bind them together to make a raft." He did just that and paddled his way safely across the span of water. When he reached the other shore he thought, "The best thing to do is lift the raft up on my head or shoulder and take it along with me wherever I want to go." Now, monks, do you think that this man did the right thing with the raft?

Not so, they replied.

"Indeed," replied the Buddha. "When he got across to the other shore he would think, 'This raft has been very helpful to me. I will haul it to dry land, or set it adrift, and then go wherever I want.' Likewise, monks, the Doctrine is similar to a raft; it is for the purpose of crossing over."

And as the Buddha spoke, as he rolled the wheel of the Doctrine at Varanasi in the Deer Park, the sound was heard by the gods of the earth, who replayed it for the gods of the four great kings of the four quarters, the thirty-three gods, and also the gods who delight in creation and the god of death. Thus the supreme wheel of the Doctrine cannot be rolled back by anyone in the world.

Moreover, even as he spoke, Kondanna saw, fully understood, and attained the Doctrine. Thus, having put away uncertainty, having attained without help the full teaching of the Buddha, he said, "May I, Lord, be accepted as a renouncer, may I receive ordination?" The Buddha replied, saying, "Come, monk, the Doctrine is fully explained; lead a life that is pure in order to attain the end of suffering." Kondanna thus became the first monk to enter the Buddha's ascetic community; this day is celebrated annually at the full moon of the month of Asalhi (June/July), two lunar months (about fifty-six days) after the Buddha's enlightenment.

The Buddha continued to teach the Doctrine to the other mendicants, and his instruction soon led to the acceptance of Vappa and Bhaddiya and then Mahanama and Assaji. There were now five mendicants in the Buddhist order of the Middle Way. Then the Buddha, eating the food brought back by the newly ordained mendicants, instructed them all that they, henceforth, should live on whatever was brought back from the daily almswalk.

A few days after the ordination of Mahanama and Assaji, the Buddha gave a second, more difficult discourse, "The Discourse on the Marks of No-Self." He opened his discourse with the following assertion: "The body, monks, is without a self." This was, indeed, a remarkable thing to say, since one of the primary beliefs at the time entailed a self or soul that was eternal and survived death. The Buddha went on to declare that if an immortal self existed it could not be identified with the body, since the body is subject to sickness, old age, and death. He then pointed out that the self cannot be identified with any of the five aggregates or groups that make up the body and our personality, namely, matter, sensations, perceptions, karmic dispositions, and consciousness.

The Buddha focused on each of the five aggregates, saying the body, as matter, sensations, perceptions, karmic dispositions, and consciousness, cannot be identified with the self because they are all conditioned and subject to decay. And when he asked them whether the five aggregates that constitute the body and personality are permanent or impermanent, the monks agreed that they were all impermanent. "Well, then," the Buddha concluded, "the truth is that all things are impermanent and there is nothing that can be characterized as the self! He who understands this leads the life of a renouncer, destroys rebirth, does what has to be done, and there is nothing for him beyond this world."

The monks rejoiced at the words of the Buddha, and when they heard his discourse they were freed from ignorance and fully enlightened.

At that time in Varanasi there lived a young man, the son of a great merchant, well educated, whose name was Yasa. He had three mansions, one for winter, one for the hot summer, and one for the monsoon where he now dwelled during the four months of the rainy season. One night he awoke before all of his retinue and saw them all asleep, openmouthed, disheveled hair, muttering in their sleep; the scene appeared to him as if he were looking at a cemetery right before his eyes. Yasa thought, "What distress, what affliction" and put on his golden sandals and headed for the door. Superhuman Agents opened the door for him, thinking, "Let there be no obstacle for leaving home into homelessness for this young man," and the same thing happened as Yasa approached the gates of the town. He then headed for the Deer Park at Isipatana.

The Buddha, as was his usual practice, had risen in the night, and pacing up and down in meditation in the open air toward dawn saw Yasa approaching in the distance and sat down on his usual seat. He noticed Yasa's distress and said to him, "Come, sit down, Yasa, I will teach you the Doctrine." Yasa took off his sandals, greeted the Buddha, and sat down at a respectful distance. Then the Buddha began a brief, graduated discourse that began with the importance of giving, the moral life, heaven, and the vanity and peril of the pleasures of the senses and the advantage of renouncing them. When he knew that Yasa was ready, uplifted, he then explained the Doctrine by means of the Four Noble Truths: existence as suffering, its cause, its cessation, and the way that leads to the cessation of suffering. And just as a clean cloth takes a dye easily, and just as he was sitting on that very seat, the insight on Doctrine arose dustless and stainless in the mind of Yasa.

In the meantime, Yasa's mother walked over to the mansion in the morning and not finding Yasa, told her husband about his absence. The great merchant, the householder, dispatched messengers on horseback to the four quarters of the world while he himself followed Yasa's footsteps to the park. The Buddha saw him coming and thought, "Suppose because of my superhuman powers, I perform a wonder so that when he arrives the great merchant does not see Yasa sitting here?" And he did just that.

When Yasa's father arrived he asked the Buddha, "Lord, have you by any chance seen Yasa, my son, the young man of my family?"

"Well, householder, sit down," replied the Buddha. "Perhaps sitting here, you may well see Yasa sitting next to us," and began using various figures of speech to talk about the Doctrine.

On hearing the Buddha's words the merchant cried out, "Excellent! Excellent! I myself go to the Buddha, the Doctrine, and to the Community for refuge. Accept me as a lay disciple gone for refuge from this day forth for as long as life lasts." Thus the merchant, Yasa's father, became the first lay disciple in the world using what would become the threefold formula for entrance into the Community.

The Buddha then thought, "Suppose I were to annul the wonder of Yasa's disappearance?"

The merchant, householder, and father saw Yasa immediately and said, "Dear Yasa, your mother is full of sadness and grief, do give her life." But as Yasa looked at the Buddha and reviewed what he had heard, his mind was freed from clinging, and the Buddha said, "Can Yasa turn back to the life of the pleasures of the senses as he did formerly as a householder?"

"No, indeed!" said Yasa's father, and he invited the Buddha with Yasa as his attendant for a meal the next day and departed, keeping his right side toward the Buddha.

Then Yasa said, "Lord, may I receive ordination?"

"Come, monk," the Lord said, "well taught is the Doctrine, lead the life of a renouncer for making an utter end to suffering." So this came to be Yasa's ordination, and now there were seven perfected ones in the world.

The next morning the Buddha, taking his robe and bowl along with Yasa as his attendant, visited the home of the wealthy merchant and delivered a discourse on the importance of giving, the moral life, and Doctrine. Hearing his words, both Yasa's mother and his former wife approached the Buddha and said, "We go to the Buddha for refuge, to the Doctrine and to the Community for refuge. Let the Lord accept us as women lay disciples, for refuge this day for as long as life lasts." Thus they became the first women lay disciples.

Yasa's mother and father and former wife served the Buddha and the venerable Yasa sumptuous foods, solid and soft, and when the Buddha had finished his meal and removed his hand from his bowl he delighted them all with a talk on Doctrine. He then rose from his seat and departed for the park.

In a short time Yasa introduced four and then fifty of his friends, young merchants, to the Buddha, and they too requested ordination. The ascetic order now grew to sixty-one perfected mendicants. The Buddha encouraged his disciples to go out separately and teach the Doctrine for the welfare and compassion of the common folk of the world; as for himself, he would head for Uruvela in order to teach the Doctrine.

The monks soon brought back from their various journeys those wishing to be ordained, and all soon found this travel to and fro very tiring. The Buddha reflected on this problem while meditating in seclusion. "Suppose," he thought, "I said to the monks, 'You monks may now yourselves go forth and ordain others in any district." Toward evening he emerged from his seclusion and addressed the monks, saying, "I allow you to ordain others in any district. You should first make them cut their hair and beard off, have them put on yellow robes, arrange the upper robe over the shoulder, honor other monks, salute with both hands, and say three times, 'I go to the Buddha for refuge, I go to the Doctrine for refuge, I go to the Community for refuge.'" From that day forward all monks were allowed to ordain others using this threefold formula.

The Buddha spent the rainy season in Varanasi and then decided to set out for Uruvela once again. He turned off the main road and headed for the woods, sitting down at the foot of a certain tree. At that time a group of thirty friends of high repute and social status along with their wives were amusing themselves in the same woodland. One of them did not have a wife, and he brought a woman of lesser standing with him. While they amused themselves the woman took their belongings and ran away.

As the entire group began looking for her, they saw the Buddha sitting at the foot of a tree and approached him, saying, "Lord, have you seen a woman passing by?" The Buddha replied, "Just what have you, young men, to do with that woman?" They then told him of their visit to the woods and the theft of their belongings. The Buddha then said, "What do you think of this? Which is better for you, that you should seek a woman or that you should seek liberation?" They all agreed that it would be better to seek liberation "Well, then," the Buddha replied, "sit down and I will teach you the Doctrine." They sat down, and hearing his words they were ordained; uttering the threefold formula, they became venerable ones.

7

The Buddha Becomes a
Wonder-Worker

The Buddha finally arrived at Uruvela. At that time three brothers,
all of them ascetics, were living there. One of the brothers was the
leader and guide of five hundred matted-hair ascetics, the second
brother was leader of three hundred, and the third was the head of
two hundred ascetics.

As the Buddha approached the hermitage of Kassapa of Uruvela,
the first brother, he said, "If it is convenient for you, Kassapa, let me
stay for one night in the ritual fire-room." Kassapa replied, "It is not
convenient, venerable one, because there is a fierce Naga, a terribly
venomous snake with superhuman power, living there. Do not let
him harm you." After repeated requests, and with the assurance that
the serpent would not harm him, Kassapa said, "As you wish," and
let him in.

The Buddha entered the ritual room, sat down cross-legged on
a grass mat with his back erect, and began to meditate. The Naga
saw him and became distressed and began to blow smoke. Seeing
this, the Buddha thought, "What if I match his fire with my own fire
without destroying any part of him?" He then enacted the appropriate exercise of miraculous power and emitted a cloud of smoke. The
Naga, losing control of his rage, emitted flames, and the Buddha
converted his body into a mass of flame, and the room looked like it
was burning with a raging fire. The matted-hair ascetics surrounded
the room and agreed that the composure of the Buddha was simply
wonderful but were certain that the Naga would do him harm. When

morning came the Buddha placed the Naga in his begging bowl and showed him to Kassapa of Uruvela saying, "Look, here is the Naga, his fire was completely conquered by my fire." Kassapa did not doubt that the ascetic possessed powerful magic in order to conquer a Naga, but said to himself, "Nevertheless, he is not as worthy as I am."

The same event happened when the Buddha asked Kassapa of the river whether he could stay in his ritual room during the moonlight night. As the Naga's fire was extinguished, the fire of the Buddha's multicolored flames continued, dark green, then red, yellow, and crystal-colored flames appearing on his body. Kassapa became thoroughly convinced of the genuine nature of the Buddha's magical power and spoke up, saying, "Stay here, I will provide you with food."

The Buddha stayed in a grove near the hermitage of the matted-hair ascetics, and the Great Kings of the four quarters illuminated the grove in glorious colored light and stood at each of the four quarters like huge fires. At the end of the night Kassapa came to tell the Buddha that his meal was ready and asked him who the beings were that had lit up the night. The Buddha told him. Although Kassapa was impressed by his magical powers and the fact that the Four Kings came to hear the Doctrine, he remained of the opinion that this ascetic was not as deserving as he was.

Then Sakka (that is, Indra), the chief of all the gods, created a glorious colored display the next night, and Brahma, the supreme creator, did the same the following night. Kassapa remained unmoved.

At this time Kassapa, as was the custom, was about to perform a sacrificial ritual to which the entire population of Anga and Magadha was invited to attend. Everyone would bring huge amounts of good food. But Kassapa was worried. He knew that if this wonder-making monk showed up at the ritual, then he would gain honor, and that any gains Kassapa might win would be lost. He absolved himself of this concern by assuring himself that the Buddha would certainly not attend the ritual the following day.

In the meantime, the Buddha knew in his own mind what Kassapa was thinking, and concentrating his mental powers traveled to Uttarakuru, the northern paradise, ate his meal at the lake there, and took his midday rest. Then at the end of that night Kassapa came to the Buddha and told him that his meal was ready and asked him why he did not come to the great ritual. He informed the Buddha that they had thought of him and set aside a portion of food for him. The Buddha replied that he had known all along what was in Kassapa's thoughts and so decided to go to the lake for the day. Although Kassapa was truly impressed with such powers of the mind, it did not change his attitude toward the Buddha.

At that time the ascetics wanted to perform an important ritual but discovered that they could not split the wood for the ritual fire. It occurred to them that this was due to the mental power of the great mendicant. The Buddha asked Kassapa, "Should the firewood be split?" "Indeed it should," replied Kassapa. In a moment all the firewood was split. But then the fire could not be kindled and later it could not be extinguished. When the Buddha asked at each occasion whether the five hundred fires should be kindled or extinguished, it happened in a moment. Kassapa remained unmoved in his opinion of the Buddha.

Then, during the cold winter nights during the dark half of the moon in February, the matted-hair ascetics of the river performed a ritual bathing, plunging in and out of the river. The Buddha prepared five hundred ovens to warm the ascetics at just the spot from which they left the river. And then a huge out-of-season rainfall created a severe flood. The Buddha thought, "Suppose I make the water recede all around me so that I can walk up and down on dust-covered ground." It was done in a moment. The ascetics rowing in boats saw this and approached the place where the Buddha walked. "Is it you?" they shouted.

"It is indeed I, Kassapa," replied the Buddha, and he rose into the air and placed himself in the boat!

There came a time when the Buddha thought, "There seems to be nothing I can do that will change this foolish recluse from thinking that although I do indeed have mental powers and supreme faculties of thought, I am not more worthy than he. Perhaps I should shake him up mentally in order to show him my superiority." So when next he met Kassapa, the Buddha said, "You, Kassapa are not worthy. In fact you have not entered the path of the Perfected Ones, nor do you walk in the path that will lead to perfection or to entering the path of wisdom and liberation from rebirth." So shaken was Kassapa that he prostrated himself in front of the Buddha with his head inclined to the Perfected One's feet and said, "Lord, let me receive entrance and ordination."

The Buddha replied, "Kassapa, you are chief of the five hundred monks, their leader, foremost among them. Go first and tell them of your intention and then let them do what they think fit."

Then Kassapa of Uruvela went to his mendicants and said to them, "I am going to lead a sacred life under the instruction of the great ascetic; you may do what you think best." They replied that they had developed a great affection for the Buddha a long time ago and that if he had decided to follow the Buddha, they too would follow the Buddha's instruction. They then cut off their hair and flung it together with all the ritual implements into the river and went to prostrate themselves before the Buddha, saying, "Lord, receive us, give entrance and ordination into the order."

The Buddha replied, "Come, monks, well taught is the Doctrine, lead the life of a perfected one for the complete extinction of unhappiness."

In the meantime, the monks of Kassapa of Gaya, the second brother, saw the hair and implements floating down the river and were sure that something catastrophic had happened to their ascetic brothers. Kassapa of Gaya dispatched some of them to find out what had happened, and when they learned what had happened they too cut off their hair and threw it together with their bundles and ritual implements into the river. Asking for ordination, they all became venerable monks on the Eightfold Path that the Buddha taught.

As the community of monks grew in size, so did the possibility of misunderstanding as the monks discussed the Doctrine among themselves and with other ascetic groups. One day the Buddha decided that it was time to clarify two issues. The first concerned wrong views. The second point had to do with the learning and use of the Doctrine.

The Buddha brought all the monks together and taught them the lesson concerning wrong views. "Wrong views," he said, "are held by most ordinary persons who have no regard for the Doctrine or the truth. They believe that what is seen, heard, sensed, cognized, encountered, sought, or mentally pondered involves a self saying, 'This is mine, this I am, this is my self.' They thus believe that something like 'This is the self, this world exists,' and therefore also believe that after death they shall be permanent, everlasting, eternal, not subject to change, endure as long as eternity. They believe that 'this is mine, this I am, this is my self.' But the monk who knows the Doctrine does not yearn for or fear what is nonexistent."

The Buddha then asked, "Monks, what do you think? Is material form permanent or impermanent?" Impermanent, they replied. He then asked, "is feeling, perception, or consciousness permanent or impermanent?" Impermanent, they replied once again. Well, then, the Buddha asked, "is what is impermanent, suffering, subject to change to be regarded as 'This is mine, this I am, this is my self?'" Not so, the monks replied.

The Buddha then concluded that any kind of material form whatever, whether past, future, or present, internal or external, inferior or superior, far or near, as well as any kind of feeling, or perceptions of any kind, and all consciousness should be seen as they are with proper wisdom; that all of this should be known as "This is not mine, this I am not, this is not my self." Knowing this, a monk becomes disenchanted with all material form, feeling, perception, and consciousness, and becoming disenchanted he becomes dispassionate. Through dispassion he becomes liberated and knows that rebirth is destroyed.

The Buddha then reminded the monks that in proclaiming this Doctrine he had been baselessly and falsely misrepresented by some ascetics and Brahmins who argued that he led people astray by teaching annihilation, the destruction or extermination of an existing being. But the monks should always remember that what he has taught both formerly and now is suffering and the cessation of suffering, that whatever arises is suffering arising, and that whatever ceases is only suffering ceasing. He reminded them that his Doctrine was known as the "Middle Path," for he taught neither "eternalism" nor "annihilationism."

He told them "that those who know the Middle Path know that birth, becoming, grasping, craving, feeling, contact, sense, name and form, consciousness, activity, ignorance, and rebirth are by nature impermanent, conditioned, arising and fading away. That is what 'All things are impermanent' means.

"Those who truly know this, who know the relatedness of this to that as causal happening and what things are as having causally happened, such as birth, becoming, grasping, and the like, do not ask, 'Did I live in times gone by? Or did I not? What was I in times gone by? Or from what being did I become that?' Nor do they ask, 'Shall I be reborn in a future time, or shall I not? What shall I become in the future? Or being what I am, shall I become what in the future?' Nor do they become confused and ask, 'Am I indeed? Or am I not indeed? What indeed am I? Or this person that I am now, whence came he, and where will he go?' They know that these kinds of questions are based upon false views, not founded upon the truth that existence is suffering, that suffering is caused by ignorance, the ignorance that all things are impermanent."

Staying at Uruvela for as long as he thought fit, the Buddha decided to travel to Bodh-Gaya accompanied by thousands of monks, including the recently ordained monks who followed the Kassapa brothers. Arriving at Bodh-Gaya, he went to a hill nearby and addressed the monks with a discourse that became known as "The Fire Sermon." This is what he said:

Everything, monks, is burning! Sensations and feelings are burning, be they pleasant, unpleasant, or neither pleasant nor unpleasant. With what is it burning? I say it is burning with the fire of passion, with the fire of anger, with the fire of stupidity; it is burning because of birth and aging and death; because of grief, sorrow, lamentation, and despair. Seeing this, monks, the instructed disciple disregards all feelings and sensations whether they be pleasant, unpleasant, or neither pleasant nor unpleasant, as well as all mental formations and consciousness of such feelings and sensations. Disregarding them he becomes dispassionate, and through dispassion he becomes free, and in this freedom he then knows, "I am free" and he comprehends: destroyed is birth and rebirth, the way is attained, done is what was to be done, and there is no more return to this world.

And while this discourse was being uttered and repeated, the minds of these thousands of monks were freed from attachment to this world, and they were freed from all desires.

8

The Buddha Meets a King and Two Brilliant Ascetics

The Enlightened One was becoming quite famous. After a stay at Bodh-Gaya, the place of his enlightenment, the Buddha decided to take a large number of monks to Rajagaha, the capital city of Magadha. When he finally arrived there he settled near the town in the pleasure garden known as the Bamboo Grove, near a sacred shrine. Rajagaha was the seat of the famous king of Magadha named Bimbisara.

The king was told of the Buddha's arrival. He was told, "This was indeed the perfected one, fully awakened, the knower of all worlds, unrivaled in the superknowledge that he had attained by himself. He makes known the truth and this world together with its gods, Maras and Brahmas. He teaches the Doctrine and explains the path that completely satisfies and is pure. Good and rare indeed is the opportunity to see such a perfected one as this."

Without hesitation, King Bimbisara decided to visit the Buddha with a vast number of Magadha, Brahmins, and householders. As the crowd reached the grove, some exchanged greetings with him and sat down near the Buddha while others shouted out their names or their family names to him; others just kept silent and sat down. Many in the crowd were curious; did the great ascetic place himself under the tutelage of Kassapa of Uruvela, or had Kassapa placed himself under the instruction of the Buddha? The Buddha, of course, understood what was going on in the minds of the crowd and turned to the venerable Kassapa and said, "What knowledge have you gained, you who at one time were called 'the emaciated one' that has led you to give up both the ritual implements and the performing of ritual fire sacrifices?"

Kassapa arose from his seat and arranged his robe over one shoulder and said, "The Lord is my teacher and I am his pupil. I have seen the obstacles to perfection and therefore no longer delight in fire sacrifices." The Buddha knew that the crowd now realized that it was Kassapa that had placed himself under the instruction of the enlightened one. He stood up and spoke to the multitude about the Doctrine and obtained the knowledge that whatever is subject to the law of Dependent Origination is subject also to the condition of cessation. And as a result of this knowledge of the Doctrine, vast numbers of the crowd declared themselves to be lay followers of the Buddha, his teaching, and the order.

King Bimbisara, who had also seen the truth of the Doctrine, crossing over uncertainty and doubt, leaned toward the Buddha and said: "Many years ago when I was a prince I made five wishes. My first wish was that I become a king. I then wished that the Lord might visit my kingdom and wished thirdly that I would be able to pay my respects to him at the time of his visit. I then wished that he would teach the Doctrine and my fifth wish was that I would understand it. All five of my wishes have now been fulfilled. Now that I have taken refuge in the Buddha, the Doctrine, and the community, may I be accepted as a lay disciple gone for refuge from this day forward for as long as life lasts? Might the Lord consent to take a meal with me tomorrow together with the fraternity of monks that are with him?" As usual the Buddha consented by remaining silent. The king, understanding this acceptance of his invitation, rose from his seat, respectfully saluted the Buddha, passed round him with his right side toward him, and went back to town.

The meal was prepared, and when the time arrived in the forenoon the king sent an announcement stating, "It is time, Lord, the meal is ready." The Buddha, together with the vast number of monks, started out for the town with Sakka, the chief of all the Gods, who had transformed himself into a young and handsome Brahmin, out front shouting to the crowd that he who they found good-looking and charming was the attendant of the Buddha in this world.

After the meal Bimbisara began to think about where the Enlightened One could stay that would be neither too far from the town nor too near, suitable for coming and going, but accessible to all the people who would want to see him, a place that would not be too crowded during the day, but also not exposed to noise and smells at night, hidden from the people and well fitted for the life of renouncers. The king concluded that there was only one place that fit all these requirements: the Bamboo Grove. He then thought, "Suppose I give the Bamboo Grove, a pleasure park, to the order of the monks with the awakened one at its head?" He decided to do it. The king sealed the donation by pouring water over the Buddha's hands into a ceremonial bowl made of gold, saying, "May I, Lord, give this Bamboo Grove to the order of monks with the awakened one at its head?" The Buddha remained silent as this acceptance of the gift transferred great merit to the king.

At that time Sanjaya, one of the most popular ascetics, with some two hundred students, lived in Rajagaha. Two of his students, Sariputta and Moggallana, were without doubt the best and brightest of them all. They were close friends and spent much time together. One day they agreed that whoever first attained liberation from the perils of existence would teach that knowledge to the other.

One morning Sariputta, on his daily alms route, saw Assaji one of the five matted-hair radical ascetics who joined Buddha in the Deer Park. Sariputta was struck by Assaji's comportment. There was something about his bearing, the way he walked, the way he kept his eyes to the ground in front of him, that made Sariputta want to meet him. Etiquette stopped Sariputta from interrupting Assaji's morning ritual for gathering alms. He waited until Assaji finished his route and then asked him, "Friend, whom do you follow in renouncing the world? Who is your teacher, whose Doctrine do you accept?" Assaji told him that it was the great ascetic, the son of the Sakya king. Sariputta then asked him about the Doctrine, but Assaji replied that since he had only recently become ordained he could not explain the Doctrine in detail, but he could perhaps give a brief description of its meaning. Sariputta told him that that would be fine. So Assaji said, "Of all existent elements which have a cause, of these the Perfect One has told the cause as well their cessation. This is the Doctrine of the Great Sage." When Sariputta heard this paraphrase of the Doctrine he immediately understood its truth about the cessation of all suffering that had remained unknown for many aeons of world cycles in the past.

Sariputta hurried to meet his friend, Moggallana, to tell him the good news. When Moggallana saw him coming, he knew that Sariputta had obtained the knowledge of liberation. Sariputta told him about his meeting with Assaji, and they agreed to go find the Buddha and become his students. As they headed for the grove Moggallana suddenly said, "Wait, friend! These 250 wanderers are staying here because of us, looking to us for guidance. Let us consult with them so that they may do what they think is right." The ascetics, hearing what Sariputta and Moggallana were about to do, said, "Look, we are here because of you, we look to you for advice, therefore if you go to the Buddha for learning, we will all go with you."

Sariputta and Moggallana then decided to tell Sanjaya what they were about to do. Sanjaya pleaded with them not to go, saying, "No, friends, do not go; we three will look after this group." Sariputta and Moggallana asked him a second and third time to come with them, but Sanjaya refused. Together with the 250 renouncers they headed for the Bamboo Grove to meet the Buddha. At that moment Sanjaya became violently ill and vomited hot blood on the earth. As the Buddha saw the large group approaching the grove, he told his monks, "The companions are coming; they shall be my most competent and distinguished disciples." The two friends approached the Buddha and asked for ordination. The Buddha said, "Come, monks, well taught is the Doctrine, lead the life that attains the complete extinction of suffering."

The rainy season was about to break open, and the Buddha decided to stay at the Bamboo Grove. As he settled in for the rainy season, the Buddha received a visitor from his home town called Kapilavatthu. Kaludayin had known the Buddha as a friend from their boyhood days. In fact, they were both born on the same day. Kaludayin was the son of one of King Suddodana's ministers, and the king requested of him that he go find the Buddha and persuade him to return for a visit. Before he made this request, Suddhodana had sent several expeditions out to find the Buddha, but in each instance the delegates, awed by the speech of the great sage, had become monks rather than bringing the Buddha back home! Kaludayin agreed to search for the Buddha under one condition: that if he found him and persuaded him to return home for a visit that he would then be allowed to enter the ascetic community as an ordained monk. The king replied, "Do whatever you will, just send me back my son!"

When Kaludayin found the Buddha, he also became a renouncer and with great skill created a context for the moment when he would try and persuade the Buddha to make the trip back home. He described their days together as young boys and became quite lyrical in his description of the countryside, doing his best to make the Buddha homesick for the land of his youth. At the appropriate time Kaludayin suggested the trip, and the Buddha finally consented to return home after the rainy season. Kaludayin was delighted and started back to Kapilavatthu with good news for the king.

9

Rules, Rules, and More Rules

The ordination of over two hundred monks into Buddha's community of ascetics had caused a great stir in Rajagaha. In fact, many of the younger men in the merchant and warrior castes enthusiastically followed the ascetics and became renouncers of the householder's life. As is usually the case in such a situation, not everyone in the town was happy with the continued growth of the ascetic community in the Bamboo Grove. For example, not all the citizens were pleased with the number of monks making their begging rounds every morning, standing silently before their homes with begging pots in hand. Moreover, many residents became angry and accused the Buddha of causing fathers to lose their sons, turning wives into widows, and destroying whole families. Upon hearing these complaints, the Buddha told his disciples to respond by saying, "Verily great heroes, Truthfinders, lead by what is true Doctrine; who will then complain, murmur at the wise who lead by teaching the truth?" As he predicted, the noisy complaints died down in seven days. Nevertheless, the Buddha rebuked those monks who behaved badly and established new rules for the proper wearing of robes, the decorum for receiving alms, and the etiquette and relations to be observed between monks, preceptors, and novices.

Now at this time disturbances appeared on the borders of the kingdom of Magadha, and King Bimbisara commanded his generals to go and search out the problem. When the order came for the army to deploy, some of the distinguished warriors reflected upon their action, saying, "Although we delight in battle we do evil, and this produces great demerit." Catching sight of the monks, it occurred to them that these ascetics, the sons of the Buddha, were indeed virtuous and led a holy life. They sought the truth and kept the precepts of morality. If they joined the monks, they would refrain from doing evil and do what was good. They then approached the monks and asked for ordination, and the monks accepted them.

The soldiers were soon missed, and the generals demanded an explanation for their absence. When told that they had all been ordained into the Buddha's order of ascetics, the generals were quite perplexed and reported the situation to the king. Bimbisara, in turn, asked the chief ministers of justice, "What punishment does someone deserve who ordains a person in the king's service?" "Sir," they replied, "such a one should have his head cut off. Those that recite should have their tongues torn out, and those who form the ascetic group should have half their ribs broken."

The king headed for the Bamboo Grove to find the Buddha. Seating himself at a respectful distance, he said, "Lord, there are unbelieving kings who would harm the monks even for a trifling matter. It would be well if the master did not let someone in the king's service become ordained." The Buddha responded with a well-formed talk about the Doctrine that gladdened the heart of the king, who then departed, keeping his right side toward the Buddha. The Buddha then addressed the monks, saying, "Let no one, monks, who is in the royal service receive ordination. Anyone who confers ordination on such a person will henceforth be guilty of an offense."

Now at that time in Rajagaha a group of seventeen boys were very close friends, and one of them named Upali was their leader. One night his parents began to discuss his future and wondered how he would live a life of ease when they died. Perhaps, they thought, if they sent him to school to learn how to write he would then live well and not be in want upon their death. But then it occurred to them that if he learned how to write, his fingers would become cramped and painful. Well, they thought, what if we send him to learn mathematics? They quickly concluded that he would end up with severe chest pains in such a career. They also dismissed the idea of sending him to learn accounting and economics, since this would only lead to sore eyes, if not blindness. It then hit them all of a sudden. "What about becoming an ascetic? Just outside of town in the Bamboo Grove there exists this large company of monks, sons of the Buddha. They are pleasant in conduct, have good meals, good beds, and shelter. If Upali were to join them, become ordained, he would surely live a life of ease and not be in want when we die."

All this time Upali was in the next room and had overheard the entire conversation. He ran out of the house and gathered his group together to tell them what he had heard. When he had finished with the story, Upali said, "Let's do it. Let's become sons of the Buddha." All of the boys answered, "If you do it, we will become ordained also." The boys each went to their own parents and said, "Please let me go into homelessness, let me become a renouncer, a son of the Buddha." And all the parents agreed, thinking, "These boys all want to do the same thing, how marvelous that they are all bent on doing what is good." With the parents' consent the boys headed for the grove and asked the monks to ordain them. The monks ordained them all.

Just before dawn the boys awoke. It had been a long time since they had last eaten, and they were quite hungry. Looking around, they found nothing to eat and began to cry out, "Give us milk, give us some food, we are starving!" Hearing this, the monks rushed over to them and said, "Wait, brothers, until daylight. If there is any food around you will eat, and if not you will then go out for alms." The young monks would have none of this and began to throw their bedding around the room, pissing on it, and yelling, "Give us milk, give us food, we are starving!"

Meanwhile, the Buddha as usual had arisen in the night and had heard this commotion just before daylight. He asked Ananda, "Ananda, what in the world was going on last night? I thought I heard noisy young boys yelling." Ananda told him what had happened. The Buddha then called for a gathering of the monks and said, "Is it true, monks, that some of you knowingly conferred ordination on youngsters under twenty years of age?" The monks confessed that they had, answering, "It is true, Lord."

The Buddha rebuked them, saying, "How stupid can you be to ordain young boys less than twenty years of age? Such youngsters cannot endure coldness and heat, hunger and thirst, the bite of insects, the injury of storms and sunstroke, the bite of reptiles. They cannot take abusive or offensive language, or suffer bodily pains." After delivering a lecture on the Doctrine he concluded his lesson by saying, "Monks, let no one knowingly confer ordination on a person under twenty years of age. He who does this is to be treated according to the rules."

As time passed, more rules were created for the governance of the ascetic order. In most cases they were established because of grievances from householders who took care that the order remained pure for the sake of gaining merit from giving gifts. As the cases arose, the Buddha announced rules that prohibited the ordination of slaves, of persons with various diseases and deformities, of thieves, deserters from the army, debtors, and murderers.

The rules also covered the acceptance into the order of nonhuman beings. For example, once when a large assembly of monks was settled in the grove a serpent, aggrieved and ashamed of his birth as a serpent, thought how he might best be released from this status and obtain the nature of being human. He immediately thought of the ascetics of the Buddha, how they led a virtuous and peaceful life, speaking the truth and living the precepts of morality. "If I could become ordained," he thought, "I could quickly be released from being a serpent and obtain human nature." Then the serpent in the shape of a youth went to the monks and requested ordination, which was conferred upon him. He was given a preceptor, and they lived at the far end of the grove near its boundary. Late one night his preceptor arose for a walk, and the serpent thought that now he was alone he was safe from discovery and fell asleep. He immediately turned into his natural shape, and the whole cell in which he lived was filled with the serpent's body; his coils hung out of the windows. Upon his return the preceptor saw the whole cell filled with the serpent's body and cried out, terrified. Awakened by the scream, the monks came running as the preceptor pointed toward the coils protruding out of the windows. The serpent also awoke from the noise and sat down on his seat. The monks said, "Who are you, friend?" "I am a serpent, sirs." "Why have you done such a thing?" they replied. Then the serpent told them his story, and they quickly ran and told the Buddha all of what they had seen and heard.

Once again the Buddha ordered an assembly in which he told the serpent, "You serpents are not capable of any understanding or growth in the Doctrine. Go away and observe the fast days and you will quickly be freed from birth as a serpent and reclaim human status." Then the Enlightened One addressed the monks, saying, "Monks, there are two instances in which a serpent manifests his true nature. The first is when he indulges in intercourse with a female serpent and the second is when he falls asleep. Monks, an animal should not be ordained; it if is ordained, it should be expelled."

On another occasion monks ordained a certain man and left him alone. As he traveled back to the monastery, the newly ordained monk met his former wife, who asked him whether he had indeed embraced the life of a renouncer. "Yes," he replied, "I have embraced the ascetic life, but it is difficult as an ascetic to obtain sex; come, let us have sex together." And they did. As a consequence he was late on arrival at the monastery, and the monks, being curious, asked, "How is it brother, that you are so late?" The monk confessed the whole story to the ascetics, who, as usual, immediately told the matter to the Buddha.

The Buddha once again assembled all the monks and told them that from henceforth all newly ordained monks should have a companion with them and that they should be informed of the four prohibitions: a monk who is ordained must (1) abstain from all sexual intercourse even with an animal as long as his life lasts; violation of the rule demands expulsion from the community of monks; (2) abstain from what is not given to him, and from theft, even down to a blade of grass as long as his life lasts; violation demands expulsion; (3) abstain from intentionally destroying the life of any living thing, from a human being, down to a worm or ant; any violation of this rule demands expulsion; (4) abstain from attributing to himself any superhuman condition that he does not possess but claims due to bad intentions or out of covetousness. Such a one is like a palm tree from which the top sprout has been cut off and cannot grow again.

One day while the Buddha and Ananda were walking through the residences of the monks, they discovered one who had fallen into his own excrement because of a severe bout of dysentery. When they asked him what his problem was, he told them about his sickness. The Buddha then said, "But, monk, don't you have anyone who tends you?" The monk answered, "I don't, Lord, because due to my illness I am no use to the monks." The Buddha told Ananda to bring water so that they could bathe him. They washed him and put him down on a couch. Then the Buddha assembled the monks and asked them if they were aware that one of their brothers was sick in one of the residence halls. They answered that they did know about it. The Buddha then asked them if anyone attended him, and they answered that no one attended him because he was of no use to them.

"Monks," the Buddha replied, "you have no mother or father who might attend you. If you do not take care of each other, then who will tend you? Whoever wishes to attend me should also take care of the sick, and do so without thought of gain, with competence in medicine, knowing what is beneficial and without revulsion to excrement, urine, or vomit, but with delight and with the purpose to gladden the sick with conversations about the Doctrine."

While staying at Rajagaha the Buddha had not prescribed any rules regarding retreats during the rainy season. The people were very annoyed and angry, saying, "How can the ascetics travel during the rainy season? As they walk they crush the green herbs and destroy vegetable life and all manner of small living things. If the birds make nests in the summit of trees and retire during the rainy season, why don't the ascetics do the same and retire for the rainy season, arranging places for themselves to live?"

Now some monks overheard this criticism and anger and returned to the grove and told the Buddha, who then announced that henceforth all monks would enter the retreat prescribed for the rainy season. They were to look after their residence, perform all rituals, and provide food and water for themselves. This rule generated cases requiring more rules to cover situations in which attendance of the sick, acceptance of gifts of land, encounters with famine, and the like called for a departure from the monastery. Moreover, how long should the departure last? The Buddha settled all such cases by establishing rules responding to them. For example, the length of time spent away from the community during the rainy season was set at seven days.

In the meantime, a number of other ascetic groups were gathering together on the fourteenth and eighth days of the half month, that is, the time of the waxing and waning moon, in order to rehearse and learn the Doctrines of their community. King Bimbisara was well aware of this. One day while meditating in seclusion he thought about this practice and realized that people went to hear about these Doctrines and were filled with favor toward both the teaching and the community, which then gained more members. The king then thought that it might be a good idea if the Buddha's ascetic community also met regularly during the month, thereby gaining interest as well as members both as monks and householders.

The king knew that the Buddha was staying at one of his favorite spots on Mount Vultures Peak, west of the Bamboo Grove and the city, and went to see him. He approached him as usual and shared his idea. The Enlightened One immediately accepted the idea and after his regular session with the monks told them that from henceforth they were to "assemble together on the fourteenth and eighth days of the half month to rehearse and teach the Doctrine." The two days were to be known as "observance days," when the monks would gather together and perform the "ritual of liberation."

The "ritual of liberation" would contain all the precepts that the Buddha had given them, and the recitation of these rules would mark the "observance day" in the ritual life of the monks. If no one had violated the rules, they should remain silent as they were recited. In the same manner, if anyone had violated the rule, they should confess it and accept the proper punishment. The Buddha informed his disciples that the "observance days" and the "ritual of liberation" would become regular rituals of purification for the community of monks.

10

The Buddha Goes Home

With the earth refreshed with monsoon rains, the Buddha decided that it was time to keep his promise to Kaludayin and visit home. It would be a long trip, some three hundred miles. When he arrived at Kapilavatthu along with a great multitude of ascetics, he was directed to Nigrodha Park for his residence. The town folk, hearing that he had arrived, started for the grove but were stopped short by a proclamation from the king stating, "No one is to go to the grove before me."

On his way to the grove, the king met a group of monks with alms bowls and asked his ministers, "Who are these renouncers?" "They belong to the prince, sir," they replied. This really troubled the king. "Had my son not renounced his royal position and left home he would be a universal king of the four quarters, having the whole world as his domain. I do not want to see them. Send them all away," he said. Several attempts were made by others, but no one could change the king's mind. Moggallana, possessed of immense powers of the mind, knew that the Buddha was thinking about sending Kaludayin. He went over and told Kaludayin about the Buddha's thoughts. But Kaludayin resisted, saying, "It is very difficult to approach and suggest anything to a king. It is as difficult as approaching a blazing bonfire, a sixty-year-old elephant, or a ferocious lion." Then the Buddha himself replied, "Listen to me, Kaludayin. You are among those who repose in the perfection of merit. You can easily placate the king; you, who have shared so much with the Enlightened One, are the only one that can do it. There is no one else."

Kaludayin consented and in an instant appeared hovering over the king at the height of a palm tree and recounted the many noble qualities of the Buddha. King Suddhodana was pleased with what he both saw and heard, and told one of his counselors to prepare a proclamation bidding "all Sakyans, to come with me and meet Gotama." The proclamation was announced at all the crossroads and marketplaces in the city of Kapilavatthu.

And so, with the roar of drums, the blare of trumpets, and great royal pomp the king in his chariot together with a huge crowd headed for the Banyan Grove to see the Enlightened One. As they approached the grove the Buddha faced a difficult dilemma. "If, on the one hand," he thought, "I welcome them all sitting down they will think, 'How can he who claims the perfection of wisdom refuse to stand and greet his father, the king, who is old and venerable?'" If he refused to stand and greet his father they would certainly take that gesture as an insult. On the other hand, it is simply impossible for a Perfected One to stand up and greet others. Seeing his father and the crowd coming closer and knowing the pride of them all, he rose up into the air to the height of a man and took a long walk without touching the ground with his feet. King Suddhodana observed this from a distance and was thrilled with wonder at such a sight. The prince was indeed a superhuman agent.

The king rode on in his carriage as far as the road allowed, and then proceeded on foot to the grove. Approaching the Buddha together with his women and escort, he bowed his head and said, "Here for the third time I bow at your feet. I did so at the time of prophecy when you were born and when the shadow of the rose-apple tree stood still for you, and now again I do so."

Then the Buddha performed an extraordinary set of magical acts known as the "magical acts in pairs." First he appeared standing in the air at the height of a palm tree. While the lower part of his body was in flames, he shot cold water from the fingers of his hands, and while the upper part of his body was in flames, he shot cold water from his feet. Next he transformed himself into a bull. The bull vanished in the east and then appeared in the west. It vanished in the west and appeared in the east. It vanished in the north and appeared in the south. It vanished in the south and appeared in the north.

Both the king and the crowd were overwhelmed by these magical acts, and when they were all seated a large rain cloud poured down a shower. Those who wished to get wet got wet, but not a drop fell on those who did not wish to get wet. Seeing this feat, the crowd was awed, shouting, "Bravo" and "It is a miracle! A miracle!" And when they finished listening to his discourse they all rose from their seats and saluted him. However, not one of them, not the king, not his ministers, or a member of the crowd said, "Accept a meal from us tomorrow" before they left.

The next morning the Buddha, along with his disciples, entered the streets of Kapilavatthu to beg for alms. The town, hearing that Gotama was going about begging for food, threw open the windows of the houses and watched with curiosity as the monks passed by. The mother of Rahula herself watched and said, "My lord, who once went about this city in a gilded carriage, in regal splendor, now goes about begging for food, carrying a begging bowl with shaven hair and beard, clad in yellow robes; does this really become him?"

Upon hearing what was taking place on the streets outside the palace, the king became extremely agitated and left the palace in great haste. Gathering up the folds of his robes, he ran out and stood facing the Enlightened One and said, "Why do you bring such disgrace upon us? Why are you going about begging for alms? Are you trying to prove we cannot feed so many monks?"

"This is our life, our tradition," said the master.

"Not so!" replied the king. "Our life is royal, we belong to the warrior caste, and our ancestors can be traced to the first king among human beings."

"That may be," said the Buddha, "but my lineage begins with Dipankara and others down to Kassapa. These together with thousands of other Buddhas have begged their daily food and lived as renouncers." Standing in the middle of the street and facing the king, the Buddha said, "Rise up! Forsake indolence, lead a life of righteousness, do not practice misdeeds, and live happily in both this world and the next."

Upon hearing these words the king took the Buddha's bowl and led the company of monks to the palace and served them all a sumptuous meal. And when the meal was over, all the women came and paid their respects to the Awakened One, all, that is, except the mother of Rahula, who told her attendants, "If there is any virtue in me, my Lord will himself come to me, and when he does I will pay him homage."

The Buddha gave his bowl to the king to carry and, with Moggallana and Sariputta, headed for the apartment of the king's daughter-in-law, telling them that nothing should be said to her when she paid her respects in whatever manner she desired. He then sat down on the seat prepared for him. She entered immediately and grasped the Buddha's feet, laying her head on them, and paid homage to him. The king then told the Buddha of her virtues. The Buddha replied that this did not surprise him, since she had the king as her guardian and teacher. He then recited the birth story of a former Buddha, got up from his seat, and departed.

On the third day of his visit the city celebrated the consecration, housewarming, and marriage of prince Nanda, the king's son and the Buddha's half brother. The Buddha wanted to ordain him and gave Nanda his begging bowl as he departed from the celebration. The bride, seeing her young groom going with him, cried out, "My Lord, where are you going! Come back soon!" But Nanda, not having the courage to tell the Buddha to take his bowl back, followed him all the way to the hermitage in the grove. And the Buddha ordained Nanda even without his explicit request to become a renouncer.

On the seventh day of his visit home the mother of Rahula dressed him in his finest clothes. When she spotted the Buddha coming on his begging route, she told Rahula, "Look, child, at that monk with a golden complexion, he is your father. He owned great treasures, but from the time he renounced home we have not seen him. Go to him and ask him for your inheritance. Say, I am your son, when I am consecrated I will become a Universal Ruler. I have need of my inheritance, give me the treasure; a son is heir to his father's property. The young lad went to the Awakened One, and with affection growing as he neared him, stood by him and said among other such statements, "O monk, even your shadow is pleasant."

The Buddha did not turn him away. After he had finished his meal and the donors had participated in the merit that is bestowed upon householders who give gifts, the master got up and departed. The young prince followed him, saying, "O monk, give me my inheritance! Please give me my inheritance!" The Buddha knew that the wealth and property he was asking for would perish in its use, bringing nothing but vexation and unhappiness. "I will give him the wealth I obtained under the tree of enlightenment thus making him the heir of an inheritance that does not perish." He then said to Sariputta, "Now Sariputta, ordain Rahula."

The king went into profound grieving when he heard about this; he had lost a son to the life of renouncers and now he had lost a grandson! Unable to bear his grief any longer, he requested a favor from the Buddha; "Lord, if it pleases you, do not receive a son into the order without the consent of his father and mother." The Buddha granted the favor, and the king on hearing the Buddha's recitation attained the permanent status of one who will attain liberation, called "the fruit of the nonreturner."

It was time to leave for Rajagaha.

II

The Buddha Receives a Gift and Befriends a King

The Buddha and the community of monks left Kapilavatthu the next day for Rajagaha. On the trip back they stayed at Anupiya, the very first town the Buddha visited after he renounced the world of the householder. What he did not know is that the most distinguished young men of Kapilavatthu had decided to renounce the world in imitation of him and to follow him back to Rajagaha.

Two brothers, Mahanama and Anuruddha, were left behind. Anuruddha, who most agreed had never done a day's work in his life, had three residences for each of the seasons: one for the cold season, one for the hot season, and another for the rainy season. During the rains he was waited on by women performing music, and he never came down from the upper story of his residence during that time.

His brother, Mahanama, felt troubled by the fact that he and his brother were the only two who did not follow the other elite young men to imitate the Buddha and become renouncers. Their family was the only family that had no one who left the householder life for the homeless state. He then thought, "Since all the others have done so, let one of us renounce the world." He then went over to his brother and told him his thoughts and said, "So either you go or I will do so."

Anuruddha said, "I am far too delicate, too sensitive. It's just impossible that I should go from the life of a householder into a homeless life. You do it." "Come on, dear Anuruddha," replied his brother, "you don't really know the first thing about being a householder. Let me tell you about what it is really like. First, you have to get your fields plowed. When that is done you have to seed them. When that is done you have to irrigate them, then weed them, and then get the crops harvested. Then you have to get transportation for the crops, arrange them in bundles, separate the straw, and winnow the chaff. And when that is accomplished you have to start all over again the next year, and the same thing all over again the year after that. The work is never done; one never sees the end of labor. Death itself does not put an end to work."

"Then you take over the duties and I will go forth from the household into the life of the renouncer," replied Anuruddha, and left to get permission from his mother. He tried three times to get her consent, but she resisted each time. Then she thought of a solution that would save her son from leaving home; she was certain that kings and princes would never renounce the world. So she told Anuruddha that if he could get his royal friend Bhaddiya to renounce with him, she would consent.

Anuruddha was delighted and quickly went over to Bhaddiya's palace and said, "My renunciation of the world, my dear friend, is being obstructed by you. If you consent to go with me, I have my mother's consent."

"No problem," said Bhaddiya, "let that obstruction be removed! On second thought, why don't you renounce the world as you wish. I just can't give up the householder life. Ask me anything else and I will do it, but not this." Anuruddha went through the whole argument once again, and Bhaddiya said, "Fine, wait for seven years and we will do it together." They began to haggle: six? five? one? seven months? At last the royal friend said, "Wait for seven days, my friend, while I hand over the kingdom to my sons and brothers." "Seven days is not very long; I will wait," came the reply.

And so Bhaddiya, Anuruddha, Ananda, Bhagu, Kimbila, and Devadatta, old friends who had always played together, together with Upali the barber, headed out of town to catch up with the Buddha. After going some distance and passing into another territory, they took off their ornaments and tied them up in their robes. They then turned to Upali and said, "Turn back for home and take these with you, they are yours." As he headed back home it suddenly dawned on Upali that the Sakyans of Kapilavatthu might be very angry when they saw him, thinking, "This is the one who persuaded the elite young men of our town to become ascetics." Why, they might even kill him. "But then," he thought, "if these young men are on their way to become renouncers, why shouldn't I?"

Upali put his bundles in a tree, saying, "Let whoever finds this take it as a gift, it's yours." When the Sakyan youths saw Upali heading toward them they all said, "What have you come back for, Upali?" He told them of his decision and what he had done with the bundles of ornaments. They all agreed that he was right, the Sakyans were indeed fierce people, and took Upali with them to find the Enlightened One and become ordained in the town of Anupiya. They all arrived at Rajagaha just in time for the rainy season.

Now it just so happened that at that time a very wealthy merchant by the name of Anathapindika had traveled from Savatthi to Rajagaha to meet his sister and brother-in-law, who was a banker. When he arrived he found the banker hard at work preparing a meal for the Buddha and his monks; the preparation was so elaborate that at first he thought it was for a wedding or the king. When he found out who it was for, he decided to visit the Buddha the next day. He was so excited about the visit that he woke up three times during the night thinking it was daybreak.

When daybreak finally came he headed for the grove. The Buddha, who was pacing to and fro, saw him coming and sat down on an appropriate seat and said, "Come, Sudatta." Anathapindika knew immediately that the Buddha was not one of the average ascetics roaming the territory for the simple reason that no one in this area knew or called him by his informal name. He was delighted and said, "I hope, Lord, that you are living at ease." And the Buddha replied, "Yes, always at ease, having attained liberation and perfect happiness. Not defiled by lust, cooled, having destroyed all clinging, averting the heart's cares, tranquil he lives, having won peace of mind." The Buddha then talked to Anathapindika about giving, the moral life, heaven, the perils of vanity, and the advantages of renunciation.

When the Buddha saw that Anathapindika was ready, he proclaimed that which is the center of the Buddha's teaching, that is to say, suffering, its origin, its cessation, and the path leading to the cessation of suffering. Anathapindika saw very clearly that whatsoever arises is liable to cessation. Having crossed over doubt, put away certainty, having attained the knowledge without another's help, he said, "Excellent! Excellent, Lord! I myself go to the Buddha for refuge, to the Doctrine for refuge and the order of monks for refuge. May the Lord accept me as a householder, as one who, from this day forward and for as long as life endures, has taken refuge in him. And may the Master consent to accept at my hand tomorrow's meal for himself and for his order of monks." The Buddha, by his silence, granted his consent. When Anathapindika understood by this that his request had been granted, he got up, bowed down, and keeping the Buddha on his right side, he passed him and departed.

The news of Anathapindika's conversion and the Enlightened One's acceptance of his invitation to a meal quickly spread throughout the town. Aware that he was a stranger in town, the womenfolk, as well as his brother-in-law and even the king, offered to help him put the meal together. Anathapindika

politely declined all the offers for help, saying, "Thank you, but I have suffi-
cient means for preparing and serving the meal."

He did indeed prepare and serve a sumptuous meal. And when they had
eaten he sat down at a respectful distance and said, "May the Lord consent to
spend the rainy season at Savatthi together with the order of monks."

"Perhaps it might be best to remind you that all Perfected Ones take pleasure in solitude," replied the Buddha.

"I fully understand that," said Anathapindika.

The Awakened One then gave his usual discourse on the Doctrine, arose
from his, seat and left.

Anathapindika completed his business and headed for his home at
Savatthi. As he set off, he told people he met that a Buddha had appeared in
the world and that he had invited him to visit Savatthi, and that he would use
this very highway to get there. He requested that since the journey was a long
one, about four hundred miles, they build rest homes along the way. Trusting
his word, they did as they were told.

When Anathapindika arrived home, he began at once to look for a proper
piece of land for the new monastery. The land should be near the town, convenient for coming and going, easily accessible for everyone who wanted to visit
the Master. It should also be peaceful during the day, and quiet especially at
night, protected from winds, hidden from people, fit for renouncers who meditate. After looking around, he found one piece of property that met all the conditions he was looking for; it was none other than Prince Jeta's lovely garden.
He met the prince and told him that he would like to purchase the pleasure
garden in order to build a monastery on it. The prince told him that the garden
was not for sale, "Not even for the total sum of money it would take if you covered the garden's ground with it."

"Fine," said Anathapindika, "I'll buy it for that price."

"Not so," said the prince. "As I said, it is not for sale."

They then took the dispute to court to determine whether a sale had been
offered or not. The justices determined that the prince had indeed established
a price whether he meant it literally or not. Anathapindika then had the garden covered in gold coins and found that the amount did not quite cover a
space near the gateway. Prince Jeta now realized this had to be an extraordinary occurrence for someone to lavish so much gold and said, "That's enough.
It will do. Let me give the uncovered space as a gift to the renouncers." The
wealthy merchant built a magnificent monastery that included cells, attendance halls, storage sheds, wells, bathrooms, terraces for pacing to and fro, as
well as lotus ponds.

When the Buddha arrived, the merchant asked him how he should transfer the new monastery to the order. "Householder," he said, "give it to the Order of Ascetics of the four points of the compass, whether now present or hereafter to arrive." Pouring water from a golden bowl over the Buddha's hands, the merchant dedicated the monastery, saying, "I give Jetavana to the Order of Ascetics of the four points of the compass with the Buddha at the head, and to all from every direction now present or hereafter to come." The Buddha accepted the gift with a discourse on the advantages of such secluded places. The dedication festival then began and lasted for several months. The monastery became the Buddha's favorite residence.

The king of Kosala lived in Savatthi and soon became one of the regular visitors of Jetavana. He and the Buddha were about the same age and saw each other often. One day King Pasenadi visited the park and asked the Buddha whether he claimed the attainment of supreme enlightenment. The Buddha replied, "If there be anyone, Sir, to whom such enlightenment might be rightly attributed, it is I. I verily am perfectly and supremely enlightened."

"Really," the king responded. "I know renouncers and Brahmins who also have disciples, who teach well-known Doctrines and are esteemed by many people. Yet when I ask them the same question, they do not claim to have perfect enlightenment. How can this be? Compared to them, Master Gotama is a young man, a novice."

"You should know, my dear king, that there are four creatures who are not to be rejected or despised because they are young. Who are they? They are a noble prince, a snake, a fire, and a renouncer. A noble prince may take revenge once consecrated, a snake may bite when young, a fire burns at any time, and a renouncer is without children, wealth, or heirs regardless of when he is harmed."

When the Buddha spoke these things, the king became enlightened as if a lamp had lit the darkness, and he said, "I, even I, Lord, betake myself to the Buddha as my refuge, to the Doctrine and the order as my refuge. Accept me as a follower, as one who from this day forward as long as life endures has taken refuge in it." The news that the king of Kosala had become a lay disciple of the Buddha and his community spread rapidly and became the topic of discussion throughout the realm; after all, it was the second-most-powerful kingdom after that of Magadha, and King Bimbisara.

From that day onward the king and the Buddha met frequently. On many occasions King Pasenadi would visit the Buddha around noon after a morning of reflection on a problem or puzzle he had been thinking about through the night. For example, he once asked the Buddha whether any born thing lives without decay and death. The Buddha told him that there is no such life. One evening as they were sitting in the eastern portico catching the evening breeze after a very hot day, the king asked, "To whom should gifts be given?" The Buddha told him that gifts should be given to whomever it pleases us most. The king was not satisfied and said, "But to whom does a gift bear the most fruit?" "Ah," replied the Buddha, "this is a very different kind of question, much more complex. A gift bears much more fruit if given to a virtuous person. Let me ask you a question. Suppose you were at war and you were enlisting men for the army. A young man arrives, noble but untrained, unskilled, timid, one who would run away. Would you keep that man? Would he be any good to you?"

"Of course not, Lord, I would not keep that man."

"Would you, sir, say the same thing if the man were a Brahmin, or a merchant's son, or the son of a working-class man?"

"I would, yes, indeed," answered the king.

"But what would you do if the youth in question belonged to any of the castes but was well trained, an expert, bold and courageous? Would you enlist that man?"

"I certainly would," said the king.

"Even so, sir, is the case of a man, no matter what his caste, who has left the world and exchanged the domestic for the homeless life. He has abolished five qualities and is possessed of five qualities. What five has he abolished? Desire for sensuous pleasures, ill will, laziness, worry, and doubt. What five does he possess? He possesses morality of the ascetic, proficiency in concentration, insight, liberation, and the knowledge belonging to one who is disciplined. Given to him, a gift bears much fruit."

On other occasions the king received comfort from the Buddha on the death of his grandmother and his beloved wife, Mallika. They also discussed the Doctrine of karma, that all living things are born, die, and are reborn in endless cycles of birth, death, and rebirth.

But the Buddha also saw fit to give him advice on a more personal level as well. Everyone knew that the king was overweight. He was, to put it bluntly, quite fat. He simply ate too much. One day after he had eaten a large quantity of curried rice he headed off, huffing and puffing, to visit the Buddha. The Buddha could hear him coming, and after he settled down told him, "Those who live a mindful life observe how much food they eat. Doing so increases their power of sense, and softly old age comes nigh, their days prolonged."

The king turned around and said to his nephew, who had come with him and was standing behind him, "Come, dear prince, learn what the Master has just said and recite it to me when you bring me my dinner. I will give you a hundred coins as a daily tip in perpetuity."

"So be it, your majesty," responded Sudassana, and carried out the king's wishes from then on.

One evening while staying at Savatthi in Jeta Grove the Buddha had a long talk with one of the monks, who was seriously questioning what the Buddha taught. The monk, while meditating alone, recalled the ten undecided questions that the Buddha asserted were irrelevant in the quest for wisdom and liberation. The questions the Buddha rejected were:

1. Is the world eternal?
2. Is the world not eternal?
3. Is the world finite?
4. Is the world infinite?
5. Is the self (or soul) the same as the body?
6. Is the self one thing and the body another?
7. Does the Perfect One exist after death?
8. Does the Perfect One not exist after death?
9. Does the Perfect One both exist and not exist after death?
10. Does the Perfect one neither exist nor not exist after death?

Pondering this list of questions, the monk decided that he wanted an answer one way or the other, and if he did not get one he would leave the Ascetic Order and return to the life of a householder. That evening he approached the Buddha, and after paying homage to him, sat down and asked him for a response to each one of the questions. Moreover, if the Buddha did not know the answers, it would seem that the straightforward response would be to simply say so.

The Buddha, as usual, responded with a question. "Did I ever say to you, come, live the renouncer's life with me and I will explain to you whether the world is eternal or not? Did I ever say I would explain to you the ten undetermined questions?" Malunkyaputta confessed that, no, the Buddha had never said that. The Buddha then told him he was misguided, that anyone who says that he would only live the life of a renouncer if the Buddha answered those questions would certainly die without being told the answer. The Buddha then related the following story.

Suppose, Malunkyaputta, a man were wounded by an arrow thickly smeared with poison, and his friends, companions, family, and relatives called a physician to attend the wound. But when the physician arrived to tend the man, he said, "I will not let the physician pull the arrow out until I know from what caste the man came from who wounded me. I also want to know his name and what family he comes from; whether he is tall or short; whether he lived in a town, village, or city; whether he used a longbow or a crossbow; whether the bowstring was made of hemp, reed, or sinew; whether the shaft of the arrow was made of wild or cultivated wood; what kind of feathers were used; and whether the arrow was hoof-tipped, curved, or barbed. This man would not discover these things, and he would surely die. Just so, Malunkyaputta, if anyone demands answers to the ten questions, they will remain unanswered, and meanwhile that person would die.

The Buddha then told the monk that he should remember what the Buddha had declared and left undeclared. Why had he left the ten questions undeclared? Because they are neither beneficial nor belong to the fundamentals of the ascetic life; moreover, they do not lead to disenchantment, to dispassion, to cessation, peace, and the knowledge and enlightenment that lead to liberation and happiness.

And what have I declared? This is suffering, this is the origin of suffering, this is the cessation of suffering, and this is the way leading to the cessation of suffering. Why have I declared that? Because it is beneficial, fundamental to the renouncer's life, and leads to disenchantment, dispassion, cessation, peace, and the knowledge that leads to enlightenment and liberation. That is why I have declared it. Upon hearing these words, Malunkyaputta was completely satisfied and delighted.

12

Meeting a Murderer, a Visit Home, and a Quick Trip to Heaven

In a few short years the Buddha had traveled hundreds of miles. Literally thousands of men had heard him teach the Doctrine and had renounced the life of the householder to become sons of the Buddha. As the community grew, hundreds of rules were established to govern the life of the layperson and the monk: rules for initiation into the community, ordination, rules for monthly confession, rules for accepting robes and the proper behavior for taking the alms-routes, rules for proper toilet etiquette, eating, bathing, and travel.

The Buddha needed a break from this seemingly twenty-four-hour-a-day life of management, decision making, and counseling.

One day while at the park at Savatthi he gathered the monks together and said, "Monks, I want to dwell in solitude for half a month. I am not to be disturbed by anyone save him alone who brings me my food." At the end of the half month he reported back to the monks, saying, "I have lived just as I did immediately after gaining enlightenment; knowing what is experienced as a result of wrong views, desires, and perceptions, and what is known as a result of right views." He then rehearsed the Four Noble Truths and the Eightfold Path with the monks.

Now at that time there was a notorious murderer in the realm of King Pasenadi whose name was Angulimala, "the garland of fingers." He had murdered many people and wore their fingers around his neck as a garland after vultures had picked the bones dry. Angulimala was a very bright Brahmin. His father had sent him to the university, and he soon became the star pupil of the senior professor on the faculty. His fellow students, quite jealous of him, told the professor that he was having an affair with his wife. Furious, the professor planned his student's ruin and told him that the honorarium for completing his degree would be one thousand fingers. Angulimala began collecting the fingers by killing people as they passed through the forest.

His mother knew that the king had formed a posse to capture him and begged his father to look for him. Her husband replied, "I will have nothing to do with such a son, let the king do whatever he wants." The mother, loving her son dearly, set out to find him and warn him of the posse. Angulimala was now one finger short of a thousand and vowed to kill the next person he met coming down the road.

The Buddha, having returned from his alms round, set his resting place in order, picked up his outer robe, and headed for the main road. Those who met him warned him not to go any farther because they had heard that Angulimala was lurking somewhere ahead along the highway. The Buddha went on walking in silence. He soon realized that there was no one on the highway; he was alone. Angulimala saw him coming and was simply delighted. "It is too good to be true," he thought. "People have come along this road in groups but still they have fallen into my hands. And now this ascetic is approaching all alone, as if driven by fate. Why not kill him?" He waited until he passed and then followed not far behind.

The Buddha, fully aware of his presence, performed a superhuman act such that even though Angulimala walked as fast as he could, he could not catch up with the Buddha walking at his normal pace. Angulimala thought, "This is indeed a fantastic, marvelous event! I know that I can catch up with a swift chariot and seize it, or even a swift deer, but now walking as fast as I can I cannot catch up with this monk who is walking at his normal pace. What is going on here?" He called out, "Stop, monk! Stop!"

"I have stopped, Angulimala, now you stop too," replied the Buddha.

"That's odd," thought Angulimala, "monks assert truth, yet this ascetic who is still walking says, 'I have stopped, you stop too.'"

"Monk," he cried out, "while still walking you tell me you have stopped; and now, when I have stopped you say I have not stopped. How is it then that you have stopped and I have not?"

"Angulimala, I have stopped forever. I abstain from violence toward all living beings, but you have no restraint toward things that live; that is why I said I have stopped and you have not," replied the Buddha.

Hearing the Doctrine spoken by the Buddha, Angulimala vowed to abstain from violence forever, and throwing his weapons over the cliff he fell upon the

Buddha's feet and begged to join the order. The Buddha accepted him, and that is how Angulimala became a monk.

When they finally returned to Jeta Grove they found the king and his troops searching the area. The Buddha asked the king whether the kingdom was threatened, and Pasenadi replied that he was hunting a violent murderer named Angulimala.

"Great King," Buddha began, "suppose I told you that Angulimala had shaved his hair and beard, put on the yellow robe, and gone forth from the house life into homelessness; that he was abstaining from killing living beings, taking what is not given and from false speech; that he was refraining from eating at night, ate one meal in part of the day, was celibate, virtuous, and of good character. If you met him, how would you treat him?"

The king replied, "We would pay homage to him, rise up for him, invite him to accept robes and almsfood, a resting place, and medicinal requisites. We would protect him."

When the king met Angulimala, he was astounded, and he marveled at how the Enlightened One tames the untamed, brings peace to the unpeaceful, and leads them to liberation. "Venerable sir," he said, "we ourselves could not tame him with force and weapons, yet the Enlightened One has tamed him without force or weapons. We must now depart, for we are very busy and have work to do."

"Do whatever you think is right," replied the Buddha.

The next morning Angulimala went into town on his almsround and witnessed a woman giving birth to a deformed child. The event confirmed the truth of existence as unhappy, and he said to himself, "How living beings are afflicted, oh, how afflicted." Upon returning to the grove he told the Buddha what he had seen and what he thought. The Buddha told him to go into Savatthi and say to the woman, "Sister, since I was born, I do not recall that I have ever intentionally deprived a living being of life. By this truth, may you be well and may your infant be well!"

"Master," he replied, "wouldn't I be telling a deliberate lie? I have intentionally deprived many living beings of life."

"Well, then," said the Buddha, "go into Savatthi and say to the woman, "Sister, since I was born with noble birth, I do not recall that I have ever intentionally deprived a living being of life. By this truth, may you be well and may your infant be well." Angulimala went into town and repeated just those words. As a protective power, monks recite this utterance even to this day for pregnant women close to delivery.

Before long, dwelling alone, withdrawn, and resolute, the venerable Angulimala realized the supreme goal for which monks go forth from the home into homelessness. He knew completely that "birth is destroyed, the holy life has been lived, what has to be done has been done, there is no more coming to any state of being." Angulimala had become one of the perfect monks.

Then one morning he got dressed, took up his alms bowl, and headed into Savatthi. Suddenly someone threw a stick that hit his body, others threw potsherds and stones. With blood streaming from his cut head, his bowl broken and robes torn, he stumbled back to the grove. When the Buddha saw him he said, "Bear it, Brahmin! Bear it! You are living here and now the results of deeds which in the future might have tortured you in hell for many years, for many thousands of years." Angulimala did indeed know that he had done what was to be done, that there is no more becoming; he had won liberation. The Buddha then decided that he would visit Rajagaha once again.

At that time a severe drought, famine, and plague had fallen on the whole area that surrounded Vesali. The stench of the dead had begun to attract hordes of animals into the city gates. After examining the dynasty of the present royal family for seven generations, it was decided that there was nothing illegal to be found in the royal lineage. The king's council concluded that it would be best to call for the Awakened One who teaches the truth for the benefit of all creatures. But they wondered, would he come? Others replied that he would indeed come, because all Buddhas are not only mighty and powerful but also compassionate.

The Buddha, together with five hundred monks, headed toward the river about fifty miles away on a newly prepared road made level and decorated with flowers by the king. Two white parasols were held above the Lord's head, and a residence was prepared at ten-mile intervals to assure a full-scale almsgiving at each resting place. The Buddha and the monks together with the king and his entourage arrived at the river in five days. King Bimbisara had two boats fully decorated with flowers joined together as a flotilla with a platform, and a throne with every kind of jewel prepared for the Buddha. As the world watched, including the deities up to the second level of the heavens, the Buddha took his seat, the monks boarded the boat, and they headed up the river for Vesali.

Traveling about ten miles up the Ganges, they crossed the boundary into Licchavi territory. The king's agents waded into the water to meet them, and at that moment a great cloud, the darkness of whose broad summit was laced with lightning flashes, began to rain down in torrents in the four directions. When the Enlightened One set foot upon the bank a lotus downpour began, and the rain continued to fall until everywhere the water flowed at least waist-deep, and all the corpses were swept into the Ganges until the land was left clean.

It took them three days to reach Vesali. At the end of each day the Licchavi had prepared a residence for the Buddha for proper almsgiving. As they neared the city, Sakka, the ruler of all the gods, heralded by his troop of deities caused most of the animals to flee the city.

As they all approached the city, a messenger informed the Buddha that his father, Suddhodana, was very ill and near death. When the Buddha reached the gate of the city, he stopped and addressed the venerable Ananda. "Learn this Jewel Utterance," he said, "and with the princes of Licchavi perform a 'Protection Ritual' in a procession around the three city walls." The Buddha then delivered the Jewel Utterance, the purpose of which was to cure the city and the people of the plague that had been inflicted on them. Then by means of his superhuman abilities, he flew through the air toward Kapilavatthu to attend to his dying father.

Ananda did what he was told to do. Armed with the "Jewel Protection Utterance," he, along with the princes of the city, proceeded around the whole town sprinkling the ritual water from the Buddha's bowl as he uttered the "Jewel Protection" verse the Buddha had taught him:

> Whatever wealth there is, here or beyond
> Whatever jewels there may be in heaven
> There is none equal to the Perfect One
> The greatest of all jewels is the Buddha
> Through this truth may happiness prevail.

As soon as the words were uttered, those wild animals remaining in the city fled toward the four gates, and the plague was cured. The city was made pure.

In the meantime, the Buddha ministered to his father in Kapilavatthu. Upon hearing the Doctrine, Suddhodana became enlightened on his deathbed and died the next day.

Mahapajapati, his stepmother, soon visited the Buddha while he stayed in the Nigrodha Grove outside the town. She approached him and said that she thought it would be "a good thing if women were also allowed to renounce their homes and enter the homeless life under the Doctrine and discipline of the Perfected One."

"Enough! Let it not please you to think so," he replied. After repeating her request twice more, Mahapajapati left the Buddha in tears on hearing the same response.

After staying in Kapilavatthu for as long as he saw fit, the Buddha, taking his time, headed back for Vesali, where he stayed at the Gabled Hall of the Great Grove.

Mahapajapati cut off her hair, put on a saffron robe, and set out with a number of Sakyan women toward Vesali. In due course she arrived at the grove, covered with dust, her feet swollen; weeping and in tears, she took her place outside and under the main porch. As Ananda approached the grove, he saw Mahapajapati and asked her why she was in such a sorry state and crying. She told him it was because the Buddha did not permit women to renounce their homes and join the ascetic community of the Perfected One.

Ananda went into the place where the Buddha was and asked whether he could sit down, and then told the Buddha what he had just seen and heard. He went on to say that he thought "it would be a good thing if women were to have permission granted to them to do as Mahapajapati desires."

"Enough, Ananda! Let it not please you that women should be allowed to do so," replied the Buddha. Ananda paused and thought that perhaps if he took another approach to the subject he might win permission.

He then said, "If women were admitted to the order and entered the homeless state, would they be capable of realizing the Doctrine and becoming perfect as ascetics?"

"They are indeed capable, Ananda," replied the Buddha.

"If then women are capable, Lord, and since Mahapajapati has proven herself of great service to the Enlightened One as his aunt and nurse, it would be well, Lord, if that woman could have permission to leave the household life and enter the homeless state under the Doctrine and discipline proclaimed by the Perfected One."

"If, Ananda, Mahapajapati is willing to take upon herself the Eight Major Rules in addition to the rules of the Order, let that be counted as her initiation into the Order."

When Ananda returned, he told the Buddha that Mahapajapati had accepted the rules, never to be transgressed for the rest of her life, and had received initiation into the ascetic order.

Although the Buddha had consented, he was not content and told Ananda that "if women had not received permission, then the Doctrine and discipline would have remained a pure religion for a thousand years. But since women had now received permission to enter the order, the pure religion would only last five hundred years. Just as houses in which many women and few men live are easily violated by robbers, or a field of rice in fine condition does not last long when mildew falls upon it, a field of sugarcane with blight, just so, Ananda, does a religion not last long once women are allowed to enter the ascetic community."

"Nevertheless," he continued, "just as a man would in anticipation build an embankment to a great reservoir, beyond which water should not overpass, just so, Ananda, have I in anticipation laid down these Eight Major Rules for the nuns, to be followed for the rest of their lives."

After returning to Savatthi, the Buddha flew up beyond the triple world to Tushita, the heavenly abode of his mother. He taught her the Doctrine, and he spent the rainy season there together with Moggallana and Sariputta. His mother, together with those deities who understood the discourse of the Buddha, became disciples of the great liberation, and he accepted alms from the chief of all the deities. Then as the rainy season came to an end, the gods stood in their mansions and watched as he descended to earth once again.

Upon his return to the Jeta Grove at Savatthi, the Buddha learned that Anathapindika was gravely ill and had requested a visit from Sariputta. The Buddha, as usual, consented by remaining silent.

Both Sariputta and Ananda dressed and took up their bowls and outer robes and headed for Anathapindika's residence. When they got there, Sariputta said, "I hope you are getting better and that you are comfortable, and that your pain is subsiding."

Anathapindika said, "Venerable Sariputta, I am not getting well and I am not comfortable. I feel as if someone is splitting my head open with a sword, and there is a violent burning in my body. I am afraid that I am not getting well, my pain is increasing."

"Then, householder," Sariputta replied, "you should train yourself so that your bodily organs do not cling to the objects or feelings of sense, or the mind or consciousness, to infinite space, or the perception of nothingness, neither perception nor nonperception. You should train yourself so that you do not cling to the world, or the world beyond. You should train yourself so that you will not cling to what is seen, heard, sensed, cognized, encountered, sought after and examined by the mind, and that your consciousness will not be dependent on all of that."

When Anathapindika heard all this, he wept. Ananda, fearing the worst, said, "Are you foundering? Are you sinking toward death?"

"I am not foundering," he replied. "Although I have served the great Teacher and the esteemed monks for a long time, I have never before heard such a talk on the Doctrine."

Sariputta then replied that "such talk on the Doctrine is not given to laypeople clothed in white. Such teaching on Doctrine is only given to those who have gone forth from living as householders, who have become homeless."

"Well, then, venerable Sariputta," said Anathapindika, "let such teaching on the Doctrine be given to laypeople clothed in white. There are householders who have a little dust in their eyes, wasting away because they have not heard the teaching; there are householders who will certainly understand the Doctrine."

Sariputta and Ananda rose from their seats and departed. Soon after they left, Anathapindika died and reappeared in Tushita heaven. When the night was well advanced, Anathapindika appeared before the Buddha as a young god of beautiful appearance, illuminating the whole of Jeta Grove, and praised the Buddha, the Doctrine, and the order along with Sariputta, who at best could only be equaled but never surpassed. Then he thought, "The great teacher has indeed approved of me," and paid homage to the Buddha and vanished.

The next morning the Buddha addressed the monks and told them what had happened far into the night. Ananda said, "Surely, venerable sir, that young god must have been Anathapindika, for he had perfect confidence in Sariputta."

"Excellent! Excellent, Ananda. You have deduced the right conclusion. That young god was Anathapindika, no one else." Ananda was both satisfied and delighted in the Perfect One's words.

13

Devadatta Attempts to Kill the Buddha

Devadatta, the Buddha's cousin and brother-in-law, seemed to envy the Buddha from the time they were children at play. When he joined the ascetic community during the Buddha's first visit home, he pledged to himself that he would acquire the special mental/ magical powers the Buddha perfected during his enlightenment and that some ascetics possessed as a part of their discipline in following the Eightfold Path. Over time he succeeded in acquiring these mental powers.

One day while at Rajagaha, the Buddha recognized certain exceptional qualities in some of the monks. He pointed out to his disciples, for example, that both Moggallana and Sariputta were models of great mental power and wisdom, that Kassapa was singular in strict observance of all rules, that Anuruddha was able to discern things beyond the senses, that Upali knew all of the ascetic rules by heart, and that Ananda had learned a great deal. He then pointed out Devadatta and said, "Do you see Devadatta walking back and forth with many of the brothers? Know that he has evil desires."

The Buddha, of course, was quite right. What Devadatta wanted more than anything else was power and fame. He thought that the best way to achieve this would be to become close friends with Prince Ajatasattu, the son of King Bimbisara. So one day, he concentrated his mental powers and took on the form of a child with a belt of snakes and terrified Ajatasattu by appearing in his lap. When he quickly assumed his proper form again, Ajatasattu was overwhelmed by his magical powers and paid him great honor. Pride, power, and renown led Devadatta to think about replacing the Buddha as master of the community. He thought to himself, "Surely, it is I who should lead the monks of the community, not the Buddha."

Now at that time a monk who had been Moggallana's attendant for many years had just died, and appeared as one of the celestial beings. Perceiving what Devadatta was thinking, he appeared at Moggallana's side, told him about Devadatta's intention, and then vanished. Moggallana then went to Kosambi and told the Buddha what he had heard.

"Are you sure?" the Buddha replied. "Have you so penetrated the mind of that celestial being that you know beyond doubt that what he says will be and not otherwise?"

"I have, Lord," Moggallana replied.

"Keep this a secret, Moggallana, for this foolish man will himself make it known."

When the Enlightened One had stayed at Kosambi for as long as he thought fit, he set out directly for Rajagaha. When he arrived he was immediately told of the lavish feasts that Prince Ajatasattu was preparing daily, both morning and night, for Devadatta. "Envy not the fame and honor of Devadatta," the Buddha replied. "Know that to his own hurt, his own destruction, has this gain and fame come to Devadatta, just as the plantain tree dies after bearing fruit. It is the fruit that destroys the plantain tree just as fame and renown destroy the evil person."

At a later date the Buddha was seated teaching the Doctrine to a multitude, including the king and his retinue. Devadatta rose from his seat, arranged his upper robe over his shoulder, stretched out his joined hands to the Buddha, and said, "The Enlightened One, Lord, is now grown old and has accomplished a long journey, his life almost run. Let the Enlightened One now dwell at ease in the enjoyment of happiness reached even in this world. Let him give up the community to me; I will be its leader."

"Enough! You have said enough!" replied the Buddha. After Devadatta had made the request a third time, the Buddha said, "I would not give over the community even to Sariputta and Moggallana. How much less then would I give it over to someone so vile, someone who has less value then spit!"

Devadatta was stunned by this rebuke heard by the multitude, the king, and his retinue. Angry and displeased, he bowed before the Buddha, passed him on his right side, and left. The Buddha then announced that the community should carry out an "Act of Proclamation" to the effect that whatever Devadatta said and did in no way represented the Buddha, the Doctrine, or the community, and that the venerable Sariputta should proclaim this act throughout Rajagaha.

Upon hearing the proclamation, Devadatta went to the prince and said to him: "In days gone by people lived a long time, but now life is short. It is possible, therefore, that you may never live to be king. So you, prince, should kill your father and become the king; and I will kill the Enlightened One and become the Buddha."

Trusting Devadatta's power and knowledge, Prince Ajatasattu headed for his father's chambers armed with a dagger. Fearful and anxious and at an unusual hour, he alarmed the attendants of the private royal quarters who seized him and took him to King Bimbisara. "Why in the world did you want to kill me?" Bimbisara asked him.

"Because," replied the prince, "I wanted a kingdom!"

"If that is what you want," said the king, "then let this kingdom be yours," and he handed over the kingdom to Ajatasattu. Ajatasattu in turn had his father imprisoned, where he slowly starved to death.

Encouraged by all these events, Devadatta asked the prince to tell his men to follow whatever orders Devadatta gave them. The prince consented, and Devadatta gave the following command: "Go, good friend, and find Gotama who is staying at such and such a place. Kill him and then come back by another path." Then on that path Devadatta placed two other men, telling them, "Whatever man you see coming along this path, kill him, and return by another path." Then on that path he placed four men, telling them, "Whatever men you see coming along this path, kill them." Then on that path he placed eight men, telling them, "Whatever men you see coming along this path, kill them." And finally he placed sixteen men on the last path with the same command.

The first man took his sword and shield and hung his bow and quiver on his back, heading for the Buddha. At a little distance from the Buddha he became terrified and anxious, standing stark still and stiff. Seeing him, the Buddha said, "Come here, friend, don't be afraid." The man then laid his weapons aside and confessed his evil intent to the Buddha, who upon teaching him the Doctrine also accepted him as a lay disciple who from that day forward and as long as life endured took his refuge in him.

The Buddha instructed the man to take a different path back into the city. In the meantime, the two men who awaited him thought, "Where can that man be who was to come along?" As they headed down the path looking for him, they spotted the Buddha sitting at the foot of a certain tree. The Buddha also taught them the Doctrine, and they, along with the other four, eight, and sixteen, became lay disciples and took refuge in the Buddha, the Doctrine, and the community.

The first man found Devadatta and said to him, "I cannot deprive the Enlightened One of life. Great is his mental/magical power, great is his might."

"That will do, friend," said Devadatta. "You need not do so. I will kill him myself."

One day the Buddha was meditating in the shade of the mountain known as Vultures Peak. Devadatta noticed him and climbed up the peak and hurled down a mighty rock with the intention of killing the Buddha. The mountain peaks, however, came together and stopped that boulder, and only a splinter falling from it hit the foot of the Enlightened One and made it bleed.

The Buddha looked upward and said to Devadatta, "Great, you foolish one, is the demerit you have brought upon yourself, bad karma will work out its effect in the immediate future." Hearing what had happened, the monks immediately began walking around the monastery chanting recitations in high and loud tones for the protection of the Buddha. Upon hearing the chants, the Buddha gathered them together and told them that "it is an impossible thing, one that cannot occur, that someone should deprive a Perfected One of life by violence, that a Perfected One should be killed by any act by anyone besides himself. Perfected Ones are extinguished in due course and thus do not require protection."

Now at that time in Rajagaha there lived a fierce man-slaying elephant named Nalagiri. Devadatta knew this and visited the stables, telling the elephant keepers that he was a relative of the king and was thus able to both promote and increase the pay of any of the workers who would let Nalagiri loose when Gotama arrived at the road. "Consider it done!" responded the elephant keepers.

Early the next morning, the Buddha dressed himself and, taking his robe and bowl, entered the road for alms. On seeing him, the elephant keepers let loose Nalagiri, who charged down the road, rushing toward the Buddha with trunk uplifted and with tail and ears erect. As the bull elephant approached, the Buddha infused it with his own loving compassion. Nalagiri put down his trunk, approached, stopped, and stood in front of the Buddha, who stroked the elephant's forehead with his right hand while Nalagiri took the dust at the Buddha's feet and scattered it over its head. The elephant then stepped back and returned to the stable.

Failure did not stop Devadatta. If his plots to become the master of the community did not succeed, perhaps he could cause a split in the community of monks. Devadatta waited for the sacred day of rituals and observances that were held twice monthly. On the particular day of the full moon, he arose from his seat and told the assembled monks that a vote should be taken in favor of five subjects: first, that monks should only live in the forest; second, that monks should only eat alms food and reject all invitations; third, that monks should wear robes made only from rags they themselves had collected; fourth, that monks should no longer live under a roof even during the rainy season, but under trees; and fifth, that monks should observe strict vegetarianism.

In attendance at that meeting were five hundred monks who had recently been ordained, and who were ignorant of the subjects being discussed. Not knowing that the Buddha had already rejected these restrictions and thinking that all was in accord with the Doctrine the Buddha taught, they voted in favor of the five subjects and at the end of the meeting departed with Devadatta for residence at the hill at Bodh-Gaya, the place of the Buddha's enlightenment. The Buddha was fully informed of this breach in his community by Sariputta and Moggallana, and he told them to follow the group and have compassion for them, and convince them of their error before they fell into deeper trouble and distress.

Devadatta was overcome with joy when he saw both Sariputta and Moggallana following them to the new residence. "See," he said to the monks, "how well do I teach the Doctrine that even the chief disciples are coming to me, approving my teaching." Knowing their profound grasp of the Doctrine and the perfection of their wisdom, he invited them to have a seat near him, which they politely turned down. Devadatta then entered into a discourse that gladdened and delighted the monks far into the night. He then told Sariputta that he needed to stretch out because of a severe backache, and that since the monks were wide awake and not drowsy at all he should address them as it occurred to him. "Very well," answered Sariputta. Then Devadatta, tired, lay down on his right side and fell asleep that very moment.

Sariputta instructed the monks with talk about the Doctrine and the wonders of the various mental powers of meditation. His talk was powerful, full of energy, which led them all to understand the nature of the Four Noble Truths, the Eightfold Path, and the basic principles of the interdependent origination and cessation of all things. Sariputta ended his discourse by saying, "We are going, monks, to the Lord. Whoever approves of his Doctrine, let him come along."

When Devadatta was told that all five hundred monks had departed with Sariputta and Moggallana and returned to the Bamboo Grove, hot blood poured from out of his mouth.

The Buddha addressed the monks, telling them Devadatta was doomed to a downfall, his mind controlled by gain, fame, honors, and evil friendships. He was doomed to dwell in Niraya hell for an aeon.

14

The Buddha's Last Days

It was well known throughout the land that both Sariputta and
Moggallana were the most powerful intellects of the Buddhist
monastic community. The Buddha often asked them to take his
place during evening teaching sessions; this was especially so during
evenings when his backaches became severe.

One day while staying at Vultures Peak in Rajagaha, and after
speaking to the assembly of monks about the mode of living that is
conducive to their welfare, he told Ananda that they should all travel
to Nalanda, the home of Sariputta, to visit him. When Sariputta
was told of their visit, he immediately went to the grove to see the
Buddha. Seated to one side, he said, "It is clear to me, Lord, that
there never has been, will be, or is not another ascetic or Brahmin
who is better or more enlightened than the Lord."

"You have spoken rather boldly, Sariputta, like a lion's roar of
certainty. Why? Have all the Perfected Ones of the past appeared to
you and were all their minds open to you?"

"No, Lord," Sariputta replied.

"Well, then, Sariputta, have you also perceived all the minds of
the Perfected Ones who will appear in the future as to their virtue,
teaching, wisdom, and liberation?"

"No, Lord."

"Well, then, Sariputta, you certainly know me as a Perfected
One, a Buddha, and do you also know, 'The Lord is of such and such
virtue, wisdom and such is his liberation?' "

"No, Lord."

"So, Sariputta, you really do not have knowledge of the minds of the Buddhas, past, future, and present. How then do you speak with certainty?"

"It is true, Lord," replied Sariputta, "that I do not know the minds of the perfected Buddhas of the past, present, and future. But I know by inference that the Doctrine is the same for all those Perfected Ones who have attained supreme enlightenment, that all the Buddhas of the future will do likewise, and you, Lord, who are now the Perfected One, fully enlightened, have done the same. I came to the Lord to listen to the Doctrine, most excellent and perfect, and so I gained insight into that Doctrine and I established serene confidence in the Teacher, the fully enlightened Buddha; also that the Doctrine is well taught by the Venerable One, and that the order of monks is well trained. I also learned that the Lord's way of teaching the Doctrine is unsurpassed. That among the topics, including mindfulness and the elucidation of the domains of sensation, we gained insight into the modes of rebirth, the telling of thoughts, the attainment of vision, the factors of enlightenment, and the modes of progress toward enlightenment."

"Also unsurpassed," Sariputta continued, "is the Lord's way of teaching the proper conduct of speech: how one should avoid not only any speech involving lying, but also speech that is ruinous or sneeringly triumphant, but should use wise words, words to be treasured, words in season. Unsurpassed also is the Lord's way of teaching the Doctrine with regard to a person's ethical conduct. One should be truthful, faithful, not using deception, patter, belittling, on the make for gain, but always watchful, active, a mediator, mindful, steady, resolute, and sensible. Also unsurpassed is the Enlightened One's way of teaching the Doctrine with regard to the modes of receptivity to instruction of which there are four: the Perfected One knows by his observation that one will, by following instructions, by the complete destruction of three fetters, become a Stream-Winner, no more subject to rebirth in the lower worlds, firmly established, destined for full enlightenment; or that one, by the complete destruction of the fetters and the reduction of greed, hatred, and delusion, will become a Once-Returner, having returned once more to this world, will put an end to suffering; or by the complete destruction of all fetters become a Non-Returner, reaching liberation from birth, death, and rebirth without returning; or by the destruction of the corruptions gain in this very life the deliverance of the mind, the deliverance through wisdom which is uncorrupted, and which one has understood and realized by one's own superknowledge. Indeed, the Enlightened One is able here and now to enjoy the surpassing happiness of dwelling in the four domains of meditation."

"Lord, if I were asked, 'Well, now, Sariputta, have there ever been in the past any ascetics and Brahmins more exalted in enlightenment than the Buddha?' I would say no. If asked, 'Will there be any such in the future?' I should say no. 'Is there any such in the present?' Again, I would say no. If, however, I were asked, 'Have there been any such in the past equal in enlightenment to the Lord?' I should say yes. But if I were asked, 'Are there any such at present who are equal in enlightenment to the Lord?' I should say no. And if I were then asked, 'Venerable Sariputta, why do you accord this highest recognition to one and not the other?' I should say, I have heard and received from the Lord, from his own lips, that 'There have been in the past, and there will be in the future, Perfect Buddhas equal in enlightenment to myself.' And I have also heard from the Lord's own lips that it is not possible, it cannot be that in one and the same world-system two Perfect Ones should arise simultaneously. No such situation can exist.

If I gave these answers to such questions, would I be telling the truth, or would I misrepresent the Lord's word by departing from the truth?"

The Buddha replied, "Most certainly, Sariputta, if you answered like this you would not misrepresent me, you would be explaining the Doctrine correctly and not laying yourself open to censure." Sariputta remained silent. He felt content.

For many years the Buddha spent the rainy season at Savatthi, staying at Anathapindika's park at the Jeta Grove monastery. On one such occasion the venerable Sariputta was once again staying at Nalanda, his home near Rajagaha. He became sick, stricken with a serious disease, and Cunda, who at one time was an attendant of the Buddha, became his nurse. In a very short time Sariputta died of that disease on the full-moon day of Kattika (October/November). So Cunda the novice, taking the venerable Sariputta's bowl, outer robe, and relics, traveled to Savatthi to find Ananda to tell him of Sariputta's death.

When Ananda was informed of Sariputta's death, he told Cunda that they must by all means inform the Buddha. They then went to the Enlightened One, saluted him, and sat down at one side. Ananda said, "Lord, Cunda has told me that Sariputta has died. Here are his bowl, outer robe, and the water strainer that holds his relics. Hearing the news, Lord, my body is as drugged, my hearing confused, and the Doctrine no longer clear to me when I heard the words, 'The venerable Sariputta has died.'"

"But tell me, Ananda," the Buddha replied, "when the venerable Sariputta died, did he take with him the elements of virtue? Did he take with him the components of concentration and wisdom? When he died, did the components of liberation, knowledge, and wisdom go with him?"

"Not so, Lord," said Ananda. "But he was my adviser, my instructor, never tiring in teaching the Doctrine. He aroused and gladdened us, supporting all those who lived the righteous life along with him. We have what he also possessed."

"But have I not on previous occasions declared to you how in all things that are dear and delightful there is the nature of diversity, the nature of separation? How is it possible, Ananda, in the case of what is born, what is become, what is compounded, what is transitory—how is it possible to have one's wish fulfilled: Oh! may it not perish! No, no, Ananda, such a thing simply cannot be!"

"Just as, from some mighty tree, standing firm and full of life, one of the great limbs falls off, even so, from the mighty order of monks standing firm Sariputta has died. How is it possible, Ananda, in the case of what is born, what is become, what is compounded, what is transitory, how is it possible, I say, that one's wish could be, 'Oh! May it not perish.' I say, No! Such a wish simply cannot be."

"Therefore, Ananda, abide in the Norm, taking refuge in none other; be self-refuged, grounded in the Doctrine. Either now or when I have died, whoever is self-refuged, taking refuge in none other than the Truth, the Doctrine, they shall be my monks, they shall be on top of the gloom, for they are anxious to learn."

No more than a fortnight had passed before news arrived that Moggallana had also died—he had been murdered by robbers. Living in Rajagaha, he took great satisfaction in ascending to the abode of the thirty-three gods to inform them all of those disciples of the Buddha who had been reborn there and also of those who believed in false Doctrines who were reborn in hell. Over time the dissenters noticed that their respect was slowly decreasing, and they hired robbers to go and murder Moggallana. When Moggallana saw them coming, he rose in the air by means of his superhuman power, evading their swords. For six days the robbers tracked him down, and on each of those days Moggallana ascended into the air to escape certain death. On the seventh day, however, the power of his past karma overcame him, and his superpower failed him. In a previous life he and his wife, disguised as robbers, decided to kill his aged parents by taking them into the forest. This bad karma remained unexhausted, like fire hidden under ashes, and overtook him in this, his last body so that he was unable to rise in the air. The robbers crushed his bones and left him for dead.

At the news of his death the Buddha assembled a multitude of monks. Observing that they had become silent, he said: "Monks, truly this company seems empty. Now that Sariputta and Moggallana have died, my company is empty of them. It does not concern us what quarter it is in which they may be dwelling. Monks, whosoever in past times has been a Perfect One, fully enlightened, each Exalted One had such a noble pair of disciples as were Sariputta and Moggallana to me, and whosoever in future times shall be a Perfected One likewise shall have such a noble pair. It is a wonder, monks! A marvel! For although such a remarkable pair of disciples has died, there is in the Enlightened One no sorrow or lamenting. How is it possible, monks, in the case of what is born, what becomes, what is compounded, what is transitory—how is it possible to have one's wish fulfilled: 'Oh, may it not perish! No, such a thing cannot be.'"

After his address to the multitude of monks, the Buddha told Ananda that he should make ready for a trip to Patalagama. When he arrived at the city the lay followers met him and invited the company to stay at their rest house. The Buddha once again consented by his silence.

The Buddha, bathed, robed, and with his bowl, went with his monks to the rest house, where he sat down facing east with his back against the central pillar. The monks sat down with their backs to the west wall, facing east and with the Lord sitting in front of them. The lay followers sat down with their backs to the east wall, facing west with the Lord before them. He addressed the assembled group with a discourse on morality, inspired them, and delighted them concerning the Doctrine far into the night. He then dismissed them, saying, "Now it is time for you to do as you think fit," and they passed by him and departed, leaving him in solitude in the empty hall.

The next day the Buddha departed and soon arrived at the Ganges River. The river was at flood level, and people were looking for boats, rafts, or anything that would serve as a raft to get to the other side. The Buddha, as swiftly as a strong man might stretch out his flexed arm, vanished from this side of the Ganges and reappeared with his order of monks on the other shore and traveled on to Kotigama. After a short stay, they went on to Nadika, where Ananda asked the Buddha about the rebirth of those who have died. The Buddha replied, "Ananda, it is not remarkable that that which has come to be as a human being should die. What is remarkable is that you should come to the Perfect One to ask the fate of each of those who have died; that is wearisome to him." He then taught Ananda how to discern the rebirths of persons at death, called "The Mirror of the Doctrine"; whether they be once-returners, stream-winners, and so on.

Continuing their journey, they reached Beluva, where during the rains the Buddha was attacked by a severe illness with sharp pains as if he were going to die. He endured it, clearly aware of it, without complaining and held the disease in check by his own mental powers. As he did so the disease abated.

Ananda then admitted to the Enlightened One that the only thing that comforted him throughout this ordeal was this thought: "The Lord will not attain final liberation until he has made some statement about the order of the monks." "But Ananda," the Buddha replied, "what does the order of monks expect me to say? I have taught the Doctrine. There is nothing more to say. Ananda, I am now old, worn out, venerable, one who has traversed life's path. I have reached the term of life, which is eighty. Just as an old cart is made to go by being held together by various straps, so the Perfect One's body is kept going by being strapped together. Ananda, you should live as islands unto yourselves, being your own refuge, with no one else as your refuge, with the Doctrine as an island, with the Doctrine as your refuge."

Continuing north, the Buddha together with Ananda reached Vesali, his favorite city. Ambapali, a courtesan of the city, heard the Lord was staying at her grove. Arriving in her best carriage, she was instructed, inspired by the Buddha, and being thus delighted she said, "Lord, may the Lord consent to take a meal from me tomorrow with his order of monks!" The Buddha consented by silence, and she departed to prepare for the meal.

The elite men of the city also heard of his arrival and, dressed in splendid colors, rushed to meet with him. Ambapali met them on the way back to the city and at great speed drove her chariot axle to axle against them. The men shouted, "Why are you driving like that?" and she replied, "Because, sirs, I have invited the Buddha for a meal with his monks."

"Ambapali! Give up this meal! We will give you a hundred thousand pieces!"

"Young sirs," she replied, "if you were to give me all of Vesali with its revenues, I would not give up such an important meal." Determined, the young elites snapped their fingers and headed for the grove.

Seeing them coming from afar, Buddha told the monks, "Monks, those of you who have not seen the thirty-three gods, just look at this troop of Licchavis! Take a good look at them, see their splendid colors, and you will get an idea of the thirty-three gods."

When they arrived the Buddha instructed them, fired them up, and delighted, they invited him for a meal. "But, Licchavis, I have already accepted a meal for tomorrow from the courtesan Ambapali!"

"We've been cheated by that mango-woman," they murmured, but then rejoicing in his talk, they passed him on the right and departed.

On the morrow the Buddha and his monks assembled at the residence of Ambapali. After the meal she took a low stool and sat down to one side and said, "Lord, I give this park to the order of the monks with the Buddha as its head." The Enlightened One accepted the park and delighted her with a talk on the Doctrine, arose from his seat, and departed.

The next morning, arising early, the Buddha dressed, took his robe and bowl, and entered Vesali for alms. Having eaten on his return from the alms round, he said to the venerable Ananda, "Bring a mat, Ananda. We will go to the Capala Shrine for our rest."

"Very good, Lord," said Ananda, and getting a mat, he followed behind.

At the shrine the Buddha sat down and said to Ananda, "Whoever has developed the four roads of power could undoubtedly live for a century, or the remainder of one. The Perfect One has developed these powers and could, Ananda, live for a century."

The venerable Ananda, failing to grasp this hint, this clear sign, did not beg the Lord: "Lord, may the Perfect One stay for a century, may the Well-Farer stay for the benefit and happiness of the multitude, out of compassion for the world, for the benefit and happiness of the gods and humans." Ananda's mind for the moment was possessed by Mara.

After repeating his offer twice more, the Buddha said, "Go now and do what seems fitting to you." And he did, and sat under a tree some distance away.

Soon after Mara came to the Buddha and said, "May the Lord now attain final liberation. Now is the time. Your mission is accomplished."

The Buddha replied, "You need not worry. The Perfected One's final liberation will not be long delayed. It will take place three months from now." And when he said this and had mindfully and in full awareness renounced the life-principle, there was a great earthquake.

Ananda, shocked by the quake, came to the Buddha and asked its cause. He was told of the Buddha's conversation with Mara and he then begged the Buddha to stay for a century. "Do you have faith in the Perfected One's enlightenment?" asked the Buddha.

"Yes, Lord," Ananda replied.

"Then why do you bother the Buddha with such a request?"

"Because," Ananda said, "I have heard from the Lord's own lips that 'whoever has developed the four powers could live for a century or for the remainder of one.'"

"Do you have faith, Ananda?"

"Yes, I do, Lord," he replied.

"Then, Ananda, yours is the fault, yours is the failure, given such a broad hint, such a clear sign. If you had persisted, the Perfected One would twice have refused you, but the third time he would have consented. Remember when we stayed at Vultures Peak? Or again at the Banyan Park at Robbers Cliff, at the Satapanni Cave or Tapoda Park, or again at the Squirrels Feeding-Ground? At all of these places I said to you, 'Whoever has developed the four powers could live for a century.' But you, Ananda, failing to grasp this hint, did not ask the Buddha to stay. The Enlightened One has renounced the life-principle and once and for all has said final liberation will not be long delayed. That the Perfected One should now withdraw such a declaration in order to live on is not possible. Now, come, we will go to the Gabled Hall in the Great Forest."

"Very good," answered Ananda. When they arrived at the Gabled Hall, Ananda summoned the monks of the area to hear a discourse and rehearsal of the Doctrine by the Buddha.

The next morning after returning from the alms round, they headed out of the city. The Buddha paused as they looked down upon the city and said, "O Vesali, this is the last time that the Perfect One will see your fair face." And turning to Ananda, he said, "Let us go now to Bhandagama." They stayed there with a large company of monks for as long as the Buddha wished, and then departed for Pava, where they stayed at the mango grove of Cunda, the blacksmith. When Cunda heard that they had arrived, he invited the Awakened One together with his order of monks for a meal. As the night came to an end, Cunda had a fine meal of solid and soft food prepared together with an abundance of "pork special." When the Buddha arrived he sat down and said, "Serve the 'pork special' to me, and serve the remaining soft and solid food to the order of monks." And Cunda did so.

Then the Buddha said to Cunda, "Whatever is leftover of the 'pork special' you should bury in a pit, because, Cunda, I can see none in this world with its gods, Mara's and Brahmins, its princes and peoples who, if they were to eat it, could thoroughly digest it except the Perfect One." Cunda did as he was told, and the Buddha departed after an inspired and delightful talk on the Doctrine.

The Buddha was then attacked by a severe sickness with bloody diarrhea and with sharp pains as if he were about to die. But he endured it all mindfully and clearly without complaint and told Ananda that they should leave for Kusinara. He told him, "Tonight, in the last watch, in the sal-grove near Kusinara, between two sal-trees, the Perfect One's final liberation will take place. Now let us go to the river Kakuttha." Arriving at the river with a large number of monks, he entered the water, bathed and drank, and emerging, went to the grove where he said to the venerable Chundaka, "Come, Chundaka, fold a robe in four for me. I am tired and want to lie down."

"Very good, Lord," said Chundaka, and did so. The Buddha laid down on his right side, placing one foot on the other, bearing in mind the time of his enlightenment years ago.

He then called for Ananda and said to him, "It might happen that Cunda the blacksmith should feel remorse, thinking, 'It is my fault, my misdeed that the Perfected One gained final liberation after taking his last meal from me!' If so, expel his remorse in this way. Tell him, 'That is your merit, Cunda, that is your good deed, that the Perfected One gained final liberation after taking his last meal from you. For I have heard from the Enlightened One's own lips that there are two almsgivings that are of very great merit, of very great result, more fruitful than any other. Which two? The one is the almsgiving after which the Perfected One attains supreme enlightenment, the other after which he attains final liberation. Cunda's deed is conducive to long life, to good looks, to happiness and fame, to heaven and to lordship.' "

15

Once the Buddha Was a Universal Monarch

The Buddha knew his career was coming to an end. After resting, he told Ananda that they should travel north to Kusinara, a town close to his birthplace. Ananda thought that that was a bad idea. Once they arrived, he told the Buddha that Kusinara was not the place to spend his final hours, that cities such as Rajagaha or Savatthi were much more appropriate. Kusinara, he said, "is a miserable little town, unheard of, in the middle of nowhere." The Buddha immediately rebuked him: "Don't call this town a miserable backwater town hidden in the jungle." He then told Ananda its history.

Once upon a time, Ananda, King Mahasudassana was a wheel-turning monarch, a cosmic king, a righteous king who had conquered the four quarters of the cosmos and chose this very town, which was then called Kusavati, for his capital. It was 120 miles long from east to west and 70 miles wide from north to south. The royal city was surrounded by seven walls and had four gates. It was prosperous, full of sounds night and day, filled with a large number of spirit beings as residents. It was, the Buddha said, just like one of the cities of the gods called Akamanda, that is to say, it was a replica of the royal city of the northern quarter called Kuru. One of the walls was made of gold, one of silver, one of beryl, one of crystal, one of ruby, one of emerald, and one of all sorts of gems. The gates of Kusavati were of four colors: gold, silver, beryl, and crystal. And before each gate were a set of seven pillars. Trees made of the same precious materials surrounded the city. For example, the gold trees had gold trunks but leaves and fruit of silver, the silver trees had trunks of silver with leaves and fruit of gold, and so forth. The sound of the wind passing through the leaves was lovely, delightful, intoxicating. Thus those who were prone to live unrestrained lives or a life of drunkenness had their desires assuaged by the sound of the leaves in the wind.

King Mahasudassana, as are all universal wheel-turning monarchs, that is, monarchs of the Four Quarters, was endowed with the seven treasures and four properties.

Once, on the fifteenth of the month known as the Uposatha, the king purified himself and went to the veranda at the top of his palace to observe this ritual day. As he did so, the superagent Wheel-Treasure appeared, and King Mahasudassana thought, "I have heard that when an anointed king sees such a wheel on the fast-day of the fifteenth he will become a wheel-turning king. May I become such a monarch!" He then arose from his seat and covering his shoulder with his robe, the king took a gold vessel in his right hand, sprinkled the wheel with his right hand, and said, "May the noble Wheel-Treasure turn, may it conquer!"

The wheel turned east, and the king followed it with his fourfold army. The king of the Eastern Quarter said, "Welcome. We are yours. Rule us, your majesty." And the Universal Monarch said, "1. Do not take life. 2. Do not take what is not given. 3. Do not commit sexual misconduct. 4. Do not tell lies. 5. Do not drink strong drink. 6. Be moderate in eating." And those facing him in the east became his subjects.

The Wheel then plunged into the eastern sea and turned south, then west, and then north and conquered all of the four quarters from sea to sea. It then returned to Kusavati, the royal capital, and stopped before the palace, where the king was trying a case, as if to adorn a royal place.

Then the second treasure, the Elephant-Treasure, appeared to King Mahasudassana. It was pure white, seven times the strength of a royal tusker, and had the magical power of traveling through the air. The king thought, "If only I could bring him under control." And the elephant submitted to his control just like a thoroughbred that had been trained for a long time. The king mounted him at dawn and rode him from sea to sea, returning to Kusavati for breakfast.

Then the Horse-Treasure appeared, black as a crow's head, powerful, traveling through the air. The horse submitted to the king's control, and they too traveled from sea to sea at dawn. Then the Jewel-Treasure appeared. It was cut into eight facets, perfect in every respect. The king took it on maneuvers on a dark night and fixed the jewel on top of his standard. The villagers, thinking it was daylight, began their daily work.

Then the fifth treasure, known as the Woman-Treasure, appeared to King Mahasudassana. She was lovely, charming, not too tall, not too short, not too thin or fat, not too dark or fair. She looked more like a goddess than a human. The touch of her skin was like cotton or silk, and her limbs were cool when it was hot, and warm when it was cold. Her body smelled of sandalwood and her lips of lotus. She rose before the king did and retired later, always willing to do his pleasure. She was not unfaithful to the king in thought and deed.

The sixth, that appeared was the Nobleman-Treasure, an exquisite house-holder who, because of his karmic legacy, possessed the power to discern where treasure, owned and ownerless, lay hidden. The king, wanting to test this power, took him on a boat trip into the middle of the Ganges. "Nobleman," said the king, "I want some gold coins." The nobleman replied that it would be best to head for either shore. "But I want it here and now!" replied the king. The nobleman then touched the water with his hands and drew out a vessel full of gold coins.

Then the seventh treasure appeared, known as the Counselor-Treasure. He was wise, experienced, and competent to advise the king on how to pro-ceed, how to withdraw, and how to overlook.

These, the Buddha said, are the seven treasures that came into King Mahasudassana's possession. And the four properties? What are they? First, the king was handsome, surpassing all other men. Second, he was long-lived, outliving other men. Third, he was free from illness and less subject to cold and heat than other men. And fourth, he was beloved and popular with Brahmins and householders; the king loved them as a father loves his children.

Once the king went out for a ride in the pleasure park, and the Brahmins and householders came to him and said, "Pass slowly, Your Majesty, so that we may see you as long as possible!" And the king said to the charioteer, "Drive slowly so that I may see them as long as possible."

One day the king decided to build lotus ponds between the palm trees he had planted. The ponds were lined with gold, silver, beryl, and crystal with staircases, posts, and railings of the same material. He then added flowers for every season and charitable posts on the banks of every pond so that the people could get whatever they wanted.

Then one day the Brahmins and householders gathered great wealth together and went to the king, saying, "Your Majesty, here is wealth, please accept it." The king replied that he had enough wealth and that they should take it back with more besides. They then considered what to do and decided to build a dwelling for King Mahasudassana. The king accepted their decision by remaining silent.

Sakka, ruler of the gods, knew what was in King Mahasudassana's mind and said to Vissakamma, "Come, my friend, and build a dwelling for the king, a palace called Dhamma." And, as quickly as a strong man can stretch or flex out his arm, Vissakamma at once vanished from the heaven of the thirty-three gods and appeared before the king and said to him, "Sire, I shall build you a dwelling place, a palace called Dhamma." The king assented by remaining silent.

The palace was about three miles long from east to west, and about one-and-a-half miles long from north to south. It was inlaid with tiles made of gold, silver, beryl, and crystal and contained eighty-four thousand columns of the same colors. It had twenty-four staircases and eighty-four thousand rooms. The gold rooms had silver couches; the silver rooms had golden couches. The beryl rooms had ivory couches, and the crystal rooms contained couches made of sandalwood. The doors contained a figure of a palm tree with leaves and fruit on them made of the same materials. The king then added a grove of palm trees all made of gold by the door of the great gabled chamber and surrounded the palace with two nets of tinkling bells made of both silver and gold, which sounded lovely, intoxicating when stirred by the wind.

When the palace was finished it was hard to look at. It dazzled the eyes just as in the last month of the rains, in autumn, when there is a clear and cloudless sky and the sun breaks through the mists in a blaze of blinding light. The king then decided to build a lake in front of the palace and surrounded it with seven kinds of palm trees. When it was all finished, and having satisfied every wish of those who were ascetics or Brahmins, he ascended into the Dhamma Palace. Seated in the palace, the king thought: "Of what past action is this the fruit, the result, that I am now so mighty and powerful?" He concluded that it was the consequence of three kinds of action in the past: giving, self-control, and abstinence.

Then the king went to the great gabled chamber and standing at the door proclaimed: "May the thought of lust cease! May the thought of ill will cease! May the thought of cruelty cease!" He then went into the great gabled chamber, sat down cross-legged on the golden couch and, detached from all sense desires, and unwholesome mental states, entered the first, second, third, and fourth levels of meditation. The king then emerged from the great gabled chamber and went to the golden gabled chamber and, seated crossed-legged, pervaded the Four Quarters, spreading the thought of loving-kindness, compassion, and joy everywhere.

The Buddha then told Ananda, "After many hundreds of thousands of years, Queen Subhadda thought, 'It is a long time since I saw King Mahasudassana. Suppose I were to go and see him?'" After seeking advice from the Counselor-Treasure, the queen, her entourage, and the fourfold army traveled to the Dhamma Palace. Queen Subhadda then went to the great gabled chamber and stood leaning against the door. The king, hearing a great noise as the sound of a great crowd, got up and headed for the door, whereupon he saw the queen. "Stay there," he said. "Do not enter!"

He then told one of his attendants to go into the chamber and bring out the golden couch and put it among the gold palm trees. The king then lay down on his right side with one foot on the other, mindful and clearly aware. The queen, noting his clear and bright complexion and hoping he was not dead, said, "Since Kusavati is the chief among all cities, make a wish, arouse the desire to live here!"

Hearing this, the king said, "For a long time you spoke pleasing and delightful words to me, but now at this last time your words are not pleasing."

"How then should I speak to you?" she asked.

"This is how you should speak: All things that are pleasing and attractive are liable to change, to vanish, to become otherwise. Abandon desires, abandon the longing to live with them."

The queen cried out and burst into tears, "Your Majesty, all things that are pleasing and attractive are liable to change, do not die filled with longing."

Soon after this, King Mahasudassana died. Just as a householder or his son might feel drowsy after a good meal, so he felt the sensation of passing away, and he had a favorable rebirth in the Brahma-heaven.

For eighty-four thousand years King Mahasudassana enjoyed boyish sports. For eighty-four thousand more years he served as the king's representative, and he ruled as king for eighty-four thousand more years. He lived the holy life of a layman in the Dhamma Palace for eighty-four thousand more, and having practiced the four levels of meditation he was reborn in the Brahma-world.

The Buddha then said,

Now, Ananda, you might think that King Mahasudassana at that time was somebody else. If you think so that would be a mistake, because I was King Mahasudassana.

See, Ananda, how all conditioned things have changed and vanished. Thus all conditioned things are impermanent, they are unstable, they can bring us no comfort, and such being the case we should not rejoice in them nor take interest in them. We should be liberated from them.

Six times I recall the breakup of the body in this place. The seventh time I ended life as a Wheel-turning monarch, a righteous king who had conquered the Four Quarters and possessed the seven treasures. But I do not now see any place in this cosmos with its gods, Maras, and Brahmas, or in this generation with its ascetics and Brahmins, princes, and people, where the Perfected One need be reborn and die for an eighth time.

16

The Last Watch and the Funeral

Settled down in the grove near Kusinara, the Buddha asked Ananda to prepare a bed for him between two *sal*-trees with his head to the north. As he lay down on his right side once again, the sal trees burst forth in abundant untimely blossoms that fell, covering his body. Heavenly coral tree flowers also fell from the sky, together with sandalwood powder, sprinkling and covering his body in homage.

As they spoke to each other the venerable Upava stood in front of the Buddha, fanning him. The Buddha told him, "Move aside, monk, do not stand in front of me." Ananda was rather shocked at this sharp command, since Upava had been an attendant of the Buddha for a long time, always keeping close at his beck and call. And now in his last hour the Lord told him to stand aside. "Why did he say that?" he thought. Ananda then asked him.

"Ananda, the gods from the various spheres of the cosmos have gathered to see the Perfect One. For a distance of about 150 miles around the *sal*-grove there is not a space you could touch with the point of a hair that is not filled with mighty gods, and they are complaining: "We have come a long way to see the Perfected One. It is rare for a fully enlightened Buddha to arise in the world, and tonight in the last watch the Enlightened One will attain final liberation, and this mighty monk is standing in front of the Buddha preventing us from getting a last glimpse of him.""

All the gods now viewed the cosmic event that was taking place, as heavenly music and song sounded throughout the skies.

As the last watch of the night approached, Ananda began to worry about the future and said:

"Lord, in years past monks have spent the rainy season in various places where we could see and listen to you. But now, with the Lord's final watch approaching, we shall no longer have a chance to do this."

"Ananda, there are four places that should arouse delight and inspiration in the faithful. Which are they? The place where the Awakened One was born is the first. The second is the place where supreme enlightenment was attained. The third is the place where the wheel of the Doctrine was set in motion, and the fourth is the place of final liberation without remainder. And, Ananda, the faithful monks and nuns, male and female lay followers will visit those places. Any who die while making the pilgrimage to those shrines with a devout heart will, at the breaking up of the body at death, be reborn in a heavenly world."

"Lord, what shall we do with the Enlightened One's remains?"

"Ananda, they should be dealt with like the remains of a Wheel-turning Monarch."

"And how is that, Lord?"

"Ananda, the remains of a Wheel-turning Monarch are wrapped in a new linen cloth. This they wrap in cotton wool, and then in a new cloth. Then having made a funeral pyre of all manner of perfumes, they cremate the king's body and they raise a memorial at a crossroads. They should deal with the Enlightened One's body in the same way. And whoever lays wreaths or puts sweet perfumes and colors there with a devout heart will reap great merit and happiness for a long time.

"There are four persons worthy of a memorial. Who are they? A fully enlightened Buddha is one, a nonteaching Buddha is one, a disciple of the Enlightened One is a third, and a Wheel-turning Monarch is the fourth. And why are these four worthy of a memorial? Because the thought "this is the memorial of a Perfected One, of a nonteaching Buddha, a disciple, or a Wheel-turning Monarch makes a person's heart peaceful and leads them to a good destiny in a heavenly world at death."

Ananda returned to his lodging and stood lamenting at the doorway. "Alas, I am still a learner with so much to do! The teacher who was so compassionate to me is passing away!"

The Buddha then inquired of the monks about Ananda's whereabouts. When they told him, the Buddha said, "Go, monks, and say to Ananda from me, 'Friend Ananda, the Teacher summons you.'"

When Ananda returned, the Buddha said, "Ananda, do not weep. Have I not told you that all things that are pleasant and delightful are changeable, subject to separation, and becoming other? Whatever is born, become, compounded is subject to decay. How then could it be that it should not pass away? For many years you have been in the Perfected One's presence, showing loving-kindness in act of body, mind, and speech; you have served wholeheartedly and unstintingly. You have achieved much merit, Ananda. Make the effort, and in a short time you will be free of all corruptions." The Buddha then called the monks together and praised the remarkable qualities of Ananda, qualities fully equivalent to that of Wheel-turning Monarchs, and told the assembly that all fully enlightened Buddhas of the past and in the future have had and will have such a chief attendant.

He then told Ananda to go to Kusinara and tell the Mallas that "tonight in the last watch the Enlightened One will attain final liberation. Come, take the opportunity to see him for the last time." The Mallas were assembled in their meeting hall on some business when Ananda entered the town and delivered the message. Hearing it, the Mallas presented themselves in such numbers that Ananda could only let them visit the Buddha in groups of families.

At that time an ascetic named Subhadda was in Kusinara and heard that the Buddha was about to attain final liberation. He was certain that the Buddha could teach him the Doctrine about which he had long been in doubt. So he went to the *sal*-grove and asked to see the master. Ananda refused him entrance, telling him that the Lord was weary. The Buddha, overhearing the conversation, called to Ananda, "Enough, do not hinder Subhadda, let him come in. He will quickly understand what I tell him." Subhadda asked the Buddha whether in fact all those who say they have realized the truth have in fact realized it or not. "Enough, Subhadda, never mind whether all or none or some have realized the truth. I will teach you the Doctrine. Listen, pay close attention." The Buddha then explained the Four Noble Truths and the Eightfold Path in which the Doctrine is found. At this Subhadda said, "Excellent, Lord, excellent! I go for refuge to the Buddha, the Doctrine, and the community. May I receive the ritual of going forth in the Lord's presence. May I receive ordination."

Although the rule called for four months of probation, Subhadda pleaded with them to allow his ordination now because of the importance of the Buddha's presence in all of their own ritual initiations into the order. Hearing his plea, the Buddha said, "Let Subhadda go forth!" The ritual took place, and in a short time Subhadda attained the status of an Enlightened One. He was the last person to be initiated into the order in the Buddha's presence.

The Buddha then addressed the assembled monks, saying, "It may be, monks, that some of you have doubts or uncertainty about the Buddha, the Doctrine, the community, or the path of practice. Ask, monks. Do not afterward feel remorse, thinking, 'The teacher was there before us, and we failed to ask the Lord face-to-face.'" The monks were silent. He asked them a second and third time and they remained silent. Then he said, "Perhaps you do not ask out of respect for the teacher. Then, monks, let one friend tell it to another." But still they were silent.

Ananda then burst out, "It is wonderful, Lord, it is marvelous! There is not one monk who has doubts or uncertainty."

"You speak from a serene mind, Ananda," the Buddha replied, "but the Enlightened One knows that there is not one monk who has doubts about the Buddha, the Doctrine, the community, or the path of practice. The least one of these monks is a stream-winner, incapable of falling into states of woe, certain of liberation. Now, monks, I declare to you: subject to decay are all conditioned things—strive on untiringly." These were the Buddha's last words.

The Buddha then rehearsed the levels of meditation, just as he performed them during the watches of the night at Bodh-Gaya. Traversing and then reversing the levels of meditation, he attained final liberation.

It was the great disciple Anuruddha who consoled them all through the night with the Buddha's teaching, that there is change and separation from all pleasant things and that everything having an origin must decay.

The next day Anuruddha sent Ananda into Kusinara to inform the Mallas who came with scents, garlands, and the cloth and robes to do honor to the body of the Buddha. On the seventh day they decided to take the body out the south gate of the town to cremate it. Eight men of the Mallas prepared to do so but could not lift the body. After several attempts at moving the body they asked Anuruddha, "Why can't we lift up the Lord's body?"

"Well," replied Anuruddha, "your intention is one thing, but the intention of the gods is quite another. It is the intention of the gods to carry him to the north of the city, bring him in through the north gate, and bear him through the middle of the town and out through the eastern gate to the Mallas shrine, and to burn the body there."

"If that is the gods' intention, then so be it." Then the gods together with the Mallas did just that, bringing the body through the northern gate, out the eastern gate to the shrine, where they set the body down and dealt with the Enlightened One's body in the manner of a Wheel-turning Monarch.

At that time the venerable Kassapa the Great was resting on the road from Pava to Kusinara with a company of about five hundred monks; when he learned of the Buddha's final liberation, he rushed to Kusinara as fast as he could. In the meantime, four ministers of the Mallas, having bathed and put on new clothes, approached the pyre in order to light the fire. They were unable to do so and asked Anuruddha why this was the case. Anuruddha replied that the Great Kassapa, a monk of great mental power and wisdom, third in reputation after Moggallana and Sariputta, was on his way to the pyre. It could not be lit until he and the five hundred monks with him paid homage to the Buddha.

When Kassapa arrived, he, together with the monks, circumambulated the pyre three times. And when this was done the Lord's funeral pyre ignited by itself. When the pyre was completely burned, only the bones of the Buddha were left. The Mallas honored the relics for a week in their assembly hall, encircling them with spears and bows.

The news traveled fast, and soon the kings from neighboring lands arrived to make claims on the relics. On hearing this the Mallas addressed the crowd, saying, "The Lord passed away in our parish. We will not give away any share of the Lord's remains." Hearing this, the Brahmin Dona reminded them that the Buddha taught forbearance, that it was wrong that strife should come from sharing the best of men's remains. He asked for peace and harmony, that they should share in friendship, dividing the relics into eight portions for memorials far and wide, that all may see them and gain serenity.

"Well, then," they said, "you divide up the remains of the Lord in the best and fairest way!"

"Very good," Dona said, and he did just that. Dona then asked for an urn, in order that he might build a memorial, and they gave it to him.

PART II

I suggested at the end of part I that you take the legends literally. What did I mean when I said this? Literal meaning is when sentence meaning and the speaker's meaning coincide. Literalness is the coincidence of language and use. When sentence meaning and speaker's meaning do not coincide, we usually interpret the use of the sentence as, for example, metaphorical, as poetry, symbolic, or a lie. Or we may conclude that what we have heard is nonsense. I speak a language, and I can use that language in a variety of ways. I can, for example, translate the language I speak into a code; I can use it to write poetry or fiction or to tell you a joke.

That literal meaning is sentence meaning can be illustrated in a variety of ways. Here is one example: When the folks at NASA announced, "The astronauts have landed on the moon," all those around the world who understood English or its translation into another language also understood the meaning of what had just been uttered. They understood the meaning of the sentence because they knew the truth conditions of the sentence. Or, to put it the other way around, to know the truth conditions of a sentence is to know its meaning. As Davidson once described it, "To know the semantic concept of truth for a language is to know what it is for a sentence—any sentence—to be true [or false] and this amounts . . . to understanding the language." To understand a language is to understand its meaning. To say literal meaning is sentence meaning is to assert that you do not have to know the context or use of the utterance in order to know the meaning, the truth value, of the sentence. You do not need to know, for example, the time, the place, or whether the announcer was lying or speaking in code to know the meaning of "The astronauts have landed on the moon."

Here is another example: We know the meaning of "It is raining, take an umbrella," regardless of whether it is spoken in your living room at this very moment, in a play at the local theater, in a novel you are reading, whether it is raining or not, or even when the speaker is lying. Whatever the uses of the sentence may be, the meaning, the truth conditions of the sentence, remain the same. In other words, to use sentences we must first of all know their truth conditions. Meaning, then, is not some object out in the world, nor is it something in our heads, or something we discover; only sentences have meaning.

As you reflect on all this, I think you will also conclude that most of the time when we speak with each other as expert translators we assume our linguistic partner is speaking literally. Moreover, it leads to the principle that the ability to speak and interpret a language presupposes that there is massive agreement between speaker and hearer about the world we live in. To disagree presupposes agreement. Thus phrases such as "people live in different worlds" or "languages are incommensurable" cannot be taken literally. Moreover, it is important to remember that literal meaning is sentence meaning. This tells us that it is confusing, if not a mistake, to talk about "hidden meanings" or "higher meanings" or "symbolic meanings"—that there are, in other words, "different kinds of meaning." Literal meaning is sentence meaning, and we can use sentences in a variety of ways.

The theoretical distinction I have made between language and its use, between language and speaking a language, is very basic to all of part II. This being the case, I want to pause here and discuss its importance.

First of all, it is important to remember that myths are language. Myths are uttered, are told, and so I shall make the same theoretical distinction for myth as I have for language: I speak a myth just as I speak a language. Thus I can make a distinction between myth as language and the use of myth.

There is nothing "unnatural," mysterious, or special about the language of myth. Although you may have found some of the names of persons and towns somewhat strange, you understood the stories perfectly well. We may find the cosmology difficult to understand, to come to grips with some of the technical points of Buddhist thought about existence, death, and rebirth, and the "no-self" Doctrine. We may find it odd that the Buddha ascended into heaven, talks with the gods, seems able to read people's minds, and can shoot water and fire out of his hands and feet, among other feats, but understanding the language was not a problem. That is to say, I doubt you had any problems understanding what was being said. You may have thought, "Well I now know what the Buddhas can do. After all, Buddhas are mythical beings, superhuman agents, and can do things that human beings cannot do. But, of course, superhuman agents do not exist! So what do I do with this story?"

It is this confrontation, this question, that often forces us into a major turn in our interpretation of myths. We now begin to look for symbolic or hidden meanings that translate the literal into a symbolic or transcendent meaning as an answer to our question, a turn away from literal meaning. In brief, we begin to think of myths as a special language with its own semantics. This translating maneuver turns my advice, "Take the myths literally," upside down. The advice now reads, "Take the myths symbolically," since taking them literally leads to nonsense if not irrationality. I think this is bad advice. It is bad advice because regardless of what we come up with, the new semantic theory will take us to either of two options: either it will contain a truth conditional semantics that is different from what we know about natural languages (and just what would that be?), or we will view myth as a language without truth conditions. The first option leads to silence, the second to incomprehension.

And, yet, religious language and myth are often identified as important examples of symbolic meaning that is different from literal meaning. In some cases this symbolic meaning is often spoken of as ineffable. It seems very odd, however, to think of a language as ineffable. Language is effable, and it is effable simply because all languages are translatable, and translation introduces us to the first level of interpretation, which is literal sentence meaning. Here I am talking not only about translating Pali into English but also, and primarily, of what occurs when you hear someone speaking, making noise that you identify as your primary native language and then without even thinking about it translating that noise into well-formed sentences. We are still not quite sure just how this is done, but we do know that all human beings have this wonderful ability, which I think you will agree is not learned. Moreover, we can posit that all languages have three distinctive properties; a syntax, a semantics, and a translation. Myths, the myths of the Buddha, are first of all language and thus share these three properties found in all natural languages.

In most books about religion the "real" meaning of religious language is often described as representational in some symbolic way. Myths "stand for" or "point to" something. For example, myths are often thought of as representations of the "sacred," which can be anything from a transcendent ultimate reality to social or political structures. Another well-known approach to the meaning of myth and ritual is to claim that the meaning of myths is expressive, perhaps nonrational, of deep biological or psychological instincts, social collective life, history, or transcendent archetypes. The task, then, is to construct a theory that will show us how to translate myths as symbolic representations of one or more of these "realities."

The history of the study of myth is a contest in which scholars of this subject have tried to convince us that one or the other symbolic representational theory is the right one, is true. Given the problems involved in such approaches to the subject, some scholars subscribe to the notion that the language of myth involves all of the preceding. The meaning of myth is then called "multivalent," that is, a language that means, that is, represents symbolically, many things at the same time.

But, this is, indeed, a very odd language. And once again it leads us to the conclusion that some people do not really know the true meaning of their language, that is, what it *really* refers to or represents. The Buddhists, for example, do not really know what they mean when they say, "I go to the Buddha, the Doctrine, and the community for refuge," or that "the Buddha was Vessantara many aeons ago." It seems that they do not know the meaning of their own language.

This puzzle led most of our intellectual ancestors to a well-known conclusion. They did not conclude, "My theory is wrong" but tried to explain this odd interpretation as "These people are primitive and underdeveloped," or "These people live in a different world," or perhaps, "These underdeveloped people should, at the least, read Durkheim, Freud, Weber or Eliade." As one scholar once put it, "If they think deeply about it," they will agree with our analysis of the meaning of their myths.

If you took my advice and read part I literally, you probably said to yourself, "But these stories just cannot be true!" I agree. People cannot fly through the air on their own, levitate in front of their parents, have former and future existences, travel to the heavens to convert their mother, and talk with the gods. We then begin to feel the pressure to resolve this apparent enigma by translating what we are reading into something we call "symbol"; we begin to look for hidden meanings. Or we say with a shrug, "What's true for them is false for us, people do in fact live in different worlds." Yet when all is said and done, we, including Theravada Buddhists, understand the legends because we take them literally, we know perfectly well what they mean. The task then becomes how to explain why people who do believe that what the myths say is true persist in holding beliefs that are false.

Putting aside, for the moment, the incoherent relativist doctrine that what is true for some people is false for us, many scholars in the cultural sciences accept a version of a theory that eventually became common sense, a good example of a theory becoming a fact. Although some people persist in believing that myths are true, so goes the theory, they persist in believing them because the myths satisfy needs that must be satisfied for the survival of both the society and the individual: religion is what it does. We will examine this popular but invalid theory in a moment. Before doing so, however, it is important to define a few crucial terms.

Many scholars either forget or overlook this requirement, often using the word "religion" or "myth" to cover just about anything or any story. To make matters worse, the words "spirituality" and "faith" are often used as a substitute for "religion," as if the substitution of one abused word for another solves the problem. Once in a while you read that "religion" and "myth" are very complex words and difficult to define, that there are dozens of definitions and very little agreement. That is, of course, also true of the word "freedom" or "community," "mind" or "consciousness." Given this situation, it is all the more important that we heed the imperative to clarify important terms. Here, then, are my definitions of "religion," "myth," and "ritual."

"Religion": Religion is a communal system of propositional attitudes and practices that are related to a superhuman agent or agents.

Explanation: "Communal system" emphasizes that religion is preeminently social and structured as a system of relations. "Propositional attitudes" stresses the cognitive and rational properties of religion. Propositional attitudes include our beliefs, hopes, values, fears, and desires. They are preeminently social, although they are not to be understood as representations, symbolic or otherwise, of social life or social structures. Durkheim was on the right track when he wrote, "We do not weep for the dead because we fear them; we fear them because we weep for them." Propositional attitudes are structured, constituted by their relations within the society and the individual. Notice that this definition does *not* assert that "religion is belief." Belief is only one of the propositional attitudes and cannot be adequately described and analyzed without the other attitudes to which it is related in a particular system. You might want to think of the attitudes as similar to the elements in a grammatical system— nouns, pronouns, verbs, conjunctions, and so on. It would be odd to think of a sentence as made up of only nouns or verbs. Similarly, it would be odd to think of religion as consisting of only beliefs. In fact, from this point of view it would be odd to think of giving belief, ritual, or myth an epistemological, ontological, or historical priority in any theory that attempts to explain religion. Thus to say that religion is essentially private, a certain feeling, hope, or value, would be starting off in the wrong direction.

"Superhuman agents" refers to agents that can do things you and I cannot do. For example, they can walk on water, levitate, and shoot fire and water out of their hands and feet, rise into the heavens, turn water into wine, and so forth. The word "superhuman" is not a synonym for "supernatural" and should not be confused with that word. The god of the three monotheistic sister religions is a superhuman agent; he certainly can do things we cannot do. But it is crucial to remember that "superhuman agent" is not restricted to the god of the three monotheistic religions. For example, it also includes "ancestors," "spirits" such as the *phi* or *nats* in some Theravada Buddhist countries, pantheons of gods and goddesses, as well as Universal Monarchs. Moreover, and especially, the concept includes the great heroic mythical figures such as Krishna, Jesus, Moses, Muhammad, and the Buddha. It is well known that Buddhism is often thought of as a religion that does not entail a belief in superhuman agents. After all, or so we are told, the Buddha was just a man. The legends you have read present massive evidence that falsify this point of view. We will look into this issue in the next chapter.

"Myth": Myth is a system of communal narrative about the deeds of a superhuman agent or agents.

Explanation: Myths are stories that have a beginning, middle, and end that describe the deeds of superhuman agents. The inclusion of the word "communal" is crucial in this definition. It signifies that the stories belong to a community, are authorless or originally given by superhuman agents, and usually transmitted orally. Thus, no story about superhuman agents, no myth. "Myth" excludes not only novels and science fiction but also Nazism, Communism, or humanism. The definition, however, raises some very interesting questions that need serious attention. What, for instance, is the difference between fiction and myth?

"Ritual": Ritual is a communal system of prescribed actions consisting of both verbal and nonverbal interactions with a superhuman agent or agents.

Explanation: Habits are not rituals. As far as we know, ants, bees, spiders, monkeys, dolphins, and, yes, cats and dogs may be very intelligent, but they do not perform rituals. They may communicate, but as far as I know they neither interact with superhuman agents nor have propositional attitudes that include beliefs, fears, hopes, and values. The ability for this kind of interaction entails a communal system that is, among other things, constituted by syntax and semantics that we call language. And just in case you are thinking of them, this definition does include ascetics, who, though in opposition to the householder, are part of the communal system. To be in opposition is a relation, defined by what it is you are in opposition to.

The operative words in each of these definitions, the words that bring them into a relation and provide them with a distinctive feature, are "superhuman agent or agents." If you page through the last three hundred years of the study of religion, you will find one central question running through the entire fascinating history: What does religion mean? Scholars in the era of the Enlightenment and the age of Romanticism who shaped the framework for the modern study of culture struggled mightily with questions such as these: What is the meaning of the goddesses and the gods? What does "superhuman agent" signify? What is the meaning of religion? What do myths mean?

The answers to these questions, it seems to me, can be divided into two general theories. The first claims that religion is rational; it entails propositional attitudes and thus truth conditions. If this is the case, then the mythical episodes concerning superhuman agents are false, and it is important to notice that the question usually changes to, Why do people persist in holding on to beliefs about stories that are false? There are a variety of answers to this question, none of which seem to be successful as explanations of either religious belief or myth because we have changed the subject by asking a new question.

You can avoid adopting the "rational but false" theory by claiming that religion is rational but its truth claims are not the same as those found in literal sentence meaning. Revelation and symbolic, hidden, or transcendental meaning are often used as the foundation for establishing this kind of response. What we need here, but what is never offered, is a "special theory of semantics" for the special truth claims. Or you can take the more modern and popular relativist view and argue that religion is indeed rational and true when viewed from the context of the language and culture in which it thrives. Thus, what is rational and true for the Buddhist may not be true for the Muslim because what is rational and what is true are given in the sense that a particular religion has in its particular linguistic and cultural context. This popular sentence, unfortunately, ends in self-contradiction and incoherence. One only has to ask, if this sentence is true, how do you know it is true? The point being, your claim seems to be the one universal claim whose meaning is not restricted to *your* language and *your* culture. In other words, there seems to be at least one sentence that is not relative to a particular language and culture! Cultural and conceptual relativism are a trap from which there is no exit. I do not know of a defense of this theory that avoids contradiction without qualifications. With qualifications the theory is no longer interesting as an alternative theory, since "people live in different worlds" is no longer to be interpreted literally.

You can avoid the traps and pitfalls of the preceding variations on the rationality and truth of religion by simply denying that religion is rational; it lies

beyond the truth conditions of literal meaning or any meaning, for that matter. In brief, religion, or more specifically religious language, does not contain
propositional conditions of any kind. This theory usually describes religion as
expressive, emotive, subjective, beyond logic. It often appeals to song, dance,
poetry, and art as familiar examples—as if song, dance, poetry, and art are
nonrational. To put it briefly, this theory and its variations claim that religion
is neither true nor false. It often claims that religion is "symbolic" in some
nonrational sense, or that if we do want to talk about "meaning," we should say
that the meaning of religion is to be found in its function of satisfying certain
needs; the meaning of religion is what it does. This "use" theory of meaning,
known as "functionalism," is very popular but quite mistaken in its logical
premises.

The notion that religion is nonrational, void of propositional attitudes,
seems clearly mistaken when confronted with the modern debates on evolution versus creationism, or the claims made during the enthronement of
Pope Benedict XVI, or the conflicts that have led to bloodshed between Jews,
Muslims, and Christians. Moreover, we seem to be in the same situation we
found ourselves in when adopting "hidden meaning" as an answer. Once again
it seems that those who are religious do not know what they are doing or talking about. They do not really understand that what they believe is "nonsense."
As I have said, this is a very odd understanding of what language is.

When all is said and done, it seems to me that the first hurdle that all theories of religion as nonrational must clear is this: they must define and describe
a theory of meaning that does not involve the truth conditions of a language,
that is to say, they must demonstrate that religious language or mythical language is a special kind of language. To put this in my words, this would entail
a theory of language of myth that does not entail propositional attitudes or
propositional content. This, it seems to me, is simply refuted on both theoretical and empirical grounds. By now the sign at the head of this theoretical path
should read "dead end." This leaves us, it seems to me, with rational theories of
myth that stress truth conditions as necessary for a comprehensive and coherent theory of meaning. From this theoretical standpoint myths are false.

Why, then, if myths are false in their content, do people persist in believing them to be true? It is important to notice that we have now changed the
question about the semantics of myth to why people believe them to be true.
The two questions are often confused. Nevertheless, the question is an important one and relevant especially for both modern, educated folk in the United
States, for example, who persist in taking Genesis 1 literally, among other stories, rather than accepting evolutionary biology, as well as for cultures we call
"underdeveloped." I do not have an adequate answer to this question, and from

what I have read I doubt that anyone else does either. But I am quite certain that to say, "They believe them because this satisfies certain needs, either psychologically, sociologically, or biologically," is an invalid or trivial claim when it is made as an explanation and not a guess. Functionalist theories rest on four basic premises: (1) A society (or person) functions adequately only if certain needs are satisfied. (2) If religion is present, then as an effect the need is satisfied. (3) The need is satisfied. (4) Therefore, religion is present. This is clearly invalid, yet many major scholars in the study of culture have made the simple mistake of "affirming the consequent": If P, then Q. Q. Therefore, P. (A complete critique of this theory can be found in the bibliographical references for this page in the notes at the end of the book.)

Part II begins the adventure of interpretation with a look at what is truly a modern, Western quest for the historical Buddha. This quest is the search for original, authentic Buddhism. It is the search for what "really" happened and remains a powerful force in our understanding of Buddhism. This quest is directly linked to the search for the authentic sayings of the Buddha, the quest for the original message or meaning of Buddhism. As you will discover, I have concluded that this quest is based on an illusion because, as someone once wrote, "every text is always-already read."

The remainder of part II consists of chapters based on three premises. First, take the myths literally; they mean what they say. When you do that, you will have no problem with the notion that the Buddha is a superhuman agent. Second, to write a biography of the Buddha is an impossible task simply because it has no beginning or end. If we take the message of Buddhism seriously, the episodes of Gotama the Buddha who "lived" in our era simply constitute one chapter in an indefinite series of lives stretching into the past and on into the future. Most modern accounts of the life of the Buddha write a biography that focuses primarily on one short chapter in his many lives, but, as you now know, the framework of the Buddha's lives is cosmological. Third, once you make the attempt to include at least some of the major episodes in his cosmological life, you begin to notice what I have called a narrative constraint, a "syntax," that provides the framework for comparison and interpretation. The basic structure or syntax, I will argue, is a set of oppositions, relations, that provide the narrative with a constraint that stamps it as uniquely Buddhist and Indian, if not Southeast Asian in general. Finally, I will argue that the basic, simplest set of oppositions that define this religion and its myths is the relation "conqueror versus renouncer," or "king versus monk," or "householder versus renouncer," a relation that is given its supreme status in the pair "Universal Monarch versus the Awakened One," both known as "the great agent" in Buddhist mythology.

In studying the legends, we must never forget that a great sage predicted that at his birth at Kapilavatthu, Gotama would become either a Universal Monarch or the Perfect Awakened One. His story, in our era, begins as a prince of the Sakyas who becomes an ascetic, and ends as an ascetic who becomes a Universal Monarch at his funeral. His funeral is a rite of passage that simply cannot be mistaken for the funeral of a renouncer. His births, deaths, and rebirths can be viewed as a series of punctuated appearances as monarch/ renouncer. And, as we shall see, it is precisely in the differences between these two great agents that they resemble each other.

It would be a major misunderstanding of what I am proposing in part II to conclude that what I call the "narrative constraint" or the "syntax" from which the myths are told is the meaning of the myths. What I do want to argue, however, is that this narrative constraint is a necessary condition for the meaning of this peculiar "biography" that has no beginning or end, and thus a requirement for a proper interpretation of the mythical language.

17

The Quest for the Historical Buddha

The modern quest for the historical Buddha is not unique. It is a variation on quests for the origin of religion that are often found linked to a grand evolutionary scale of stages in the history of human culture. The motto reads: "If we can explain the origin of religion, we will be able to explain its meaning." Many scholars in the romantic age, for example, believed that language began as poetry and symbol. Myth and ritual were often thought of as primary, original expressions that contained their own self-referential meaning. Religion was often, and still is, thought of as dramatic, poetic, a symbolic expression of primal experiences (perhaps an "oceanic feeling") that is prior to rational or discursive uses of language for objectifying our world. From this point of view we might say, "In the beginning, language, culture, religion are literally a drama."

If, however, you think that poetry, ritual, myth, and religion entail linguistic structures—syntax and semantics, for example—then the "dramatization" theory of religion will not be persuasive. You might, as did some scholars, beginning with the Enlightenment, presuppose an evolution of knowledge through time, from animism to science, with religion exhibiting a prescientific stage of knowledge. You would conclude that although religion is "prescientific" and thus false in its attempt to explain the world, it is nevertheless rational, not irrational or nonrational. We sometimes forget that if we believe something that is false, this does not mean we are irrational.

There are a variety of origin theories of culture, society, and religion, and it is not a surprise to find them applied to the study of Buddhism. If the broad evolutionary theory of knowledge is far too conjectural and biased, you might think of religion as basically ethical in origin. Thus, in your resolve to find the original meaning of Buddhism you would look for texts in which the Buddha stressed the development of moral life and then attempt to show that these texts are the earliest, or original, texts in the canon. Or you might settle on religion as originally mythical and ritualistic and look for descriptions of ritual in the *Vinaya* sections of the *Tipitaka* as evidence of the earliest and therefore authentic meaning of Buddhism.

If you found none of the preceding explanations of the origin of religion satisfactory, you might look for a philosophical or metaphysical system, perhaps some early brand of idealism, existentialism, or pragmatism, as the origin. If so, texts on the Doctrine of the "interdependent origination of all conditioned things" or the *Dhammapada* could become the focus as obvious evidence for the original teaching of the Buddha.

Explanations such as this are not absurd. They are quite imaginative and remain a powerful influence in the contemporary study of Buddhism. They have one thing in common: they all use the Pali Buddhist scriptures. This presupposes a huge leap of faith from the second or third century A.D. back to about the sixth or fifth century B.C. and the magical transformation, sometimes called "demythologization," of documents that are clearly mythical into documents that are or reflect actual historical events and developments. Moreover, it is a fallacy, I would argue, that to be competent in a language or adequately understand a religion it is necessary that you know its history or origin. Competence in speaking a language, reading a myth, or understanding the performance of a religious rite or the playing of a game does not presuppose knowledge of their history or origin. You can be or become a competent speaker of English, that is, understand its meaning, without taking a course in the history of the English language.

One of the most fascinating chapters in the history of Buddhist studies is the continued quest for the historical Buddha. It is not accidental that the origin of this search parallels the similar quest for the historical Jesus. Both quests are variations on the historical origins theory of explaining the authentic or original words and acts of the Buddha or Jesus.

Why is it that Jesus and Buddha seem to get all the attention and not, for example, Krishna and Rama, two of the great superhuman heroes of Hinduism? After all, the geographic locations of both Krishna and Rama are well known. You can visit the birthplace of Krishna, view the very place where as a newborn he parted the waters of a river, and you can stand on the spot where he danced with the cowgirls by the light of the moon. Blood has been shed at Ayodhya over the defilement of the birthplace of Rama. Yet as far as I know, there never has been a serious quest for the historical Rama or Krishna.

I think we would find it rather odd if someone asserted that it is absurd for anyone today to deny the historical existence of Rama or Krishna. The question, then, is this: Why is the quest for the historical Buddha any different? Furthermore, why is this quest so important to the Western study of Buddhism? And why have we not learned anything from the continued failure of such quests? Most South and Southeast Asian Buddhists have no problem whatsoever with Buddha's "biography." Of course, they take the stories literally and thus do not doubt his former births, the traditional Western dates of his life in our era, 566–486 B.C., or his miracles.

The reason for the continued failure of the quest seems quite simple. The primary issue in all quests for the historical Buddha is the question of evidence. Anyone interested in writing a historical biography, be it Gotama the Buddha, Shakespeare, or Abraham Lincoln, requires three kinds of evidence to write such an account: documents relating to the person, the person's own writings or recordings, and records of the social conditions of the time. Such documents are easily available for Shakespeare and Lincoln, but what about Gotama the Buddha?

As anyone who has studied the history of Buddhism in India knows, no evidence of this kind exists. The earliest extant texts are from the second or third century of our era, or perhaps even later. When we read about this subject, we must constantly keep in mind that these texts are dated at least five hundred years after the supposed life of the person scholars keep insisting "must have lived," and claim that "the bare outline" of his life is a fact. When we read such assertions, it is best to keep in mind what Collins, one of the leading scholars of Indian Buddhism, wrote several years ago: we must, he says, "move away from an outmoded and quixotic concern with origins" and the notion that the Pali canon equals early Buddhism, and we must remember that "we have no evidence *of any kind* which can be securely dated before Ashoka" (i.e., ca. 250 B.C.; italics mine).

You have read these texts in part I; they are clearly mythical in content and form. Furthermore, we have no written records that describe the social conditions in India at about 550 to 450 B.C., the approximate time that Gotama "must have lived." Anyone who uses these texts for discovering history must believe that they can be decoded or interpreted as symbolic representations of actual social conditions and events, that is to say, the myths conceal a hidden message or content. If, however, we have learned anything at all from the debates on the meaning of myth it is this: be very careful about using myths as representations of actual social life because they are often exactly the opposite. The ancient texts and myths of India remain the best evidence for observing this advice. Reginald Ray has it right when he says, "In approaching Buddha Sakyamuni, it is invalid and finally impossible to separate, as some have tried to do, the man from the myth." Most scholars know this.

K. R. Norman, one of the best philologists of ancient Indian languages, put it this way in a 1988 symposium concerning the chronology of the Buddha: "It is clear that we must guard against trying to use uncritical material critically.... References to a long or short chronology only make sense in a context where we think that the numbers are meaningful, i.e., correct." Sound advice. As far as I know, no scholar thinks that the texts used in part I of this book or other versions of these texts in various other ancient traditions of Buddhism are "critical," that is, accurate, historical accounts and chronologies. And yet there is a constant slippage back into using the texts as critical, as evidence, in arguments concerning what really happened back then.

The basic problem throughout all the debates regarding the "historicity" of the biographies of the Buddha is this: there simply is no key that allows us to unlock and separate myth from history in the documents that we possess. Most assertions that Gotama "must" have existed simply proceed as if such a key exists without a sentence of explanation for why they believe this imperative to be true. I shall call this elusive certainty the "received tradition."

The received tradition was firmly established by the time of the Seventh World Sanskrit Conference, held in Leiden in 1987. At that conference a well-known scholar of Buddhism said, "In the nineteenth century, not all European scholars were even prepared to accept that such a historical person as Gotama the Buddha ever existed; ... though such an extremity of skepticism now seems absurd." Perhaps the audience agreed. After all, who wants to be considered absurd? But no matter how loudly such sayings are uttered, they are not arguments or evidence; in most instances statements such as these, including conjectures as to what "must" have been the case, are distress signals.

The view that it would be absurd for anyone at the present time to deny the existence of a historical Buddha implies that something new, something since the nineteenth century, has been discovered that makes such a belief absurd. What is it? Frankly, I do not know. What we find is the repeated assertion, without explanation or evidence, that there simply "must" have been such a person as Gotama, otherwise we cannot explain the existence of Buddhism. As far as I know, no one has argued that there simply must have been a historical Krishna or a Rama in order to explain the existence of Krishnaism or Ramaism in Hindu India.

A critique of the received tradition that gives us a detailed analysis of its assumptions has yet to be written. A few examples taken from well-known scholars of Buddhism and introductory texts must suffice as illustrations of the tradition and its problems. You will soon notice that my use of the word "tradition" is not metaphoric.

In 1927 a book on the legends of the Buddha appeared that is still widely quoted. It is a classic in its balanced judgments and civility, and still worth reading. E. J. Thomas concluded, "Whatever additions to the legend there may be, the further we go back the less do we find...anything but the view that he was a historical personage, a great religious reformer and moral teacher, and the proclaimer of the Noble Eightfold Path." Thomas at least made it clear that his argument rested on two quite different questions. The first is the question about the historical existence of Gotama the Buddha: Did he or did he not exist? The second, quite different, question is this: Are the stories told about him credible as historical evidence? An answer to this question seems to depend upon the lawlike principle that persists to this day, that the earliest or original text is the authentic, credible text. Thus we can understand why the quest for the historical Buddha ends up becoming a quest for the "original" message or text. What remains elusive if not circular in this argument is the notion that these "earliest" or "original" documents are, or at least reflect, the actual history of what occurred or was said. Clearly, what scholars take to be the earliest or original texts are the result of constructions built out of theories regarding language, the development of language, and the basic premise that we can uncover the truth with regard to what this language reflects or refers to. We must remind ourselves that the data for such constructions are taken from the stories you have read in part I.

After raising these important questions, Thomas mentions David Strauss's *Life of Jesus* and then moves into a very short as well as cryptic comparison of the scholarship on the life of Jesus and on the Buddha. Thomas was well aware that the parallel quest for the historical Jesus also rested on the exact same questions. Thus, if you want to answer the first question concerning historical existence, you must answer the second question about the credibility of the texts as history. However, you can answer the second question only by finding documents that are "authentic," "credible" as the actual words of Jesus or, in our case, the Buddha. The task, then, is to devise a method that will allow you to determine which texts, if any, are authentic history or original sayings. If this approach seems impossible, can we come up with a method that allows us to decode the original meaning that is hidden in symbolic or mythical language? An important point bears repeating: the quest for the historical

Buddha is a variation on the quest for the origin of religion. The quest for the origin of religion is a variation on the quest for the meaning and development of religion.

After a lengthy and balanced discussion of the debate concerning the historical Buddha, Thomas turns to the fundamental question of "whether...it can be said that we possess the actual words of the Founder. In one sense it can.... We possess a large number of discourses, poems, and other sayings that claim to be Buddha's own words. There can be no reasonable doubt that the community started not merely with a code of monastic rules devised by the Founder, but also with a body of doctrinal utterances."

I think we all agree that a great deal, if not most, of the narrative in part I "claims to be Buddha's own words." In this sense, the literal sense, we can all agree that according to the texts we have read, "we possess the actual words of the Founder." It is the next question that causes problems: "Who is the Founder?" The text informs us that he is a superhuman agent, and as far as I can tell Thomas agrees.

The issue here is, are the words in the text the words of a historical person? Clearly, the only sources we have for an answer to that question are late Buddhist texts. We can now see how right Thomas was when he raised the fundamental question: "Do we possess the actual words of the Founder?" That is, "are the texts authentic, credible," the records of historical events, the actual discourse of a person named Gotama? The answer, as scholars know, is no.

After assuring us that there can be no reasonable doubt about the historical question, Thomas seems to take it all back without realizing it. He tells us that according to the textual tradition even the early Buddhists had serious difficulties in determining just what the Buddha said. He then drops the bombshell: "For us, even with stricter methods of criticism, it is still more difficult to make a clear distinction between what may have been gradually incorporated and the original nucleus. But the nucleus is there, even though we may never succeed in separating it, or in deciding what the earliest form of it may have been." The question now becomes, if we cannot separate it out how then does Thomas know "that the nucleus is there"? How do we know what it is? What does Thomas mean when he tells us that "the further we go back the less do we find anything but the view that he was a historical personage...?"

It seems not to have occurred to Thomas that one of his fundamental assumptions, that the "earliest saying" is at least closer to the "authentic" or "original saying," presupposes what it has set out to confirm: that there is an original nucleus there. The question once again is, What is the evidence for this basic assumption? It seems clear that since we may "never succeed in separating" the text from the original nucleus, the evidence cannot be based on the text of the Pali canonical *Tipitaka*. It must come from a source that is external to the canon. As we shall soon see, there is such evidence even though it too is late, and it contradicts the main argument of the "received tradition."

The question that must be kept in mind throughout all the debates concerning the quest is, What is the evidence? What is the proof, the warrant that provides us with the certainty expressed so easily in many books on Buddhism, a certainty that allows some scholars to claim that to deny his historical existence is an absurdity?

Étienne Lamotte, certainly one of the outstanding scholars of Indian Buddhism, begins his classic *History of Indian Buddhism* with the confession that "to write about the life of Gotama is a desperately difficult task." He then says, "It remains nonetheless a fact that Buddhism could not be explained if it were not based on a personality powerful enough to give it the necessary impetus and to have marked it with its essential features which will persist throughout all history." This "factual" claim is repeated again at the end of the book: "Buddhism could not be explained unless we accept that it has its origins in the strong personality of a founder." Notice that Lamotte, as is true of most of the "received tradition," has reduced the explanation of the existence of Buddhism to a question about the origins of this religion. "It is a fact," he says, "that we could not explain Buddhism were it not based on a founder." Lamotte is not thinking of modern hypotheses about the origin of Buddhism. He is thinking of hard facts, empirical facts as evidence, and he believes that he has found it in Buddhist texts. "Even though it is true that the codification of the writings came later," he states, "it is nonetheless a fact that, in order to appreciate early Buddhism the only valid evidence—or indication—which we possess is the basic agreement between the Nikayas on the one hand and the Agamas on the other."

He is, of course, quite right. When we compare the content of the Nikaya, a section of the Pali canon, with the *Agama*, Sanskrit texts later translated into Chinese, we find that there is, indeed, a great deal of agreement. It is this fact that has led many scholars to posit two hypotheses: first, the existence of a lost text as the source for both the *Nikaya* and the *Agama*, and second, that parts of both the Sanskrit and Pali versions of this lost source reflect or "indicate" an original or earlier text of Buddhism.

Lamotte seems to know better than to push this argument too hard. He backs down from the "fact" in the very next paragraph: "For anyone who is willing to take it [the basic agreement] into consideration, it appears from this that Sakyamuni [i.e., Gotama], after Enlightenment, discovered the noble truths which could lead his disciples to the end of suffering and to Nirvana." Notice the argument is no longer based upon a "fact" but on our "willingness" to take the basic agreement into consideration. And if we are willing, then it "appears" to be the case that the texts represent or indicate a basic outline of the Founder. One thing is clear, when Lamotte writes about "the fact that Buddhism could not be explained" without a founder, he is not thinking of a "superhuman agent." However, that is the only factual evidence he has.

We have no trouble finding the received tradition as described by Thomas and Lamotte, in A. K. Warder's account. Note, however, that there is nothing in the following passage that would indicate that his description is pure conjecture. Warder, an authority on Pali Buddhism, tells the story of the origin and development of Buddhism this way:

> The popularization of Buddhism was by now based very largely on the legend of the Buddha. The Doctrine itself could be presented symbolically through this legend, and however far the wandering teachers of *dharma* (in all the senses of that mightily ambiguous word) went in expounding the Four Truths and the eightfold way, and the ideal society, they evidently found that it was generally easier to make the first impression on their multiracial audiences by means of narratives rather than the dialogues of the *Tipitaka*. The greatest of these narratives was the story of the Buddha himself, and the more wonderful it could be made, the more surprising its incidents, the more effective it seems to have been.

Warder goes on to say:

> All these biographies agree in their main outlines and essential episodes, but differ completely in their actual texts, styles, and innumerable details. Whatever borrowing there was between the schools took place not in the period of formation of their common original *Tripitaka* in which no such biography occurs, but much later, when the Sthaviravadins [a Buddhist school] and probably some others had closed their *Tripitakas* against further traditions. In a sense the legend of the Buddha belongs not to the schools but to the popular Buddhism of the ordinary laity in which the doctrinal differences which split the schools count for practically nothing—in short to Buddhism as a religion, not to Buddhism as a philosophy.

Notice that Warder says "in a sense" the legends belong to "popular Buddhism," that is, the householder.

You cannot miss Warder's judgment concerning the value of religion versus philosophy, or the laity versus the monks. The distinction being made here between philosophy and religion is a distinction that is certainly not evident in the canonical texts themselves. Nevertheless, for Warder the legends are not only late developments in Buddhism but also the product of the house-holder for whom philosophy "counts for practically nothing." This important judgment is based on a premise that is sheer conjecture: that in the begin-ning there existed a single source, now lost, that was common to all Buddhists monks in which legends of the Buddha were absent. We must keep in mind that the idea of a "single lost source common to all Buddhists in which legends of the Buddha were entirely absent" is a hypothetical construction. We must remind ourselves that all the *evidence* for this conjecture is based upon the very texts that Warder has judged to be not only late but also the product of the influence of popular Buddhism, the Buddhism of the pious householder. This construction soon became a historical fact that secured the foundation of the received tradition.

William LaFleur repeats what is by now a tradition. He tells us, "At the end of the nineteenth century, many European scholars were skeptical as to whether such a person had, in fact, ever lived." He assures us, "Today, how-ever, there is general agreement that we need not be quite so skeptical," that although there were many additions and revisions produced orally and by "the imagination of pious people," the different biographies "seem to have been based on one lost one that was composed a little more than a century after his death." We are told that it is no longer necessary "to sort out the different lev-els of credibility." All we need do is "grasp the basic outline of the story of the Buddha that has captured the imagination of the Buddhist community…[and that] still serves as the paradigm of ideal human existence."

Peter Harvey also leaves little room for doubt. Although he agrees that the legends of the Buddha are late, "the details are in general agreement, but while they must clearly be based around historical facts they also contain legendary and mythological embellishments and it is often not possible to sort out one from the other. While the bare historical facts of the traditional biography will never be known as it stands it gives insight into Buddhism by enabling us to see what the *meaning* of the Buddha's life is to Buddhists." Just how Harvey knows that "they must be based around historical facts" when it is also a fact that "the bare historical facts will never be known" is never explained, nor is the notion "that the details are in general agreement" made clear.

Michael Carrithers begins his account in *Buddha: A Very Short Introduction* by saying that there are good reasons for doubting the compressed account of the life of the Buddha that he sketched in two brief paragraphs. "But," he con-tinues, "at least the outline of the life must be true: birth, maturity, renunci-ation, search, awakening, and liberation, teaching, death." Once again, what is the evidence that makes a scholar assert that "the outlines of the life must be true," the fact that the outlines agree? Carrithers does not tell us. But in stating this he makes a very important point that is seldom made explicit: it is not just that the outlines agree, but that the outline "must be *true*." That is to say, the outline corresponds or refers to actual events in the life of a historical person.

The outline, then, is not about a fictional character or a myth. But, as usual, Carrithers has a problem: How did what the Buddha taught to an elite group get spread out to "people in the world"? How did Buddhism transform itself from an ascetic, elite, movement into something called "popular Buddhism"? Carrithers thinks that we can identify accounts of the Buddha's life that are bare and simple narratives. "It is easy," he says, "to accept that these have an ancestry... actually imparted to his monks." But there are other narratives that "evidently took form some generations after the Buddha's death, and are full of mythical detail. They are therefore far from trustworthy." They illustrate how a "personal liberation was metamorphosed into a mission to the world at large." Who is doing this "metamorphosing" seems to be the proper question at this point.

Rupert Gethin, at the beginning of *The Foundations of Buddhism*, tells us "that the subsequent Buddhist tradition founded upon and inspired by the teaching of a charismatic individual who lived some centuries before the beginning of the Christian era can hardly be doubted." He quotes Lamotte: "Buddhism cannot be explained unless we accept that it has its origin in the strong personality of its founder," and then says, "Given this premise, none of the bare details of the Buddha's life is particularly problematic for the historian." There is no reason, in other words, for undue skepticism about the historical existence of the Buddha. What we must pause and ask here is, what are the "bare details" that are not problematic for the historian? Since when do historians deal with, find, or write about bare details? Is it not the case that for historians the notion of bare details is a contradiction?

What Gethin then says is worth quoting at length, since I think it describes the assumptions of the received tradition better than anything else I have come across:

> Of course, as the Buddhist traditions tell it, the story of the life of
> the Buddha is not history nor meant to be. The whole story takes
> on a mythic and legendary character. A wealth of detail is brought
> in capable of being read metaphorically, allegorically, typologically
> and symbolically. Much of this detail is to modern sensibilities of a
> decidedly "miraculous" and "supernatural" kind. The story of the
> Buddha's life becomes not an account of the particular individual
> circumstances of a man who, some 2,500 years ago, left home to

become a wondering ascetic, but something universal, an arche-
type; it is the story of all those who have become Buddhas in the
past and all who will become Buddhas in the future, and, in a sense,
of all who follow the Buddhist path. It is the story of the Buddhist
path, a story that shows the way to a profound religious truth. Yet,
for all that, many of the details of his early life given in the oldest
sources remain evocative of some memory of events from a distant
time. If we persist in distinguishing and holding apart myth and
history, we are in danger of missing the story's own sense of truth.
Furthermore, the historian must recognize that he has virtually no
strictly *historical* criteria for distinguishing between history and
myth in the accounts of the life of the Buddha. And at that point he
should perhaps remain silent and let the story speak for itself.

It would seem, given Gethin's own words, that he has just trashed the
received tradition.

The preceding statement is an excellent example of how a major premise
about a set of historical events that needs to be proved, the bare details, a lost
source, becomes the primary interpretive principle of texts compiled centuries
later for the events and hypotheses that need proving. Thus Gethin, assuming
that the "bare details" are not problematic, says, "The whole story takes on a
mythic and legendary character." Not so. The stories do not *take on* anything;
they *are* mythical. Once he assumes that the main premise is true, he can then
tell us that a "wealth of detail is brought in *capable* of being read metaphori-
cally, allegorically, typologically and symbolically."

Indeed it can. But let us remember who is doing this kind of reading.
It certainly is not the Buddhist. Once the assumed basic outlines, the bare
details, are in place and the legends "take on" a mythical character, the scholar
with a great deal of imagination can begin the search for the hidden message
as allegorical or symbolic in meaning. But the scholar of religion and myth
has been deceived here. It is not the basic outline that takes on the character of
myth, but the myth from which the basic outline is extracted that has taken on
the character of history! The motto of the received tradition, "the outline must
be true," is clearly based on the "metamorphosis" of myth into history.

What I find absolutely puzzling in all this is that from Thomas to Gethin,
scholars of the received tradition admit that, in Gethin's words, "The historian
must recognize that he has virtually no strictly *historical* criteria for distinguishing between history and myth in the accounts of the life of the Buddha."
If this is true, and I believe it is, then how can one say that these sources,
among others, give us the evidence in outline that Gotama must have existed

as a historical person? A scholar such as Lamotte may have a strong conviction that such a person must have existed as an explanation for the origin of Buddhism. Such a conviction in itself is not absurd. But the important critical questions are these: Why do scholars believe this is the case, and what is the evidence that serves as a warrant for such a conviction? Why would scholars continue to believe that the basic or bare outline is true even though they know that none of the sources can be used as evidence, that the evidence they have does not allow them to distinguish between myth and history? Why has it not occurred to them that the "bare outline" is itself not historical evidence but a construction, an abstraction taken from mythical stories about a figure named the Buddha? In fact, the "bare outline" in itself could describe any ascetic in India. It is indeed bare, providing us with no historical content whatsoever.

There are always exceptions. Not all introductory books on Buddhism are full endorsements of the received tradition. In fact, we might view these exceptions as small cracks in what once was a solid wall. For example, the evolution of the fifth revised edition of *The Buddhist Religion*, a very popular text, indicates that the received tradition concerning the life of the Buddha is beginning to lose force. "The quest for the historical Gautama," the authors tell us, "is predestined to a measure of failure. We cannot get behind the portraits drawn by the early communities; their reports are all we have.... Although the historical truth of the accounts may never be proven, the accounts themselves are undoubtedly of historical importance, as they have inspired Buddhists by the millions over the past two and one half-millennia." No one will disagree with the assertion that the legends of the Buddha are of historical importance for an understanding of the development of Buddhism.

The assertion that the quest is "predestined to a measure of failure" should come as no surprise. In 1958 Lamotte lamented that "according to tradition, the Buddha lived for eighty years, but the date of his Nirvana, that is, his decease, has still not been established with certainty." Thirty years later, Heinz Bechert summed up the work of a well-known 1988 conference entitled "The Problem of the Determination of the Date of the Historical Buddha" as follows: "There is no information on the dates of the historical Buddha...universally accepted by scholars, nor have scholars been in a position to arrive at a general agreement concerning this question." Bechert himself knows that "we have no convincing evidence whatsoever of reliable chronological information"; he concludes his introductory essay by saying, "We cannot provide a new chronology approved by all or most experts.... Opinion remains strongly divided."

This conclusion in itself should alert anyone interested in Buddhism to the many problems involved in discussing history and the Buddha. The conclusion should also warn us about taking a date "corrected by Western scholars" as fact, as if "Western scholars" had reached a consensus on this subject. And yet Warder, quoting the authority of Bareau and Eggermont, accepts the date 486 B.C. as "practically certain," and Schumann, in *The Historical Buddha*, agrees. Carrithers tells us that Western scholars have corrected the preserved date in Sri Lanka, yielding a date of 483 B.C. for the Buddha's death. He mentions the "actively debated" question and locates the problem as typically Indian, since "they were very little interested in chronology but much exercised over philosophy." LaFleur simply states that the Buddha lived "roughly between 560 and 480 BCE" and adds the important point that Indian Buddhists did not regard him as the one and only Buddha but as one among many Buddhas. Harvey thinks that there is a "consensus" on the "earlier dates" (448–368 B.C.) and offers that "something approaching the later dates is seen as more likely, perhaps, c. 480–400." As Bechert stressed in 1988, this is all speculation; a reader unfamiliar with the history of this subject, however, would never know it.

Buddhists in South Asia, in the meantime, took action on the issue of the Buddha's dates in the first World Buddhist Congress in Colombo in 1950. At that meeting it was agreed that 1956 would mark the twenty-five hundredth year of the Buddha's death. To make this clear the congress also adopted a resolution stating that "the World Fellowship of Buddhists adopt the year 2494 as the established year of the Buddhist Era as of date (i.e., 1950 AD) and...that a copy of this resolution be circulated to all known Buddhist organizations and societies for information and acceptance." The resolution was also adopted at the Third World Conference in 1954. In other words, the World Fellowship of Buddhists continued to maintain the tradition of 624–544 B.C. as marking the "Buddhist era"; in Southeast Asia the year 1956 would be known as 2500 B.E.

What would happen to our view of Buddhism if we put the perennial quest for the historical Buddha to one side? Once we reject the notion that the Pali canon or any of the other texts either literally contain or can be decoded as containing the "kernel of original" Buddhism and place them in the context of Sri Lanka at around A.D. 200, we are forced into thinking about the mythology of the Buddha in the context of a cosmology that gives us detailed information on his former lives.

But why focus on the former lives of the Buddha? Because the texts and the Asokan evidence tell us, "prove," that the *Jataka* stories, the stories of the Buddha's former lives, were well known and an essential part of his "biography." I believe it is safe to assume that a long tradition existed before artists depicted scenes of the Buddha's former lives on famous pilgrimage sites such as the gates of the memorial shrines at Sanci. It seems safe to assume, therefore, that legends of the Buddha's former lives are not to be put aside as late developments, as "the imaginative embellishments of the pious."

If this simple conjecture is reasonable, then there is much more that can be said. For example, no one doubts that the Ashokan inscriptions as well as other inscriptions about donations of material to the great shrines at Sanci give us some of the earliest hard evidence for the existence of Buddhism. What does this evidence tell us? For one thing, that the donations of posts, crossbars, balustrades, railings, architraves, and so on were made not just by laypersons but also by nuns and monks in significant numbers, and that these ascetics were not just the run-of-the-mill ascetics but specialists in specific sections of what became the Pali canon. They are, as Schopen calls them, "doctrinal specialists." They are fully participating in an activity that the received tradition has identified as late, as an aspect of "popular" or "kammatic" Buddhism. Not only that, but the inscriptions tell us that they are participating in this ritual because these monks and nuns believe that such gifts will produce great merit not only for themselves but for their parents or relatives who have died, or for the welfare of all beings.

We can identify the great shrine at Sanci as an explicit representation of a well-developed system of beliefs and practices that we identify as Buddhist, a system of beliefs that includes the legends of the Buddha together with his former lives, as well as the cosmology in which they appear. And lest we forget, it also includes a belief in karma, a Doctrine about causes and existences in the past and present, suffering and the liberation from suffering. And it clearly includes the Doctrine that gifts to the Buddhist community, a community that included both householder and renouncer, produce great merit, and that the giving of gifts was not the exclusive obligation of the householder. From this point of view the legends of the Buddha are not the product of "popularization," a late symbolic development to help householders understand a difficult Doctrine, but the very structure that constitutes Buddhism as a religion. As Collins puts it, "The idea of future (and past) Buddhas is intrinsic to the logic of Buddhism."

Thus Warder is quite right when he says that "all [the] biographies agree in their main outlines and essential episodes," but also quite mistaken in his conjecture that "in a sense the legend of the Buddha belongs not to the schools but to the popular Buddhism of ordinary laity in which the doctrinal differences which split the schools count for practically nothing—in short to Buddhism as a religion, not to Buddhism as a philosophy." If this is true, then why were significant numbers of "philosophical" monks giving donations for the construction of memorials as a means for the transfer of merit? Given what little evidence we do have, it would seem that the legend of the Buddha belongs to both "popular" and "philosophical" Buddhism, if that division makes any sense in the study of religion. It would be best to simply drop the notions of "popular" versus "philosophical" Buddhism as aids to an adequate under-standing of this religion.

We know that the canonical texts do not contain a complete legend of Gotama the Buddha. The absence of the legend in the texts has led many scholars to conclude that this is evidence that the episodes we find scattered in the texts is a late development. Nevertheless, we are told, the texts seem to reflect a bare or basic outline of a figure or person that "must" have existed, that Buddhism could not have persisted as a religion without a historical foun-der at the foundation of its origin—in fact, it would be absurd to deny it. But, we must continue to ask, What is the evidence?

None of the scholars who are committed to the apparent historical ver-ity of the Founder actually set out to prove it. As they say, "It must be true." This assertion seems to be taken as self-evident, something we must simply take as granted. What we must never forget is the question that Thomas him-self raised in looking at the legends: "The question remains for consideration whether we are justified in selecting from this legend the portions that appear credible, or whether the whole legend is not the invention of a period."

We must also take for granted the assumption about a lost core story, a single text that is the basis of all the variations we now possess in the various "versions." No one has put this as boldly as LaFleur, who asserts that the differ-ent biographies "seem to have been based on one lost one that was composed a little more than a century after his death," and that it is "no longer necessary to sort out the differences of credibility," since all we need to do is "grasp the basic outline." The task, then, is to work out an interpretation that seems to verify both the existence of the apparent lost text and the original historical event based on texts that appear hundreds of years later. As Roy Harris has pointed out in a different but related context on the study of Indo-European languages, this is "like standing the historicist method on its head."

The irony here is that the more you try to verify these self-evident proposi-tions, the more unhistorical your conclusions become. Take, for example, the constant appeal to the bare (or basic) outline as the foundational evidence for a historical Buddha. As I have already noted, the bare outline is not a piece of history. It is clearly a construction or an abstraction taken from Buddhist legends. In fact, as you reflect on the outline, "birth, maturity, renunciation, enlightenment...," you suddenly note that it is anonymous, bare of any his-tory. The moment you attempt to put flesh and blood onto the outline, give it proper names, a birthday, and so on, you find yourself in mythology rather than history. In brief, the bare outline that supposedly provides the founda-tion for discussing a historical Buddha provides no historical information whatsoever.

Let us go to one of the most quoted sections of the Pali canon, *The Long Discourses* (the *Digha Nikaya*), for a final illustration of the problem. This section contains "The Great Discourse on the Lineage." This is followed by "The Great Discourse on Origination," which describes the doctrine of the interdependent origination of all conditioned things, and the discourse on "The Great Passing of the Buddha's Last Days."

The discourse on the lineage begins, as we expect, with an introduction by Ananda: "Thus I have heard. Once the Lord was staying at Savatthi in Anathapindika's park." After telling us where this particular discourse took place, Ananda announces what caused it. He tells us that a number of monks had gathered together in the Kareri pavilion after the alms round and meal. While they were talking there arose a serious discussion about the actual existence of a person's various lives in the past. Ananda then says that because the Buddha had superhuman powers that were beyond the capacity of any human being, he knew what the monks were talking about and walked over to the pavilion. The monks tell him about their discussion, and he asks them whether they would like to hear a proper discourse on past lives. They are delighted to hear it. What follows is an abridged version of what he told them.

First, he told them that ninety-one aeons ago, the fully enlightened Buddha Vipassi arose in the world. Thirty-one aeons ago the Lord Buddha Sikhi arose; then in the same thirty-first aeon the Lord Buddha Vessabhu arose. And in this present fortunate aeon the Lord Buddhas Kakusandha, Konagamana, and Kassapa arose in the world. He then told them, "In this present fortunate aeon I too have now arisen in the world as a fully enlightened Buddha."

The Buddha then describes what caste and clan the Buddhas were born into. The first three Buddhas were born into royal/warrior castes, the next three were born into teaching/ritual specialist castes, and he, of course, was also born into a warrior caste. He goes on to inform them about the life span in each of the seven Buddha eras. In Vipassi's era the life span was eighty thousand years; in the time of Sikhi it was seventy thousand; in Vessabhu's sixty; in Kakusandha's forty thousand, in Konagamana's thirty, and in the time of Kassapa it was twenty thousand years. "In my time," he says, "the life span is short, limited, and quick to pass: it is seldom that anybody lives to be a hundred."

He next informs them about the different trees under which each gained enlightenment. He tells them about the pair of noble disciples each of the Buddhas enjoyed, including his own, Sariputta and Moggallana. He notes the number of assemblies each has: Vipassi had three, one of them containing 6.8 million monks. He has only one, consisting of 1,250 monks who are all of the highest rank. He names the attendants of each Buddha, naming Ananda as his own, and then gives the names of each Buddha's father and mother.

Ananda then tells us that the Buddha rose up from his seat and went to his own lodging.

The monks, the text tells us, were simply delighted and thought his powers of recollection were awesome. They wondered how he came by this knowledge of the past, whether, for example, some god told him about it. The Buddha, of course, knew what they were talking about and once again came to them and asked them what they were discussing and whether they were interested in hearing more. They were, indeed, eager to hear more.

The Buddha tells them that all perfected ones know these things by their own penetration into the principles of the Doctrine, but that the gods can also inform them about it. He then gives them a detailed description of the life of Vipassi and makes it very clear throughout his description that these details are not unique to Vipassi but are "the defining rule" for all Buddhas. He repeats what he has already said about Vipassi and then adds that Vipassi, the Buddha-to-be, descended into Tushita heaven and from there, fully aware, complete in all his faculties, entered into his mother's womb, protected by the four great kings of the four quarters. He was born pure, stainless, facing north, taking seven steps, and scanned the four quarters of the cosmos, saying, "I am supreme in the world, I am the eldest. This is my last birth, there will be no more rebirths."

Vipassi is then taken to his father; the Brahmins present in the palace note the thirty-two marks on the Buddha's body and tell the king that this newborn infant is indeed a "Great Agent" whose life will be open to two paths. If he lives the life of a householder he will become a ruler, a Universal Monarch, a conqueror of the four quarters. But if he becomes an ascetic, becomes homeless, he will become a Perfected One, a fully enlightened Buddha. The Buddha adds that it is owing to the results of past karma that Prince Vipassi had superhuman vision.

His father builds three palaces for Vipassi. After living in them for thousands of years, he decides to take a pleasure trip and inspect a park; he sees an old man and returns to the palace. A thousand years later he decides to take another pleasure trip and comes across a sick man; another thousand years later he sees a dead man. On a fourth trip he sees a shaven-headed man wearing a yellow robe. The charioteer tells him that this is someone who truly follows the Doctrine, who is at peace, does good actions, performs meritorious deeds, is harmless, and truly has compassion for all sentient beings. Vipassi tells his charioteer to go back to the palace. He shaves his head, puts on yellow robes, and begins a life of homelessness.

Alone in a secluded spot, he discovers the Doctrine of the interdependent origination of all conditioned things. Fully enlightened and after god Brahma appeals to him on three different occasions, he is persuaded to teach the Doctrine to all who will hear it. His first converts are his half brother Prince Khanda and the chaplain's son Tissa, and then eighty-four thousand are newly ordained at the Deer Park. He tells the newly ordained monks, "Wander abroad for the good of the many, for the happiness of the many, out of compassion for the world, for the welfare and happiness of the gods and humans. Teach the Doctrine that is lovely in its beginning, middle, and end, and demonstrate the ascetic life fully complete and perfect. There are beings with little dust in their eyes who are perishing through not hearing the Doctrine; they will become knowers of "the Doctrine." He then travels to the gods of the Pure Abode, who repeat the biographies of the seven Buddhas. "And so it is," the Buddha said, "that the Perfected One, by penetrating the fundamentals of the Doctrine, remembers the past Buddhas who have exhausted the round of rebirths and attained final liberation."

As a detailed description of the life of Vipassi this legend does indeed follow the narrative constraint, or outline, if you will, that defines a Buddha's life. What must be emphasized here is that what Carrithers and others have called the bare or basic outline fits not just Gotama but all seven of the Buddhas. Carrithers, you will recall, describes the basic outline this way: it included the Buddha's birth, maturity, renouncing, search, awakening, liberation, teaching, and death. He then goes on to assert that this "outline must be true," that the outline depicts a historical fact, a person who actually exhibited those features in his life that were then projected into the development of the legends.

It should be clear by now that this premise in the received tradition is anything but obvious. If the bare outline is true for the Buddha, why is it not also true for all the other Buddhas whose lives have the same outline? The focus on Gotama by scholars who are interested in the quest for a historical Buddha misses this crucial point. The point is not that the bare outline is true of someone who must have existed historically, but that it is the outline for all Buddhas, including Vipassi, who in the Buddhist cosmological scheme of things existed ninety-one aeons ago. After all, Carrithers has not constructed his basic outline from historical documents about the life of a certain Indian named Gotama but, as have we all, has extracted the outline from the myths that are Buddhist religious texts. The proof, therefore, that the outline is true is not based on the fact that history confirms it, but because it is an accurate synopsis or condensation of the legends in the Pali texts. And this is exactly the argument Lamotte used in his explanation of the deification of Gotama.

In fact, Lamotte uses the legend of Vipassi as his basic evidence for the development of Buddhism. He notes that the legend of the Buddha Vipassi contains "detailed indications about [his] life from his conception until his deeds as a Buddha." It is this biography, repeated again and again for all the Buddhas, that is also reproduced in detail for the life of the Buddha Gotama. Here is how it happened. "In short," Lamotte writes, "everything occurred as if the devout biographers, unaware of the precise details of Sakyamuni's coming into the world, had after the event attributed a marvelous conception and birth to him, by applying to him a legend intended to glorify the Buddhas and cakravartin [i.e., universal] kings, a legend the themes of which were fixed in advance."

Lamotte is well aware of the fact that this is conjecture, not an explanation based on historical evidence. He knows there is another perfectly sound conjecture that is just the opposite of what he has argued. Lamotte adds the following footnote to his argument: "It is true that, theoretically, we could uphold the opposite thesis and claim that the life of Sakyamuni served as a model and point of departure for the legend in the Mahavadanasutra [i.e., Vipassi]. This would mean that at the same time we would have to accept blindly all the miracles of the golden legend of Buddhism." Skipping over the word "blindly," it would also mean the end of the received tradition.

If we follow Lamotte's important alternative, we can correct the received tradition by using "The Great Discourse on the Lineage" as a basic source for insisting that when we talk or write about the biography of Gotama the Buddha we emphasize three points. First, the biography of a Buddha entails the framework of a cosmology and the belief in karma. The Buddha begins his discourse with an account of a Buddha who existed ninety-one aeons ago and continues to describe others in an ever-decreasing cosmological time scheme. Second, a biography of Gotama the Buddha always entails the lives of *all* the Buddhas. Third, the biography of a Buddha is about a superhuman agent whose birth is a miracle, who performs miracles, and who will renounce the life of the householder, become enlightened by his own efforts alone, and decide to teach the Doctrine to all beings, including the gods, and then gain final liberation from the rounds of rebirth. It is these three points that establish what I have called the "narrative constraint," for describing a Buddha's life. If Gotama the Buddha has anything unique about him, it is because of these relational constraints that define him.

The characters and events that are defined by this narrative constraint are obviously not based on history, on what many of us assume is the "really real." The imperative that is embedded in the Western quest for the historical Buddha, "it must be the case that...," is also a narrative constraint, a constraint, it would seem, whose absence would constitute the collapse of scholarship if not an absurd world.

In "Pali Buddhism" elements of history, time, and geography are swept up into a mythical narrative and transformed into a story that gives structure and systematic significance to what we identify as the history and development of Buddhism. I suggest that we view the myths of the Buddha, given the preceding framework, as containing the syntax of Buddhist thought and practice, the grammar through which Buddhists think, develop their distinctive beliefs, perform their rituals, and live their lives day by day and year by year. From this perspective the maps produced at the beginning of books on Buddhism for the purpose of locating the travels of the Buddha should not be taken as a road map marking the geographic origin and history of Buddhism in India but should be read, as we shall see in the next chapter, as a geo-cosmological map, a cosmography, marking the Buddha's journey of the "four cosmic continents."

18

The Cosmological Structure

Some scholars say that the cosmology in part I is a joke or an ironic story. I agree with K. R. Norman, a leading philologist in the study of early Buddhism, who says, "Joking is not a well-known or highly approved Buddhist pastime." Be that as it may, the one thing we do know is that the Buddhist tradition did not take the account as a joke. So let us take the tradition seriously and read the cosmological story literally as a story about the history and structure of the cosmos and the beginning of society. Just remember that when you read "Buddhists" or "the Buddhist religion," "Buddhists think that" or "Buddhism teaches," I am referring to Theravada Buddhism, the Buddhism of the Pali texts of South and Southeast Asia, the myths of part I.

There are at least three basic differences between the Buddhist cosmology and the cosmologies of the three monotheistic religions most of us are familiar with. Buddhists do not think that the cosmos has a beginning or end. Thus the Buddhist religion does not have a cosmogony, a myth such as Genesis 1 that describes how the cosmos began. The first sentence of the text you read does not begin with "In the beginning God created the heavens and the earth." For the Buddhist, the cosmos is a process that has no beginning or end; it evolves and devolves in a pulsating rhythm throughout vast, endless cosmic aeons. This conception of the cosmos is clearly in opposition to myths of the cosmos that do have a beginning and end, such as those described by Judaism, Christianity, and Islam in which the

Doctrine of creation out of nothing is often argued in theological debates. This difference, together with our modern Western emphasis on history as the anchor to which existence and meaning is tied, may well account for the lack of interest in the Buddhist cosmology and the sustained quest for the historical Buddha.

The second difference you confront when you study Buddhism is that since it has a cosmology that does not entail a cosmogony, it does not require a creator god. To put it bluntly, God is irrelevant in the Buddhist cosmological scheme of things. Thus theology as we know it in the West is absent in Buddhism. When you study Buddhism, you will find no cosmogony, no God, and thus no theology.

These major differences falsify the notion that "all religions say the same thing," that they are in fundamental agreement. The absence of an omnipotent and omniscient god in Buddhism became a serious problem in the study of religion in general and the study of Buddhism in particular. After all, how could Buddhism be classified a religion if God is not a primary element in its doctrinal set of beliefs? Because religion is often defined as "belief in god," it became impossible to take Buddhism seriously as a religion. This is especially the case when this is linked to the Buddhist denial that there is such a thing as an immortal soul or self, that in fact the belief in immortality is a basic cause of suffering. These differences are often erased by translating "perfect happiness" (*nibbana/nirvana*) either as godlike, an "ultimate reality," "being itself," an "unconditioned state," or as "nihilism."

The Doctrine of karma is the third difference that must be mentioned before we take a look at the Buddhist cosmology. The Doctrine of karma tells us that we and we alone are responsible for our actions, and that most of our present actions are conditioned by our actions in the past and will condition our actions in the future. Existence, then, reflects the cosmology in that it too has no beginning and no end. Karma is often described as a wheel that depicts existence as a repetition of birth, death, and rebirth. As we shall see, karma is a necessary component of the Buddhist cosmology as well as Buddha's biography. It is a necessary Doctrine, a right belief, in the Eightfold Path of the Buddhist religion. Sujata and Cunda remain the best exemplars of the Doctrine, and Vessantara and all the Buddhas are perfect examples of it.

Max Weber was certainly right when he called the Doctrine "the most rational solution to the theodicy problem." Most solutions to the problem of evil and suffering in human life, especially in monotheistic traditions, "solve" the problem by claiming that "God's way is not our way," or, as Job was asked, "Where were you when I created the world?" The Doctrine of karma in India leaves no mystery; you and you alone are responsible for the condition you find yourself in today. It is, when you think about it, an awesome if not awful doctrine.

Good deeds, the giving of gifts, produce merit and reward in a future life. Likewise, the causal efficacy of bad deeds will inevitably manifest itself sometime in the future as confirmed in both the lives and deaths of Moggallana and Angulimala. It goes without saying, of course, that the doctrine of karma is simply assumed in the lives of the Buddhas and Universal Monarchs. Birth → death → rebirth is the lawlike sequence of karma. The Buddha's quest for enlightenment entails both an explanation for this sequence and a solution to its inevitable consequences. As we know from the legends, the doctrine of the interdependent origination of all conditioned things is the explanation of both what action is and why it exists. Both the Eightfold Path and the Doctrine are embedded in a cosmological framework.

The Doctrine of Karma has often been misunderstood as leading both Hinduism and Buddhism into a fatalistic view of life. It is true that the Doctrine leaves us without excuses. We and we alone are responsible for our status in life at the present time. We are what we are because of our past karmic legacy. However, we can do something about it. The point to be made is that the doctrine does not say "my life or history is what I will it to be." It would be more accurate, I think, to say that "although life or history happens as a result of individual actions it does not happen as we will it." Thus the Doctrine of karma is not reducible to my individual will or intention. It is this notion that is captured, I think, in the Buddha's command to Angulimala after he was beaten by the crowd, "Bear it, Brahmin! Bear it!"

It is true that we cannot find a text in the Pali canon that gives us a complete description of karma or the cosmology. Nevertheless, as the myths in part I fully demonstrate, they are always presupposed, sometimes explicitly, as basic elements that constitute the structure of the myths. They constitute what I have called the "syntax" or structure of Pali Buddhist discourse—no cosmology, no Doctrine of karma, no Buddhism. The remainder of this chapter will demonstrate what I mean by this assertion.

A description of the complexity of the cosmology is made more difficult because of differences in the text about some of its details. It is not just the fact that names change, but also of who did what, where, and when. We can nevertheless construct an accurate description of the structure of the cosmology that is in agreement with the texts as a whole, a master framework or grid that is in agreement with the Buddhism represented by the redacted texts and the commentaries. Moreover, it is also in basic agreement with many of the classical texts of Hinduism. We may say that the cosmology is pan-Indian.

The cosmology, as do all cosmologies, entails two elements: space and time. Space in Buddhism is divided hierarchically into three spheres, each of which contains several domains. They are called the Formless Sphere, the Sphere of Form Only, and the Sphere of Sense-Desire (see figure 18.1). The meditation of the Buddhas and the Universal Monarchs encompasses all three spheres. What the Buddha discovers in his meditation during the three watches of the night is that there is no enduring substantive self, no immortal

I. The Hierarchical Levels

1. The Formless Sphere
2. The Sphere of Form Only
3. The Sphere of Sense Desire
   A. The Six Heavens
      1. CATUMMAHARAJIKA
      2. TAVATIMSA
      3. YAMA
      4. TUSITA
      5. NIMMANARATI
      6. PARANIMMITTA VASAVATTI

   B. The Human World
   C. The Subhuman World
   D. The Hells

II. COSMOS VIEWED FROM ABOVE MOUNT SINERU

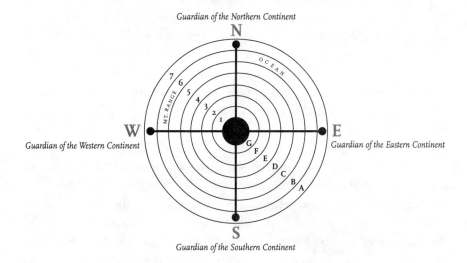

1-7 = MOUNT RANGES OF THE COSMOS
● = FOUR CONTINENTS
A - G = OCEANS OF THE COSMOS
⬤ MOUNT SINERU THE LOCATION OF TAVATIMSA HEAVEN.
THE SUMMIT IS THE ABODE OF SAKKA AND THE 33 GODS.

FIGURE 18.1 Cosmology I

soul, to be found in any of the cosmological domains. What he discovers is the radical notion that "all things are impermanent, and subject to decay, death, and rebirth" in the three spheres of the cosmos as described in "Cosmology and the Great Declaration."

Our world is a subdivision of the Sphere of Sense-Desire; it is below the six heavens, which are listed in the figure so that you may locate the various heavens mentioned in part I.

The Formless Sphere, the highest of the three spheres, contains sixteen levels that are described in terms of the four highest levels of meditation. It is a sphere, therefore, known only to those who have reached these levels. The first level has a "temporal duration" of 20,000 aeons. The fourth and highest level has a temporal duration of 84,000 aeons. The main point to be emphasized here is that even the highest level is not eternal or changeless. All things, even the highest abode of the cosmos, have a birth, death, and rebirth; all things are conditioned and change. Being, substance, is nothing more than a characterization of a becoming, contingent, conditioned process.

The third sphere, the Sphere of Sense-Desire, consists of four hierarchically arranged worlds (see the upper portion of figure 18.1). Starting from the top, this sphere includes the six heavens, our human world, the subhuman worlds made up of ghosts and animals, and the domain of the hells. The sixth heaven is the highest heaven, where the maximum length of life is 9,219,000,000 human years. Tushita is the fourth heaven, in which Gotama's mother lived and to which the Buddha ascended to convert her. It is also the heaven from which Buddhas descend into our human world. The maximum life duration there is 576,000,000 human years. The third heaven, Yama, is where Mara lives; the duration of life there is 144,000,000 years. The second heaven is Tavatimsa, the home of the thirty-three gods, Sakka, Moggallana, and Sariputra. Life in Tavatimsa lasts 36,000,000 human years. The first heaven, the lowest, is the dwelling place of the Four Great kings or guardians of the four quarters, where life's duration is given as 9,000 human years. It is also the domain of the famous Universal Monarchs.

Built into these cosmological, hierarchically arranged, spatiotemporal spheres is a complex geographic structure (see the lower portion of figure 18.1). Mount Sineru (Mount Meru in Sanskrit) is at the center of this structure. This cosmic axis is surrounded by seven concentric mountain ranges, each separated by an ocean. Four continents are located at the cardinal points of the outermost mountain range and ocean. The four guardians dwell in the lowest heaven located immediately above the four continents. As I have already mentioned, Sakka, also known as Indra, the king of the gods or commander in chief, reigns over the Four Great Kings and the thirty-three

Gods in the second heaven, Tavatimsa, which is located at the tip of Mount Sineru.

Although there may be no beginning or end to the cosmos, although life is a process of birth, death, and rebirth, notice that there is a beginning and an end for each specific life lived in the various spheres of this complex cosmology no matter how long that life is calculated. All things, even the spheres themselves, are governed by the law of the interdependent origination of all conditioned things: all things are born, die, and are reborn.

This structure reflects what may be called a South Asian structure of the cosmology from Tibet to Indonesia. It can be reduced to a simple diagram that represents the cosmology of Buddhism as confirmed by evidence from both text and material culture. The diagram in figure 18.2 represents most South Asian descriptions of the cosmology. It is known, for example, in the Vedic Brahmanas: "For this reason one must not sleep with his head toward the west,

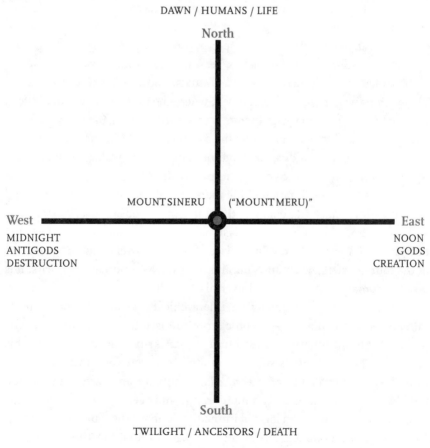

DAWN / HUMANS / LIFE

North

MOUNT SINERU   ("MOUNT MERU)"

West   East

MIDNIGHT   NOON
ANTIGODS   GODS
DESTRUCTION   CREATION

South

TWILIGHT / ANCESTORS / DEATH

FIGURE 18.2 Cosmology II

for one would then sleep stretching [feet] toward the gods. The southern quarter belongs to the ancestors, and the western one to the snakes. That faultless one [the east] is from where the gods ascended. The northern quarter belongs to men."

The main difference involves the central axis. In some Hindu Puranas, for example, Mount Sineru (Mount Meru) is replaced by the four-faced creator god Brahma, who is seated on a lotus and creates the four cardinal points, the four Vedas, and the four beings and times of the day from the mouths of his four faces. With few exceptions, Hindu temples face east. The magnificent South Indian temple compounds with their four great gates are a microcosm. One cannot miss the significance of most Buddhist temples in Thailand, Cambodia, and Burma as representations of the cosmos. Borobudur, the great Buddhist monument (stupa) in Java, is a spectacular replication of its cardinal and hierarchical structure as portrayed in the abstract diagrams in figures 18.1 and 18.2.

The diagram in figure 18.2 is an abstraction of a very complex cognitive structure: space, time, geography, and mythology. It can be reduced to a simple set of oppositions, an "oppositional syntax" or rule, which we can represent as A : B :: C : D. This can be read as North : South :: East : West, or "North is to South as East is to West," "human is to ancestor as gods are to antigods," "dawn is to twilight as noon is to midnight." We may also interpret the set of oppositions as life : death :: creation : destruction.

It is absolutely crucial that you not misunderstand what is being said here. The structure does *not* tell us the meaning of the cosmology or the myths of Buddhism. It is not a semantic code for the hidden meaning of the myths. It is simply a hypothesis that gives us the logical structure of the cosmology or myth. It is an interpretive hypothesis that avoids viewing the legends of the Buddha as "popular Buddhism," that is to say, the product of a degeneration of Buddhism from reason (philosophy) to religion (mythology). This structure may help us explain why certain things occur or are being said in the story about the Buddha. It describes the structure of what I have called the "narrative constraint" in which or through which the legends are told. The meaning of the myths remains the literal meaning of the sentences.

Moreover, the schema is not to be viewed as a theory about Buddhist cosmology or mythology. The algorithm is a hypothesis for solving a puzzle or problem that we find in the legends. It tells us that the myths are constituted by a set of oppositional relations that are necessary for understanding the meaning of the myths, just as the syntax of English is necessary for understanding the meaning of English as a language. We would not say, for example, that the syntax of English is the meaning of English sentences, yet no one would deny that the syntax of English is a necessary condition for the semantics of English. In like manner, I am positing that this oppositional structure is a necessary condition for the Buddhist legends.

Here are two examples in addition to the legends you have read that will illustrate the presence of the templates throughout the texts in part I.

The first example is taken from *The Long Discourses*. The setting is the Brick House at Nadika where the Buddha describes the various rebirths of the citizens of Nadika. He tells the monks how many of the citizens attained liberation or had at death become "Once-Returners" or "Stream-Winners" certain of winning liberation. The lay folk of Nadika, of course, are delighted at the news. After hearing all this, Ananda becomes curious about the rebirths of devotees from Magadha, especially King Bimbisara, who devoted himself to the Buddha and his teaching until his dying day. Upon arising the next morning, Ananda goes directly to the Buddha and asks him about it. The Buddha meditates and perceives the destiny of each of the devotees of Magadha. In the evening he tells Ananda how Bimbisara, in his rebirth in the heaven of the thirty-three gods, appeared to him. Bimbisara told the Buddha that in "earlier days, long ago on the fast day at the beginning of the rainy season in the full-moon night," all the thirty-three gods were seated in the Great Sudhamma Hall together with a great host of superhuman agents. The kings from the four quarters were not only in attendance but they together with the multitude of superhuman agents were seated in an explicit order and orientation.

"There was the Great King Dhatarattha from the east known as Pubbavadeha at the head of his followers facing west; King Virulhaka from the southern continent called Jambudipa was at the head of his followers facing north; the Great King Virupakkha from the west called Aparagoyana at the head of his followers facing east; and the Great King Vessavana from the northern continent known as Uttarakuru with his followers facing south" (see figure 18.3).

The template or structure of the cosmology as outlined in both figures 18.1 and 18.2 gives us the structure of the myth. The meeting is within a cosmological framework: Vessavana : Virulhaka :: Dhatarattha : Viruppaka just as North : South :: East : West. The meaning of the myth is quite clear. We take it literally. The population of gods is increasing due to their adherence to Buddha's teaching in their former lives, while the population of the antigods (the *asuras*) is declining: "The thirty-three gods were pleased and happy, filled with delight and joy, saying, 'The god's hosts are growing, the antigods hosts are declining.'"

Why were the gods pleased that the antigods were declining? Because, as we know from the myths of India, the gods and antigods are always in a perpetual battle for the drink of immortality (a foolish act from the Buddhist

FIGURE 18.3 The Cosmography

point of view). That conflict is often mentioned in passing in the legends of
the Buddha. The myth is also well known in Hinduism and it marks a very
important geographic location on the banks of the Ganges at Allahabad, where
millions of Hindus participate in the ritual known as the Kumbha Mela, a ritual primarily for the initiation of Hindu ascetics and the production of merit.
The place marks the spot where a drop of the elixir of immortality landed, as
it spilled from the pot the gods carried as they rushed back east to their abode
after a battle with the antigods from the west. The gods in Buddhism as well as
in Hinduism are in perpetual conflict with the antigods, the *asuras*.

The second example is interesting because it is one of several texts in the
Buddhist canon that explicitly function as *paritta*, or "protective verses," which,
when chanted, guard against danger and affliction. It is, in short, a magical
text, one that continues to be recited for protection in contemporary Buddhist
countries in Southeast Asia. It is also an excellent example that illustrates the
crucial distinction between meaning and use; the meaning of the protective

verse is not to be confused with its use for protection. It is also interesting to note in passing that the Buddha apparently did not know about these magical verses and their magical power. They seem to belong to the Universal Monarchs as protectors.

The setting is Rajagaha. The Four Great Kings had set up a defensive guard to watch over the four cosmic quarters. As night drew to a close they, along with their entourage, decided to visit the Buddha, lighting up the entire Vulures Peak as they descended. King Vessavana, the guardian of the North, tells the Buddha that the majority of *yakkhas* (a class of superhuman agents) do not believe his Doctrines. This situation, he said, "places both monks and laypersons in a precarious situation if the *yakkhas* should ever turn against them." If the Buddha learned the magical verses it would give them "confidence and allow them to live guarded, protected, unharmed, and at their ease." The Buddha agreed!

With the Buddha's consent King Vessavana began to recite the verses. They begin with praise for previous Buddhas and famous monks and then turn to a description of the four continents and kings, each verse ending with the following:

> Often asked, do we revere
> Gotama, the great conqueror?
> We reply: "We do revere
> Gotama, great conqueror,
> In wisdom, trained, in conduct too,
> Buddha Gotama, we hail!"

The continent of the north, Kuru, receives the longest verse. It is described as a continent of happy people. They possess nothing and have no need to plow or scatter seed; ripened corn presents itself for eating, and the finest rice is free from mildew and husk. Well-built cities soar into the skies. Fruit trees are forever blooming and full of birds. It is a land where peacocks scream and herons cry, where the cuckoo gently calls, the *jiva* bird cries "live on," and mynah birds mimic man.

After reciting the verses, the Four Great Kings vanish, and the Buddha recites them to the monks, telling them that they are for their benefit and the well-being of the lay followers.

Using our diagram, we find that Kuru is clearly the opposite of the continent in the south described as a place where ghosts, murderous thieves, and greedy folk dwell. The eastern continent, the first, a domain of daylight and "the mighty sons" of Dhatarattha, who "though not human" honor the Buddha, is opposite the western quarter, the last, the domain of night, "the shrouder." The template of the cosmos is the framework or narrative constraint of the protective verses. But there is more to be found in this important section of the Pali canon.

The north, Kuru, is a paradise. The description clearly reflects the story in chapter 1 of the evolution of society before greed destroys peace and happiness. Rice and fruit, for example, are always plentiful without labor, and ownership is unknown.

We have also come across this paradise in the legend of Vessantara. Vessantara travels north with his family toward the wilderness. Once the family arrives deep in the forest, they live in a bark hut they do not own and live off food of the forest that they have not planted. What is at first feared, exile and the terrors of the wilderness, is transformed into liberation and happiness, a life in paradise, the domain of the north. The framework, the template, is clearly there in the story—they travel north. The city is opposite the wilderness, paradise is opposite the world of desire and possession, and the ascetic life is opposite the life of the householder. The practice of giving, the perfection of giving, leads to asceticism that, cosmologically speaking, is to the north.

There is an interesting similarity between the northern quarter as a description and domain of paradise and asceticism. The hallmark of the ascetic life is a life that is sexless and without possessions. This description also fits those "mind-born" beings at the beginning of the evolution of society as well as Vessantara toward the end of his exile. Life in paradise is a form of asceticism, a genuine, true poverty. His biography can be interpreted as the opposite of the Buddha's; he becomes a Universal Monarch, the Buddha becomes the great renouncer. But the point to be emphasized here is that both reach their goals by means of an ascetic life.

Notice that Vessantara does not understand why he must leave his royal life. "Why do they want to banish me?" he asks his father. The Buddha, however, is fully aware of why he must depart his palaces after living an innocent life, unaware of old age, sickness, and death. It is "all through the night" that Vessantara and his family discuss life in the wilderness and then depart at dawn. Gotama, however, decides not to talk to his family and departs from home at night.

In order to gain the perfection of virtues and wisdom, Vessantara travels north. If we refer to figure 18.3, we note that the Buddha travels in the opposite direction to gain the perfection of wisdom. He travels south, alone, to Bodh-Gaya from his birthplace in the north, toward the night, to the domain of death and an encounter with Mara. Vessantara takes his wife and children to the wilderness. Gotama forsakes his wife and children before he enters the forest. Sakka intervenes and assists Vessantara in the final act in the perfection of giving—the gift of his wife to the decrepit old Brahmin. And to drive the point home, it is Vessantara who performs the water ritual of donation to validate the gift of his wife, while it is kings who perform this ritual in giving gifts of property to the Buddha's community. Moreover, in the legends of the Buddha it is Sakka who is assisted by the Buddha in gaining wisdom and becoming a follower of the Doctrine. Sakka, however, assists and grants Vessantara's wishes for becoming a Universal Monarch. In the legend of Vessantara it is Vessantara's father who travels north to the forest to reunite with his son and family, but in the legend of the Buddha, it is the son, now a Buddha, who travels north to his father's palace for an unsuccessful meeting with his family.

It is in these remarkable cosmological oppositional differences that the two legendary heroes resemble each other. We must remember that aeons ago the Buddha was Vessantara; Vessantara is a chapter in the Buddha's biography. Second, both are born into royal families, and both become ascetics, although for opposite reasons. Third, both reach the perfection of giving and wisdom for the welfare of the people; thus giving is not incommensurable with wisdom.

The cosmological set of oppositions is also explicit in the Buddha's quest for liberation. Recall that the Buddha's quest begins in the palace at night. In order to "gain freedom from rebirth," he leaves the palace by means of the east gate and crosses a river into a forest. He tells Chandaka that he must return and inform his father that Gotama has entered the forest to put an end to birth, death, and rebirth, not because of "some yearning for paradise, lack of affection, or anger." As dawn appears Gotama notices the deer "sleeping in perfect trust and the birds sitting at peace." We must remember this series of events when we finally arrive at the end of his life. At his funeral, during the day, he is taken out of the east gate, not as an ascetic but as a Universal Monarch. The Buddha's funeral is a royal funeral!

After years of failed radical techniques for gaining liberation and the encounter with Sujata, Gotama follows the road the gods have prepared that leads him to the tree of enlightenment. The legend in chapter 5 tells us that his awakening took place at the full moon night in the month of Visakha. At first he stands on the south side of the tree facing north. As he stands there, the southern half of the world sinks as if it would reach one of the hells, and the northern half of the world rises to the highest heavens. He is obviously standing on the wrong side of the tree. Walking around the tree, he stands on the western side facing east. The world once again tilts as if a huge cartwheel was lying on its side and someone has stepped on its rim. He then moves to the north side and faces south. The earth pitched once again as before. Finally, he moves to the eastern side and faces west. This is the side all Buddhas choose, the side that neither sinks nor rises. He turns his back to the trunk of the tree, faces east, and makes his great resolution. At this moment the sun sets, and he begins his meditation through the three watches of the night. He will have attained enlightenment by sunrise. As the story reminds us, "And as he reflected upon his liberation the sun shown brightly over the eastern horizon." The famous watches of the night are in perfect synchrony with the cosmology.

Emphasis on the "historical Buddha" passes this by as mythical, as fiction, the imagination of the Asian mind. If, however, we concentrate on the cosmological framework of the myth, which itself tells us from beginning to end that it is a story about a superhuman agent, it may be possible to unravel some of the puzzles we confront as we read it.

Once again, the meaning of the myth, its literal sense, is not too problematic. The meaning of this episode is exactly what it says. We might have trouble with the notion that someone can tip the world up or down by standing at various points around a tree. And we might also have trouble with the notion that either the Buddha or we ourselves have existed in other forms of life in the far distant past. We may have trouble with it because we just do not believe it. Our disbelief is due, first of all, to the fact that we understand the meaning of the myth perfectly well. The fact that we do not believe what it asserts is another matter.

The meaning of the myth is exactly what it says about the actions of the Buddha. When, as usual, we have trouble with its truth content, we begin to look for symbolic or hidden meanings. And the problem with this attempt to "save meaning," to save truth, is that it assumes a very strange notion of semantics. It assumes that the folk who tell the myth or believe it do not know the meaning of it. In brief, they speak a language whose meaning they do not understand. We have to tell them just what the hidden or symbolic meanings are. That is not only a strange outcome but also a contradiction of what language is as a system of communication and cognition.

If we use both figures 18.1 and 18.2 as a template, we first note that the Buddha has become, or is, the pivot of the four quarters. We can interpret this framework as follows. Just as Mount Sineru is the axis of the cosmos, the mediation between the four cardinal points, so Buddha in the night of his enlightenment becomes the axis or mediation between life and death, creation and destruction, birth and death. He has his back to the west, to night and destruction, while facing east, day, creation, and the gods. His meditation takes place from within a specific cosmology in both its horizontal and vertical dimensions; he is not only seated at the axis of the cosmos, we are told that his meditation throughout the watches of the night take him through the hierarchical levels of the cosmos into its highest spheres and then back again into the sphere of sensation and desire, this world. This cosmological journey is taken once again before his death, and we have good textual evidence that Universal Monarchs take the same journey in their meditation.

The cosmological framework is made explicit once again at his funeral, omitted in most introductory books on Buddhism. The myth gives us his last words and then tells us that he entered the levels of meditation just as he performed them at Bodh-Gaya while Anuruddha consoled the monks throughout the night. We are then told that on the seventh day they decided to take his body out of the south gate of the town to cremate it. This was the proper ritual procedure. The south is the domain of death, twilight, the domain of the ancestors. In India both the plans of towns and houses in classical architectural texts and the Brahmanic texts that prescribe the rules for properly performing rites of passage, mark the domain of the south as the domain of death, sunset, and the ancestors. Towns, temples, and homes are microcosms built on this cosmological grid marked by the cardinal directions.

The story of Buddha's funeral then tells us something quite remarkable. We are told that the eight men who were selected to carry the body out of the south gate could not lift it. According to the legend the gods and the Mallas then take the body through the north gate, bring it back again through the north gate and out through the eastern gate to the Mallas shrine, and cremate it there.

Now let us place this mythical funeral scenario on the cosmology in figure 18.2. If we retrace the funeral procession, it takes the body out of the city and brings it back in through the north gate, that of life, dawn, the human domain. The procession then goes through the city and out of the east gate, that is, creation, the domain of the gods, noontime. The procession is clearly marked by the cosmology. The funeral procession in this remarkable schema tells us it is, as we have already noticed, a funeral for a Universal Monarch, a superhuman agent, else he would have been taken through the south gate at twilight into the domain of death as is the case with all human beings. This episode also repeats the ritual of his birth and his enlightenment as episodes whose narrative constraints are also cosmological in their structure and thus a necessary framework for their significance. The map is a cosmology on which India is transformed into a geo-cosmography, a transformation that takes place today in all Indian pilgrimages (see figure 18.3, where the four cosmological regions and their towns are included to mark the four cardinal points of the cosmos and the Indian continent as the framework of the Buddha's journey).

The legend of the Buddha seems to fit the cosmological framework on a grand scale. If we take figure 18.2 as our cosmological grid or template and place it on a map of ancient India, we discover that the Buddha's birth at

Kapilavatthu is at the northern end of his travels. His enlightenment at Bodh-Gaya marks the most southern location. Regardless of how we arrange the various episodes of his travels, they follow a north-south axis between life and death.

It should come as no surprise to discover that the "biographies" of Vessantara, Gotama, and Mahasudassana, for example, can be compared as narratives that are constituted by the same structure; they repeat a structure that can be defined as sets of oppositions. As we have already noted, Vessantara travels north with his family and becomes an ascetic living in the wilderness that is transformed into a paradise. He returns victorious with family and wealth after his ascetic journey. In brief, Vessantara goes into exile as an ascetic and returns home as a Universal Monarch.

Mahasudassana's habitat, however, is just the opposite of Vessantara's. Sakka builds him an immense palace in the city, and the events that take place during his ride to the park are just the opposite of Gotama's. Also, it is his wife who leaves the palace, and his mediation and withdrawal from royal affairs takes place in the great hall. It is also his wife who pleads for him to live and who weeps at his death. Gotama, on the other hand, leaves both family and the palace for the forest and meditates in the forest under a tree.

One of the interesting themes that the schema highlights is the following: asceticism is a necessary stage in the successful biography of each hero. Vessantara, Mahasudassana, and the Buddha, for example, all begin as princes or kings but then become ascetics, renouncers in different modes, before they become teachers, Universal Monarchs, or die and reach heaven. As we shall see in the next chapter, asceticism is the central phase of their rite of passage toward liberation. In the last chapter we will develop the theme that the gift is also a mode of asceticism in the life of the householder. This motif can be seen very clearly in the story of Vessantara; the more he gave, the less he possessed until at the end of his life in the forest he had nothing left to give away, which is the exact state of an ascetic.

The dominant cosmological orientation in two of the myths is a north-south axis, the opposition between life and death, dawn and twilight, humans and ancestors. Vessantara travels north, to life, a paradise, and then south again at the end of his exile. Mahasudassana, on the other hand, travels the four quarters before returning to his palace in the center of the cardinal points and then enters into the great palace chamber for meditation. The central phase of the Buddha's rite of passage is identical to both Vessantara's and Mahasudassana's, that of ascetic, homeless, without family. His journey after his departure from the palace, however, is the opposite of both Mahasudassana's and Vessantara's. The Buddha travels south into the wilderness, to encounter Mara and death, then travels the four quarters during his life as teacher, then north once again during his final days.

The cosmological/narrative constraint is not only at work in the biographies of the "Great Persons." It is also at work in the conception of the Buddhist ascetic community. There are, for example, several places in the canonical texts where the Buddha speaks of the community as the ascetic order of the "four quarters/continents" or the "four directions."

Here is an example from chapter 11. The wealthy merchant by the name of Anathapindika had decided to buy a fabulous piece of property from Prince Jeta and give it to the Buddha. After a sumptuous meal he asks the Buddha how he should go about transferring the property to the Buddhist order. The Buddha replies, "Householder, give it to the Order of the Ascetics of the four points of the compass whether now present or hereafter to arrive."

In another version of this story Anathapindika sees the monks coming into town from every direction to begin their morning alms gathering. He asks them whether it would be possible for him to build dwelling places for them. They go to the Buddha for consent, and he gives it to them. "The great merchant of Rajagaha" builds sixty dwelling places for the order and asks the Buddha to come over for a meal. After the meal he tells the Buddha that he has built the sixty dwellings "because I need merit and heaven," and asks the Buddha how he should go about dedicating and establishing the dwellings in the name of the order. The Buddha replies, "Dedicate the sixty dwelling places for the use of the order of the four directions, now present and to come." He thanks the merchant and departs.

On another occasion a monk who had collected "much property and a big supply of a monk's requisites" died. The monks of the order asked the Buddha what they should do with these things. The Buddha replied that they were allowed to give the robes and bowl of a monk who has passed away to those monks who tended the sick because "they are of great service." But "the many other things and requisites belong to the order of the four quarters, for those who have come in and for those who have not." The phrase "order of the four quarters" is also found on numerous plaques of dedication concerning gifts and merit at major shrines and memorials.

I do not think that these episodes in the life of the Buddha refer to the order as it was established in India or "the world," as most translations put it. Rather, the framework for these narratives allows us to interpret the order as having cosmological significance. The order, in other words, is a community known throughout the four continents of the cosmos ruled by the four kings and Sakka. And if it is history that we want to use as a reference point for the narratives, then it is a cosmic history, a history that is calculated in hundreds, millions, and billions of aeons.

It is this same cosmology in which, during a full moon at the beginning of the rainy season, the great god Brahma addressed the thirty-three gods who were seated in the great hall together with a multitude of deities including Sakka and the Four Great Kings from the four continents, seated at their appointed thrones at the north, south, east, and west. That audience also included various deities "who, having lived the holy life under the Buddha, had recently appeared in the heaven of the thirty-three, out [shining] the other gods in brightness and glory." Brahma teaches them the Doctrine taught by the Buddha during the three-month retreat during the rainy season, only here it takes place in the heaven of the thirty-three gods and the Great Kings of the four quarters. It is this cosmological constraint, unmistakably Buddhist, often erased by the scholarly effort spent in the quest for the history and origin of Buddhism, that constitutes the oppositional "syntax" or structure of the legends of the Buddha.

The legends tell us that the Buddha was at Kuru when he told his followers what some scholars believe to be one of the most important sections in all of the Tipitika. Walsh, beguiled by realism, tells us that some scholars think that Kuru was near what is now modern Delhi! If that turned out to be true, would it help us make sense out of what the Buddha said? Why not read this particular discourse in the context of the mythological framework itself, which tells us that Kuru is the northern paradise of one of the four continents of the cosmos as described throughout the legends. We often forget, as Walsh did, that there is no sharp line that we can draw between geography and cosmology in myth.

It should come as no surprise when I say that maps of the "land of the Buddha" are tricky, if not illusory. There is, indeed, a realistic style to the beginning of each section of the episodes. We can, after all, locate Varanasi, the Ganges River, and Rajagaha, just like Bethlehem or Mecca. But can we find Kapilavatthu, Buddha's birthplace or, Pava, Cunda's home? But then, geography, without notice, becomes transformed into cosmography before our eyes as we read that the "miserable little town" called Kusinara was "really" jewel-bedecked golden Kusavati aeons ago when the Buddha was Mahasadussana, a Universal Monarch, and that India is located in Jambudipa.

Part I richly verifies the transformation of history and geography into myth. There is no immunity against this dramatic intrusion into the events of history and the solid markings of geography by mythical narrative. Mythical narrative always requires the pollinating gift of facts.

19

The Legends as Rites
of Passage

Most significant human actions, events, and classifications in
the history of religions are rituals. For example, birth, death, sex,
naming, eating, education, marriage, war, time (the day, the week,
month, and new year), travel, and space (building, boundaries) are
at one time or another constituted by ritual. And because all rituals
entail belief and the presence of superhuman agents, they also entail
a language; they are communal, thus social. As you will recall, I
defined ritual as a communal system of prescribed actions consisting of both verbal and nonverbal interactions with a superhuman
agent or agents.

Sometimes a theory becomes a fact. Early in the twentieth century Arnold van Gennep proposed a theory about ritual in a book
he titled *Rites de Passage*. Years later the book was translated into
English, but by that time "rites of passage" had become a common
phrase in the English language. Unfortunately for van Gennep, no
one refers to his book anymore when the phrase is used; it is a fine
example of theory becoming a fact. His book marked another small
step forward in our understanding of ritual and religion.

Van Gennep's theory tells us that every ritual is made up of
three parts. He called the first part "preliminal," the second part
"liminal," and the third part "postliminal." Rites of passage are specific kinds of actions that either take you or the community from one
point to another or transform you into a new status. Van Gennep
found that not only did each ritual have three parts, but that it also

included specific rituals that marked the actual separation and reincorporation of the individual or community back into the world from which they had initially been separated.

Rituals, then, provide the rules that constitute the passage from childhood to adulthood. Rituals transform you from being single to being married, from being human to becoming an ancestor. Rituals mark the transition from secular life to religious life, from being a son or daughter to becoming a wife, husband, monk, nun, king or queen, teacher or doctor. Taking a pilgrimage such as the hajj in Islam is a fine example of the liminal. Mardi Gras continues to echo the liminal voices of a passage from one year to the next, a rite of separation in preparation for lent, death, and resurrection in Christianity, a colorful "time out," "betwixt and between" ordinary social life.

Figure 19.1 presents a schema that depicts what this theory looks like when it is applied to Buddhist rituals that transform a Buddhist householder into a Buddhist renouncer; substitute "bachelor" for "householder" and "married man" for "renouncer," and you have the schema for a traditional marriage with the traditional "honeymoon" as an excellent example of part of the "rite of reincorporation."

This approach to the structure of rituals tells us that the initial preliminal stage, marked "A," is to the liminal, marked "B," as the liminal "B" is to the

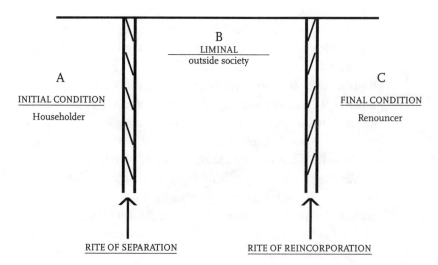

A = PRE LIMINAL (SEPARATION)
B = LIMINAL
C = POST LIMINAL (REINCORPORATION)

B
LIMINAL
outside society

A
INITIAL CONDITION
Householder

C
FINAL CONDITION
Renouncer

RITE OF SEPARATION   RITE OF REINCORPORATION

FIGURE 19.1 The Structure of Rites of Passage

postliminal stage, marked "C." Thus A : B :: B : C. Moreover, A is the inverse of C. Rites of passage are sets of oppositions. Rituals, then, are entirely logical—they entail a structure that is completely rational. And we must never forget that rituals as actions are always related to complex belief systems and myths. My holistic definition of religion as "a communal system of propositional attitudes and practices that are related to superhuman agents" can now be more fully understood.

Several years ago Victor Turner paid tribute to van Gennep's discovery by concentrating on the liminal stage of ritual, that is, the actual ritual itself, describing it as "betwixt and between" the preliminal and postliminal stages of life. Turner focused on "liminality" as the heart of ritual. He viewed liminality as "antistructure," describing it in terms that emphasize contradiction and the nonrational. Although this view of ritual remains quite popular, it turns out upon examination to be a mistake. Liminality is indeed in opposition to the preliminal and postliminal, but to say that the liminal is opposite the preliminal or postliminal does not entail that it is therefore antistructural or nonrational. Turner was quite right in calling liminality "betwixt and between." But he was wrong, I think, in describing it as opposite rationality, logic, and structure. In the history of India's religions, for example, the liminal is often described as the "wilderness" or "forest." In the legends of Vessantara and the other stories you have read in part I, the forest is both a paradise and a terrifying, horrible place.

We often find that liminality in some rituals stresses an ambiguous state or domain where the initiant is described as neither male nor female, neither child nor adult. It is an action where time is suspended ("time out"), where death and birth are often emphasized. What Turner missed in his emphasis on antistructure and the nonrational is that the significance of the liminal is given in its structural and oppositional relation to both the pre- and postliminal stages of which it is a part. The liminal stage of a ritual is like the phoneme "o" in the word "dog." "O" by itself has no value or significance except in its relation to other phonemes. We can see that by itself "o" is arbitrary, having no phonetic value. We might say that by itself it is nonrational, meaningless; its significance is due to the relations it enters into with /d/ and /g/ to produce the words, "dog" and "god," that are meaningful when used in English sentences.

Here, briefly, is an example of a rite of passage. According to classical texts that describe the rites of passage in the life of a Hindu, every Hindu male of the upper castes must go through the ritual of being twice-born (dvi-ja). The lad is "born again"! This ritual is a necessary condition for his next rite of passage, marriage. It also introduces him into a stage of student life where he learns the sacred details of his tradition. The age for the ritual differs depending on the caste that the young boy belongs to. On the appropriate day, determined by the family astrologer, the young boy has a last breakfast with his mother, a ritual clearly signifying separation. The family's Brahmin ritual specialist then performs rituals that correct any mistakes of past rites of passage (birth, naming, and so on) to make certain that this ritual is pure. The boy then steps into a ritually prepared circle divided by the four cardinal points with his Brahmin ritual specialist. They stand to the north of the center facing each other, the boy facing west, the Brahmin facing east. The Brahmin will eventually give the boy his name and the most sacred verse of all Hindu scripture. As each is given to him, he walks around the center, ending up at the north side of the circle. He does this except for one event in the ritual, the one in which he is given his name. At this point in the ritual he walks around the center, ending up north of it but facing east, and the Brahmin declares, "You have become born!" The ritual ends with several declarations and a gift from the newborn to the Brahmin. He is now born again, "casted," an adult, and as such he has all the responsibilities and values of an adult male Hindu. He will become a student. His next rite of passage will be marriage. At death he will be cremated, not buried. The rites of separation and reincorporation are clearly marked by the last breakfast the boy has with his mother and the declarations and gift to the Brahmin, given by the newly created adult, at the end of the ritual.

The orientation of all "life-giving" rituals in Hinduism is north, in the morning, to life. Rituals of death and cremation are oriented south, the domain of the ancestors, at twilight. Moreover, all but a very few Hindu temples are built on an east-west axis, with the entrance to the temple from the east. Hindu classical texts on house architecture always show the house built on an east-west axis. With the diagram of the cosmology in hand, on which side of the house would you find the front entrance? Quite right. The East side.

Is there a similar rite of passage in Buddhism? There is, but its description needs a preface. A monk in Buddhism is a "son of the Buddha," and to become a son of the Buddha is a merit producing act par excellence. Anyone contributing to the performance of the ritual of initiation into monkhood is a recipient of merit, and merit produces a good karmic legacy for the future. In South Asian Buddhism, to become a monk is a rite of passage required of almost every young Buddhist boy, the equivalent of confirmation in Christianity or a bar mitzvah in Judaism. Thus, just about every male in South East Asia is a son of the Buddha. The ritual is usually performed just before what scholars have called the "Buddhist Lent," the time before the monsoon. Lent is marked by the full moons in July and October.

The following is a brief description of this important rite of passage in Thailand that often takes two days. The day before the ritual is a day of preparation given over to festivities involving relatives and friends at the house of the initiate, and the gathering together of the articles that will be necessary in the life as a monk. Early the next morning, the first day of the ritual, the initiate is taken from his house to the monastery, where his head is shaven. He is taken back to his house wearing the white cloth of the layperson. The ritual at this point is entirely made up of relatives and friends and is performed by the elders of the town. The ritual emphasizes merit, the initiate's biography, and his responsibilities to the family and community. Monks, who have been absent until now, enter the ritual for the first time and chant protective verses from the *Tipitaka* to protect the initiate as he is ritually changed from householder to renouncer. This use of the verses in the *Tipitaka* for ritual purposes should not be new to you, since you know the story of the utterance of verses as protective in the legends of part I.

The magical use of words in ritual contexts is as perplexing as it is familiar to most students of religion. It is a performance in which most of the people present, including the initiant, are not familiar with the language being used. It is a use of language that is clearly not intended for communicative purposes, a clear instance of the use of language in which truth conditions are intentionally absent! If this is so, it seems clear that the use of Pali scripture in this ritual is meaningless to all those present at the ritual that are not monks. (This, of course, assumes that all monks know Pali, an assumption that is not always true.) It is an instance in which the householders hear a language they do not understand, an example of an important use of language known to exist in the performance of rituals in many religions. (Is it possible that we still hear an echo of this use of language in the modern "languages" of the academic, professional, and scientific disciplines?) We have yet to come up with an adequate theory that will explain this important use of language in ritual performances. To say that the rituals are performed because they satisfy certain needs may be a heuristic device to allow us to move on, but it is not a valid explanation.

Early in the morning of the second and last day of the ritual, parents, relatives, and friends take food to the monastery. A procession is formed in town that will carry the boy, dressed in royal robes, to the monastery. Once there, he takes his robes from his parents and puts them on with the aid of teacher monks. He requests ordination and recites the triple refuge and the ten precepts. He is then given his alms bowl and is examined by his mentors on his qualifications for becoming a monk. Satisfied, the mentors report to the assembled monks and request his admission. He is given a new name, usually in Pali, and informed of the rules he must obey as a monk. The monks then chant verses regarding the splendors of monkhood, and the new monk performs a ritual for the transference of merit to parents and relatives. He is now a true monk, a beggar, in liminality.

The ritual ends with a feast for the monks, relatives, and friends, provided by the parents of the newly ordained monk. Ideally, he will live as a renouncer and student until the full moon of October, when he will then disrobe in a ritual that introduces him to his social world as an adult. In some versions of the ritual he is met by a young virgin at the gate of the monastery. There is absolutely no stigma attached to leaving monastic life for the world of the householder at the end, or even before "Buddhist Lent." If at some later date this son of the Buddha wishes to return to monkhood, he may do so by establishing an auspicious date for his full ordination. We must remember that throughout all these rites the cosmology is always present in the microcosmic structures, both temporally and spatially, in which the rites are performed. The rite takes place at the center of the four continents.

The new life of the young man while a renouncer is temporary and liminal, lasting a few months. It is only when a decision is made later in life to become ordained as a monk that liminality becomes permanent, that a rite of passage becomes a rite of initiation into the life of a renouncer as a permanent mode of existence.

Perhaps something closer to home may make the structure of a rite of passage more vivid. Universities and colleges at one time were fully religious institutions; some still are. I have often thought of the four-year liberal arts college as a "modern rite of passage." Here, then, is the secular version I observed for many years at Dartmouth College. It always takes place in September, a most auspicious month in the history of religions and not therefore simply to be explained by the completion of agricultural work in a farming culture years ago. The grand rituals performed in September in many religions (or in the spring) marked the beginning of a new year.

Before classes begin each fall term, first-year students are put through a rigorous, carefully designed "orientation period," a true rite of separation from parents and the past. Among a host of important things, they also learn the sacred songs and history of the college and meet some of the high chiefs of the institution. Then on the first day of classes the college celebrates convocation, truly a collective ritual made up of students and faculty that marks the new year and the beginning of a long, long, liminal period (four years) for the new initiates. The initiates are taught the sacred beliefs and values from within a cosmological framework, marked by the sacred space of the quad and the library, the font of all knowledge and tradition. In fact, many campuses are a distinct microcosm, and some, reflecting Eden, even have a river running through the campus. At Dartmouth, the library, with its tower reaching high into the sky, marks the center of the campus.

During liminality, when certain rules are violated, the initiates are punished and sometimes expelled. And although there are many collective "rituals" throughout the year (homecoming or winter carnival, for example), the students are put through a discipline of examination and rigid scheduling. The end of liminality is marked by commencement, a new beginning, where the student will emerge into the "real world." The "unreal" world, the world of the ivory tower, has its own rules, a world where the police and the law are for the most part out of bounds. It is clearly "betwixt and between" the matrix in which everlasting friendship is forged. And how do we know liminality is over? The rite of "reincorporation" is called "commencement," an elaborate ritual that lasts several days. And to reinforce this rite, after commencement these new human beings hear, "Welcome to the alumni club. How much can you give?" They are adults now. The framework is there; I did not make it up. The problem with this interpretation, of course, is that the superhuman agents are no longer efficacious, at least for the most part, even though they are often evoked. Nevertheless, it remains a fascinating instance of a rite of passage gone secular, where the structure or "syntax" but not the old content persists.

With the structure of rites of passage and a few examples in hand, let us now take a look at the legends of Mahasudassana, Vessantara, and the Buddha. That they should contain rites of passage should come as no surprise once we focus on the structure of religion as communal systems that consist of two basic complex elements, myth and ritual. Do not interpret this as an attempt to update the old theory that myths are the libretto of rituals. That theory has been laid to rest, more or less, and it is best to leave it there. It is not a question of which came first, rituals or myths. What I find of interest is that the legends not only contain ritual but also seem to be framed by the *structure* of a rite of passage. This kind of approach may lead to a more adequate alternative to the quest for the historical Buddha, an original Buddhism, leaving us with unacceptable interpretations of the legends as signifying an original ascetic Buddhism, otherworldly, that degenerated into a popular folk religion or a schizoid religion made up of two contradictory parts, one emphasizing enlightenment and withdrawal from the world, the other stressing devotion and the production of good karma.

With this in mind let us take a brief look at the legend of Mahasudassana. It begins and ends, as you will recall, with elaborate rites of passage that should remind us of the beginning and end of the legends of the Buddha and Vessantara. Kusavati is the capital city in which Mahasudassana's extraordinary palace is located. It is a microcosm, surrounded by seven walls and four gates, a replica of Kuru, the paradise of the northern quarter of the cosmos, a reminder of the palaces built for the young Gotama.

The first rite begins when Mahasudassana purifies himself and then mounts the stairs of the veranda to the top of his palace. This ritual clearly marks a rite of separation and an entrance into liminality. It is the fifteenth of the month, and the king is about to perform the Uposatha ritual, which is central in the life of all Buddhist monks. He is alone. It is in this period of "betwixt and between" that Mahasudassana not only receives the Seven Wheel-Treasures and the Four Properties of a Universal Monarch but travels the length and breadth of the four corners of the cosmos.

The king then returns to life in the city as a Universal Monarch. We are told that he rides slowly in the pleasure park so that people may view him, and he provides for their every need an episode that is quite the opposite of Gotama's afternoon rides to the park. After returning gifts of wealth and a great deal more, he decides to build a fabulous lotus pond, and Vissakamma constructs a magnificent palace for him called the Palace of Dhamma. His wife leaves him, taking with her a huge entourage. Once again this episode is the exact opposite of Gotama leaving his family and the palace at night for the wilderness.

After completely satisfying all the wishes of his people, the king reflects upon his fantastic success. "It is," he concludes, "the result of giving, self-control, and abstinence." He then enters the great gabled hall and begins the fourfold meditation that is so well known in the legend of the Buddha's own awakening, passing through the hierarchy of the four levels of meditation and traversing the four quarters of the cosmos. Mahasudassana then leaves the hall and spreads unbounded loving-kindness, compassion, and joy throughout the four quarters: the equivalent of the Buddha's career as a teacher after his enlightenment.

The queen, absent after many hundreds of thousands of years, decides to return home. The king forbids her entrance into the golden chamber of the palace, and the second and final rite of passage is about to begin. The king leaves the chamber, goes into the palm grove, and lies down on a golden couch, lying on his right side and adopting the "lion posture" with one foot on the other, mindful and clearly aware. After teaching the Doctrine of impermanence to his wife, he once again enters the fourfold meditation and is reborn in the highest attainable world.

This is a story that is both strikingly different and yet quite similar to Buddha's life and death. For example, to identify only a few episodes, it is Mahasudassana's wife who leaves him while the king remains in the palace;

the people ask him to drive more slowly so they can view him as he rides in the pleasure park, and it is the palace rather than the forest that becomes his paradise and place of meditation. His final meditation takes place in a grove of the palace and leads to the highest attainable world. Giving, self-control, and abstinence are the karmic legacy of both the Buddha and Mahasadusanna. A rite of passage marks both the beginning and the end of their lives. The most striking feature of their legends is that both are renouncer/ascetics even though they live in opposite environments: a luxurious palace and the wilderness. Both the Buddha and Mahasudassana begin their lives as royal princes and through rites of passage become ascetics who attain the highest level of enlightenment and then in turn teach the Doctrine (the *dhamma*) to either an estranged wife (Subhadda) or a determined stepmother (Mahapajapati). The final scenes of Mahasudassana with Subhadda and the Buddha with Ananda bring the relations between a Buddha and a Universal Monarch to a rich comparative ending. It is indeed in the differences between the characters and the two episodes that we discover the resemblances.

Vessantara is introduced to us after an involved set of rebirths and marriages that include Sakka, the king of the thirty-three gods and chief of the guardians of the four quarters. The pregnancy is miraculous, and Vessantara is born in the merchant section of the city (note how this is opposite of the Buddha, who is born in a grove outside the city). After a brilliant life as a student, Vessantara marries Maddi, who gives birth to a son and daughter. During a drought Vessantara gives the rain-bestowing elephant away to a group of Brahmins, who finally meet him at the South gate of the city. They leave through the North gate with the elephant. The details of the Brahmins' departure are the exact opposite of the Buddha's funeral procession through the East gate. The people become enraged and demand that Vessantara be exiled from the kingdom.

When we view this legend as a rite of passage, it seems clear that this marks the end of Vessantara's preliminal life. The legend tells us not once but twice that rather than being sent into exile immediately, he was allowed to spend the night with his family. It also makes sure that we understand that he is innocent of any wrongdoing. After agreeing to enter exile, Vessantara "made it clear that it was not because of an offense but because of a gift of an elephant that he was banished. This being so, he asked that he be given one day's delay to give the gift of seven hundred."

The rite of separation then takes place. "All through the night the royal family talked about life in the wilderness. And as they conversed the dawn appeared along with the rising of the sun." Vessantara, Maddi, and the two children then bid his parents farewell. The departure marks the beginning of the liminal phase of his life. He leaves the city and heads for the wilderness. Notice that he heads north. He gives away his horses and carriage and begins the long trip to the forest with his family. They finally reach the hermitage deep in the forest that has been built for them by Vissakamma under orders from Sakka.

We are told that Vessantara entered the hermitage alone, took off his sword and bow and outer clothes, and put on the dress of a hermit together with a staff. He then walked up and down the path Vissakamma had made, then went up to his wife and children, "calm and composed as one who by himself has found Enlightenment." He tells them that they are now to live as hermits and asks Maddi, his wife, not to make contact with him, since "a woman is a stain on a life of renunciation." He is described as having "no possessions, no wealth or grain." At this point Vessantara has reached the center of liminality. He is "betwixt and between" the pre- and postliminal phases of his life. He has traveled north to the forest that is clearly opposite the south and the civil city. The forest is ambiguous. It is both to be feared and a place of peace and quiet. Vessantara is with his family in the forest, yet he is alone.

Meanwhile, a Brahmin endures the hardship of the forest, the home of fierce wild beasts, and cries out from a tree when he has lost his way, yet a local hunter describes the hermitage as located in what can only be called a paradise. It is a place without dust, where a person knows no hunger, thirst, or discontent. Recall that the children played in it without fear, and Maddi gathered its fruits without effort, just as Kuru is a land without labor or civil strife. Moreover, sexual desires are overcome; Vessantara has not "touched" Maddi during their life in the forest. Vessantara's hermitage is a paradise, as is Mahasudassana's Kusavati or the Buddha's place of meditation; they all resemble Kuru, the kingdom of the North described at the beginning of part I as "passionless, without wives, they have no need to scatter seed, or to draw the plow, of itself the ripened crop presents itself for men to eat." It is a place where "giving, self-control, and abstinence" are achieved.

It is at the midpoint in the liminal period where the perfection of giving takes place. First, Vessantara gives both his children away. They become the vehicles for Vessantara's perfection, synonymous with the Doctrine and truth that the Buddha will discover in the perfection of wisdom. Vessantara says, "Come, fulfill my perfection. Be a steady boat on the sea of becoming. I shall cross to the further shore of birth, and make the world with its gods cross on it also." The image of a boat crossing the sea of suffering to the shore of liberation is a popular metaphor for the four noble truths and eightfold path, the Doctrine that the Buddha taught.

When Maddi returns from gathering food, she misses the children and believes they are dead. Maddi goes out into the wilderness three times in search of the children while Vessantara remains silent. She returns and loses consciousness, and Vessantara caresses her body and brings her back to awareness. Maddi agrees with him that the gift was indeed a proper one, and the earth trembles once again as a witness. The next ordeal takes place when Sakka, disguised as a decrepit old Brahmin, asks Vessantara for his wife. Vessantara, "indifferent," "unattached," "his mind clinging to nothing," gladly consents. Pouring water over his hands, he gives Maddi to the Brahmin. Maddi consents without resentment or sorrow and says, "Let him give me away or sell me, let him kill me!" Sakka, king of the gods, declares this as an act of great merit, and that such acts bear fruit in the Brahma heaven. He then reveals his disguise and returns Maddi to Vessantara. Rising into the air, he grants Vessantara eight wishes, the wishes of a Universal Monarch.

The emphasis throughout the legend is on giving. But we should not overlook the fact that throughout the legend we are reminded that Vessantara is a "Great Agent," a superhuman agent who possesses the Buddhist virtues of "giving, self-control, and abstinence." During his life in the wilderness he is able, through the power of his mediation, to make the fierce animals of the forest live in harmony with each other, and he walked "as one who by himself had found enlightenment." The difference between the Buddha and Vessantara is the difference between the two paths each has chosen.

In the meantime, Vessantara's father ransoms the children and makes ready a royal road to the forest, arriving there with a great entourage. A great ritual of reincorporation is about to begin. At first Vessantara meets his father alone; he then bathes, changes clothes, and puts on his sword in preparation for his reincorporation with the social world. The celebration takes place outside the forest for a month and marks the ritual ending his liminal life as an ascetic. He will return home perfect in giving, a king, and at death will be reborn in the Tushita heaven. Vessantara's life as a rite of passage is a life that begins as a prince who becomes an ascetic and ends as an ascetic who becomes a monarch. The reunion of father and son is quite in contrast to the reunion of the Buddha with his father.

At this point in our analysis of the legends a brief review of the Buddha's life as Gotama will help demonstrate the usefulness of the structure of rites of passage in comparative analysis. When asked to compare, we usually look for similarities. In this chapter we are reversing this comparative procedure, looking for differences, for oppositions. It is in the *differences* between the Buddha and the Universal Monarchs that we will discover the resemblances.

The Buddha's birth, youth, and marriage obviously mark the preliminal stage. Born "bright as the morning sun," he surveys the four quarters of the cosmos and declares his mission. The emphasis in his youth is on a happy life, one that is lived in innocence of suffering, pain, and death. The ritual of separation is very clear in the story, marked by his departure at night through the eastern gate. He cuts off his hair, exchanges his royal regalia for the clothes of an ascetic, and heads south for the wilderness and a homeless life. The liminal period is a struggle with radical asceticism and combat with Mara and death. His awakening takes place during the three watches of the night as he faces east. As the sun rises in the east, he has gained the knowledge of the cause of and liberation from death and rebirth.

The rite of reincorporation lasts one month, in which the Buddha meditates on his liberation and is protected by the king of serpents. He then decides to teach the Doctrine. Leaving Vesali at the end of his teaching career, he turns around and views his favorite city, saying, "O, Ananda, this is the last time that the Awakened One will look upon Vesali." They then head north for Kusinara. His death repeats the night of his liberation, and his funeral is a ritual for a conqueror, a royal person, a Universal Monarch.

This structure of the lives of the three superhuman agents, as a series of rites of passage, brings into focus some very interesting elements of the myths. The two Great Agents never appear together; that will only occur at the end of our aeon. They must choose one career or the other. As Great Agents all three begin as royal figures, as kings or princes, become ascetics, and are memorialized as Universal Monarchs. They are separated from their families in strikingly different patterns. Mahasudassana's wife leaves for another country while Mahasudassana remains at the palace, Vessantara leaves the palace, his mother and father, and takes his immediate family with him, eventually giving them away while living as an ascetic in the wilderness, and they are reunited at the end of the legend. The Buddha abandons his family, leaves the palace alone at night heading south for the wilderness and eventually gaining liberation facing east under the tree of enlightenment, remaining alienated from his family. He heads south into the wilderness, alone. Vessantara's trip is just the opposite. He heads north with his family. The Buddha will eventually accept both his stepmother and his son into the ascetic community he has created. Although they live in separate quarters, Vessantara lives with his family in the dwelling built by Vissipassa and will give them away.

Asceticism, the act of renouncing the life of the householder, is the common feature in all three of the legends. However, it is important to note that the liminal state of each is quite different. Although Mahasudassana is separated from his wife and children, his life as a renouncer, his meditation, takes place

in the palace, in the great inner chamber. Vessantara is exiled after spending
the night with his parents and family; he leaves in the morning and heads north
for the wilderness. His life as a renouncer and his meditation take place in the
wilderness with his family, who live separated from Vessantara. The Buddha
leaves his family at night, travels south, and finally wins enlightenment after
a contest with Mara, in opposition to Vessantara, who also conquers desire
by giving away members of his family. As we shall see in the next chapter,
there are many more such oppositional contrasts in the three legends. But the
point throughout all these complex myths is this: all three become conquerors
through a nonviolent ascetic life, one that renounces the domestic mode of life
of the householder. And this ascetic life is very specific in its structure both in
action and in belief. It is defined from within a cosmology, a community, and
two crucial doctrines, the doctrines of karma and impermanence.

The popularity of Vessantara in the lives of contemporary Southeast
Asian Buddhists should not come as a surprise. Recall, first of all, that the
Buddha identifies himself as Vessantara in a former life. Second, every novice who enters the monkhood as a young boy imitates not only the Buddha
in his departure from the normal routines of social life but also Vessantara.
There is nothing in the biography of Vessantara or Mahasudassana, or in the
Buddha's telling of the story, that would indicate in any way that their rites of
passage are somehow of lesser value than the Buddha's own life as the awakened one. There is not the slightest indication in the stories that Vessantara's
or Mahasudassana's choices, or their wishes, including the wish for passage
to heaven at death, are somehow of lesser value than the Buddha's own awakening; the content of the awakening in all three of the Great Agents is the
same. Their identification as Great Agents cannot be overemphasized. It may
well be a mistake to overemphasize the "initiation" of every Buddhist lad's ritual rebirth as a "son of the Buddha." That is certainly true; however, it is also
true that this initiation creates the possibility of a choice. After reincorporation the lad at some point in his life will make a choice: he will either become
a renouncer, a monk, or he will continue on in life as householder. That is to
say, he will follow the path of either a Buddha or a Universal Monarch. Stress
or focus only on the Buddha, Buddhacentricism, prevents us from grasping
this double feature of the religion we have labeled "Buddhism." The popularity of Vessantara is not an accident or arbitrary feature in this religion. He is a
necessary element in the grammar and semantics of both myth and ritual in
Buddhism.

A good case can be made for interpreting the stories of both Mahasudassana
and Vessantara as reaching the wisdom of enlightenment in their meditation.
Where they differ, it seems, is in the karmic legacy that must, by its very law,

work itself out as in the case of Moggallana and the Buddha himself. Not even Moggallana and Sariputta, the greatest intellectuals of all the Buddha's disciples, were judged by the Buddha to have gained final liberation from their own karmic legacy when they died. Yet if anyone understood what the Buddha taught, it was clearly Moggallana and Sariputta. If I am not mistaken, the only person besides the Buddha himself who is clearly judged as having gained final liberation (nibanna) is Mahapajapati, the Buddha's own stepmother, to whom the Buddha at first denied ordination! If I am right, then this, together with the Buddha's resistance to her entrance into the ascetic community, requires further analysis, since it is not solved by asserting, "Ah, yes, but these episodes are a late addition to the text."

I have used the tripartite form of a rite of passage for three primary reasons. First, it helps highlight the differences between the major superhuman agents in the legends of Buddhism. Second, its use also highlights the essential similarities between Buddhas and Universal Monarchs, the two appearances known as Great Agents. The third reason for its use is that it may help us overcome the emphasis on narrative in the received tradition. We might call this tradition "our narrative mode of thought," a mode of thought that is dominant in our culture. It assumes that the good life entails self-identity, and that this self-identity involves a narrative, an unfolding story about who we are—that if we are to make sense of our lives, that if life is meaningful, we must possess a narrative of ourselves. In our culture a meaningful life entails narrativity, the unfolding of a story about the self, narrative as actually lived. When we lose our narrative of the self, we seek therapy, which attempts to discover it and reproduce it; Freudian psychoanalysis is a perfect example of this mode of thought, as is the popularity of biography.

According to the legends of the Buddha, however, the quest for biography is useless; it is arbitrary if attempted and false in many of its representations. Moreover, it is precisely this quest for the self that is the cause of suffering. Thus, I do not think it is accidental that we do not find "biographies," or narratives of the self, in Buddhist scripture. In brief, narrativity presupposes a self that can be identified in the past, the present, and the future, a self that persists, develops, and is identified in narrative form. The Buddha clearly denies the ontology of a self. It would seem, then, that if there is no self, there is also no narrative; self, narrative, and biography are fictions, if not false from the very beginning. Given the basic foundations of our own education, this is, indeed, a radical set of premises.

Be that as it may, the doctrine of karma now becomes more intelligible. Karma is episodic action of the past in the present without the intervention of an enduring self. The legacy of karma, for example, is like the legacy of practicing the piano in the past. You would not say that that practice is now literally present in your performance of a Beethoven sonata. Nor would you say that your performance now *is* literally a repetition of your practices in the past. Nevertheless, that practice is "present" and has an effect on your performance of the prelude now; indeed, practice does have consequences.

The legends seem to be the reverse of how we go about managing our lives. The quest for the self, self-identity, and the quest to produce a narrative of the self are the sources of unhappiness; according to Buddhism it is a quest based on wrong views. Buddhism is a clear falsification of the worn-out cliché that "all religions say the same thing," or, "all religions are true."

At the beginning of the legends of the Buddha we are told that it was predicted that he would become either a Universal Monarch or an Enlightened One. Although his father dearly wanted him to become a Universal Monarch, (what parent wouldn't?), we know the outcome. The point to be made, however, is that the texts do not seem to treat one as of higher value than the other, and the Buddha made this crystal clear at the time of his own death with regard to his funeral. Both the Universal Monarch and the Buddha teach the same Doctrine and have the same compassion for the welfare and happiness of the world. I now want to take a look at the relation between these superhuman agents.

20

The Great Agent

Universal Monarchs and Buddhas

The Western usage of "Buddhism" as the word for identifying a religion may contribute to some of our problems in understanding it; "Buddhism" may be far too "Buddhacentric" as an adequate identifying marker. It follows the theologically defined Christocentric nature of "Christianity" and the attempt to identify Islam as "Mohammadanism," an attempt that was quickly rejected by Muslims as outright blasphemy.

Be that as it may, a comparative analysis of the two legendary characters, the Universal Monarch and the Buddha, is necessary because concentration on the Buddha as the central figure in this religion has almost obliterated the fact that large sections of the Buddhist canonical texts have to do with Universal Monarchs. The "Great Agent" known as a Universal Monarch completely disappears in most introductions to Buddhism because of the Buddhacentric focus of Western scholarship. This focus, in turn, stems from our own Western narrative constraint in understanding religions, a constraint that considers the mythical as of less value than history and that stresses the value of the individual, the person, the self.

From this perspective the Universal Monarch is a mythical product of South Asian imagination, vivid, fascinating, but nevertheless unreal or absurd. History, on the other hand, is the way things really are, and our task is to uncover the historical agent that is clothed in that rich imaginary dress in the style of the Buddha. The Universal Monarch is myth; the Buddha is history, a founder. The one is fiction, the other is a historical person, real. A great deal of ink has been used to write about the Buddha and kings, the Buddha and his relations with royal families, his popularity among royal families at mealtime, and the close relation between the renouncer and royal households with regard to property. What is often forgotten, or simply suppressed, is that although these events do at times strike us as very realistic, thick with history, "real time," they clearly take place within a mythical framework that is not reducible to political, socioeconomic, or historical contexts. Part I of this book should provide overwhelming evidence to confirm this.

The fact that some scholars actually wonder in print why such legends are in the scriptures in the first place—"What are they doing in there?"—indicates how far off target our understanding of Buddhism may actually be. Collins, for example, agrees with Gombrich, who advises us not to accept too literal an interpretation of these stories. "From the rest of what we know of him," writes Collins quoting Gombrich, "we cannot think that the Buddha believed that one day people would literally be no more than ten years old and go hunting each other like beasts." I won't go into "what we know of him" again, but even if we did know, we could also ask such questions as whether the Buddha believed that there really was a Vessantara, or a Mahasudassana in a previous existence, and that the Doctrine of karma is true, or that Mara, Sakka, and the gods exist? Better yet, did he really believe that Universal Monarchs exist? I think Collins would agree.

Given the "received tradition" regarding Buddhism, Stanley Tambiah, one of the first to take the Universal Monarchs seriously, thought they were an "intriguing problem." "Why," he asks, did the "early Buddhist canonists in the midst of their preoccupation with renunciation of the world find time to dilate upon the worldly figure of the *cakkavatti* [Universal Monarch]?" He then mentions that there are six narratives in *The Long Discourses* alone that deal with him, a section of the canon that Buddhist scholars agree is "one of the earliest strata of the Pali canon." He separates the problem into two questions: the first is doctrinal, and the second is sociopolitical. Both involve an "interlocking" of the renouncer-king relation by means of the doctrine and ethics of nonviolence. In other words, Tambiah is interested in the *use* of the legends in Buddhist history, and he is one of the first to stress the importance of the "interlocking" of the legends. The problem with his initial approach to this subject is his agreement with the "received tradition" on the definition of Buddhism as "otherworldly." This leads him into inevitable contradictions with regard to the logic of "interlocking" of the Buddha and the Universal Monarch, as ideal models for the renouncer and householder; as usual, Tambiah is aware of this problem, and his essay is a great step forward.

This chapter concentrates on the relation between Universal Monarchs and Buddhas in the legends themselves. Vessantara, as I have stressed, is as popular in the tradition and in many modern Buddhist countries as the Buddha himself. There is a sense in which one is of no greater value than the other. In studying Buddhism, remember that both are called "Great Agents." I want to suggest that it is the relations between these two mythical characters that signify who they are. If I am right, or at least on the right track about this, then the trashing of the legends, or translation of the Universal Monarch into parable and metaphor, produces a distortion in our perception of the Buddha, the Universal Monarch, and Buddhism as a religious tradition.

Chapter 15 introduced you to one of the most popular Universal Monarchs, Mahasudassana. In this chapter I want to introduce two additional texts, which are among the longest narratives we have in Pali Buddhist scripture. Both of these texts reinforce what I have to say about this mythical character and the importance of the relation between Buddhas and Universal Monarchs who turn the universal wheel of justice and truth.

The first text is called "The Marks of a Great Agent," or, as the phrase is usually translated, "The Marks of a Great Being." Maurice Walshe, who provided us with a new translation of *The Long Discourses* (*Digha Nikaya*), has this to say about it in his introductory note to the chapter: "This Sutta may seem the most uninteresting and unedifying of the entire Nikaya." Walshe quotes Rhys Davids, the founder of the Pali Text Society, as saying that "most of the marks are so absurd, considered as marks of any human being, that they are probably mythological in origin." Rhys Davids thinks that the chapter seems "gravely ironical in the contrast it makes between the absurdity of the marks and the beauty of the ethical qualities they are supposed...to mean," as if the marks were the equivalent of the latest hairstyles.

These remarks, in a footnote, are excellent examples of the confusion that has taken place in our perception of Buddhism. Rhys Davids and Walshe have clearly confused texts that are about myths with texts that are about human beings and history. Notice, also, how "irony" appears as the interpretation of choice once the confusion takes place. This false move to the use of irony, farce, or symbolic meaning in the interpretation of myth is usually due to an error in our theory of meaning. It takes place when fright overcomes us, when we find ourselves in the language of myth and feel compelled to make a hasty retreat to sure foundations, the firm ground of reality, "the real world," as the reference for the meaning of the myth. Rhys Davids is right, though, in thinking that the marks are not the marks of any human being. They are indeed "mythical in origin."

The interpretation of the text as a "joke," "irony," "farce" or "symbolic meaning" usually presupposes a theory of representation, reference, or background that is assumed to be the external foundation of the text. That is to say, the meaning of a myth corresponds, in some sense of the word "correspond," to what we believe is real, original, or foundational. For example, real kings, and the political and economic realities of social life sometimes become the reference for interpreting the myths of Universal Monarchs based on the author's own implicit criteria of verisimilitude, or rationality. However, as the saying goes, once you take this step "the joke's on you!"

Even if we could propose such a theory of meaning without incoherence, it seems clear that such a move outside of the myth is impossible in this case. To repeat once again, we simply do not know what, in fact, "is the case" about kingship and social structure in the fifth century B.C. The irony or joke here, if there is one, is not in the text but in the attempt to explain the significance of Universal Monarchs of the four quarters by reference to historical kings of India. The belief that the meaning of myth, corresponds to, or is constituted by its reference to some "reality" external to its own structure is as unfortunate as it is popular. It ignores the explanation that the text itself makes clear, that we can identify both Universal Monarchs and Buddhas by the marks on their bodies. The thirty-two marks on the Great Agent are caused by past actions, or karma. They are the effect of a past karmic legacy. But, then, many of us may think that the Doctrine of karma is as absurd as the thirty-two marks. Confronting the problem of absurdity, we try to solve it by turning the story into a joke that is supposedly its "original meaning" or a symbolic code that needs to be deciphered. Thinking that we have now solved the problem, we have in fact only made it worse.

As I have insisted all along, meaning is "literal meaning." This theoretical premise does not deny that "what the Buddha taught" contains humor, wit, and metaphor. It should come as no surprise to discover that superhuman agents suffer pain, enjoy a good laugh, and are capable of using language as we do. What this premise together with others denies is that the meaning of a language, including the language of myth, is representational. It denies that languages, or words, produce meaning by "standing for" or naming some object. It denies that meaning is produced by a correspondence between language and the world; that the meaning of our language is due to some "fit," "conceptual schema," or "symbol system" that produces meaning. Only sentences have meaning.

Durkheim thought that the meaning of myths and religious language were symbolic, that they referred, or corresponded, to the real social life of a society that he called the "collective." Freud, as we know, sought the correspondence, the reference for meaning, in the deep recesses of the unconscious life of the individual. Marx, on the other hand, thought that the meaning of mythical language was a projection he called "ideology" based on the material infrastructure of human existence. Rudolf Otto persuaded many students of religion to think of religion as a symbolic reference to the "Sacred," a transcendent, metaphysical reality that is "wholly other." Lévi-Strauss, who was certainly influential in the creation of what became known as "structural anthropology," knew better. For one thing, he knew that the content of many myths is just the opposite of the social life in which they are found. Yet, when it came to the question What do myths mean? he concluded that if they have meaning at all, it must be because they refer to something! What could it be? He concluded that it must be the human mind and its logical structure.

Once again, and very briefly, meaning and truth have to do with sentences, sentences that we take literally. Donald Davidson put it this way:

> Nothing, however, no *thing*, makes sentences and theories true; not experience, not surface irritations, not the world, can make a sentence true. *That* experience takes a certain course, that our skin is warmed or punctured, that the universe is finite, these facts, if we like to talk that way, make sentences and theories true. But this point is put better without mention of facts. The sentence, "My skin is warm," is true if and only if my skin is warm. Here there is no reference to fact, a world, or an experience, or a piece of evidence.

There is, it seems to me, wide agreement on three important distinctions that we should keep in mind when we talk about language and meaning. Very briefly, it is perfectly correct to say, "I speak a language." When we speak, we utter a language. Utterance entails both meaning and use, but these two important terms, meaning and use, should not be confused. We must keep in mind that speaking a language and talking or thinking *about* a language entail three different things: language, using a language, and talking about language and use. With this in mind, let us take a look at the text regarding the physical marks of a Great Agent.

The story opens with the usual introduction. We are told that the Buddha was staying in Jetavana, at Anathapindika's park with a group of monks. The Buddha begins his talk with these words: "There are, monks, thirty-two marks that are unique to a Great Agent." Anyone who knows anything about the Buddha knows that his body has thirty-two distinct marks on it. What we often forget, however, is what the Buddha went on to say: "There are only two careers open to a person who possesses those marks. If he lives the life of a householder he will become a ruler, a wheel-turning monarch who secures his realm and possesses the seven treasures." He not only conquers the four quarters but does so "without stick or sword." But if such a person should "go forth from the household life into homelessness he will become a fully enlightened Buddha who draws back the veil of ignorance from the world." What is important here is that *both* are given the title "Great Agent," and *both* have the identical thirty-two marks as a consequence of their past actions.

Taking modern linguistics as our guide, it would be a mistake to focus on each of the thirty-two marks, as if they had meaning as such, or in themselves. The marks, as such, are meaningless. Think of a word in a sentence, the famous "The cat is on the mat," for example. Words have meaning in relation to other words in the sentence, just as the phonemes, c/a/t have no value except in the relation they have with other phonemes. The same holds true, we learned, in the study of totems. As Lévi-Strauss taught us, totems have no intrinsic meaning as such. For example, in studies of totemism, we at first focused on the totem itself, looking for its reference. Thus, the bear totem means "strength," or the eagle totem means "sharp eyesight." This was a mistake. It assumes, first of all, that the solution to what something means is to be discovered by determining its reference given in experience: seeing is believing. Thus, the bear "stands for" strength. Second, it mistakenly assumes that an individual object has or bears a meaning. Following the advice of Saussure, the father of modern linguistics, Lévi-Strauss demonstrated that the significance of a totemic object is found in the relations it has with other elements in a very complex cognitive system. I would suggest that we approach the thirty-two marks on the body of a Great Agent by following this holistic principle. The marks are, first of all, the unique marks that identify all Great Agents. The significance of the individual mark on the body of a Great Agent, or the number of marks, as such or in themselves, is arbitrary.

I have argued that the householder is not of lesser value than the renouncer, that "securing the realm and possessing the seven treasures" is not to be ranked below "becoming a fully enlightened Buddha" who "draws back the veil of ignorance from the world." If this is an accurate and fair interpretation of the legends, then it becomes clear that the persistent Western Buddhacentric understanding of the legends is a distortion of this religion: the householder and the renouncer are of equal value. Moreover, neither the householder nor the renouncer, the Awakened One or the Universal King, is an ideal "model" for living. They are, lest we forget, superhuman beings; they can do things we cannot do, and have power we do not have. They also have knowledge that transcends our knowledge. What is important, defining, given their karmic legacy, is that both have become Great Agents who bear the thirty-two marks.

Since the text on the thirty-two marks is seldom included in books on the Buddha, because it is thought to be absurd and uninteresting, it is all the more important to quote at least part of the introduction. The Buddha lists the thirty-two marks and then says:

> These, monks, are the thirty-two marks unique to a Great Agent. There are only two careers open to a person who possesses those marks. If he lives the life of a householder he will become a ruler, a wheel-turning monarch who secures the realm and possesses the seven treasures, conquering the world without rod or sword. But if such a person should leave the life of the household and enter into homelessness he will become a fully enlightened Buddha who draws back the veil of ignorance from the world. And sages of other communions know these thirty-two marks, but they do not know the karmic reasons for the gaining of them.
>
> Monks, in whatever former life, former existence or dwelling-place the Perfected-One, being born a human being, undertook mighty deeds to good purpose, unwavering in good conduct of body, speech and thought, in generosity, self-discipline, observance of the fast-day, in honoring parents, ascetics and Brahmins and the head of the clan, and in other highly meritorious acts; by performing that action (kamma), heaping it up, lavishly and abundantly, at the breaking-up of the body at death he was reborn in a happy state, in a heavenly world, where he was endowed beyond other gods in ten respects: in length of heavenly life, beauty, happiness, splendor, influence and in heavenly sights, sounds, smells, tastes and contacts. Falling away from there and coming to be reborn on earth, he acquired the first mark of a Great Agent: feet with level tread, so that he places his foot evenly on the ground, lifts evenly, and touches the ground evenly with the entire sole.
>
> Being endowed with the mark, if he keeps to the household life, he will become a wheel-turning monarch.... Conquering without rod or sword, but by justice, he rules over the world as far as its ocean-boundaries, a land open, free of bandits, free from wilderness, powerful, prosperous, happy and free from perils. As a ruler how does he benefit? He cannot be impeded by any human foe with ill intent. That is his benefit as a ruler. And if he goes forth into homelessness, he will become a fully enlightened Buddha.... As an Enlightened One how does he benefit? He cannot be hindered by any enemy or adversary from within or without nor from greed, hatred or delusion, nor by any ascetic or Brahmin, any god, by Mara or Brahma, or any being in the world. That is his benefit as a Buddha.

There is only one significant difference in benefits, and it should not come as a surprise. If a Great Agent chooses to become a renouncer, he will become fully enlightened and liberated from death and rebirth. This difference is emphasized in different ways in each of the legends of wheel-turning monarchs. Most of them die and are reborn as they wish in one of the heavens. However, Sankha, as we will see, seems to be an exception; he renounces his kingship and becomes an enlightened monk. Sankha has a unique position in the grand scheme of the evolution of the cosmos, since he is the only Universal Monarch who appears with a Buddha; in a future aeon Sankha and Metteyya appear together, marking the maximum benefit for the welfare of mankind.

To begin our comparisons of the two agents we must go back to the first chapter on cosmology. As you will recall, the story tells us that in its evolution the world contracts and then various beings are mind-born, they feed on delight and are luminous, traverse the air, and live for many aeons. At that time, there is just water, no sun, or moon or stars, nor night, nor day, years, or seasons. Moreover, neither male nor female exists; "beings are just identified as beings." As evolution continues, the beings grow coarser as they feed on various foods, including rice that grows without cultivation.

At a certain point in the cosmic evolution, male and female sex organs develop, together with sexual desire, and houses are built to cover indulgence in sexual activity. Desire and laziness lead one of the beings to decide to gather rice all at once for many meals. This practice in turn leads to greed, stealing, lying, and violence. The people "rebuked him, censored him, hit him with their fists, stoned him, and beat him with sticks." They lament the evil that has arisen because of "taking what is not given, censuring, lying and punishment."

Steven Collins has argued that, if you keep the Buddhist ascetic mode of life in mind, as described in the *Vinaya*, you will discover that the "fall" from a paradise entails a step-by-step transgression of Buddhist monastic rule. Although I think it is unfortunate that he uses this discovery to argue that the story is really a moral parable, full of jokes, and not a cosmology, I think he is quite right about its stress on the transgression of monastic rules. The fall is indeed caused by a violation of monastic rules. But it is not just that the Five Precepts are violated: (1) do not deprive a living thing of life, (2) do not take what is not given, (3) do not have sex, (4) do not lie, (5) do not desire sense objects. Collins finds that the whole Buddhist ascetic life has been violated in both its etiquette, eating, for example, and its mode of existence, having sex, storing food, building houses. I think he is quite right. Remember also that paradise in the Buddhist scheme of things is identical with the homeless/ascetic life as described in the *Vinaya*. (We need to take great care here, as we remember the complex sense of "paradise," that we do not slip back into the quasi-historical mode of interpretation by insisting that the *Vinaya* texts are the template for translating the Buddhist cosmology because we think they are the earliest texts we have or contain "original" Buddhism.)

What Collins has discovered is that for the Buddhist tradition life in paradise is semantically equivalent to ascetic life. But, once again, this is not to say that the ascetic, the monk, is of greater value in the Buddhist scheme of things. To think this way, as Collins points out, is to take the first step in making Buddhism an ascetic, "otherworldly" religion. This distortion takes place when we focus on only one pole of the bipolar set of elements, the renouncer, as defining Buddhism. The quest for the historical Buddha is one version of this Western, Buddhacentric focus. We shall take a close look at this bipolar relation in the last chapter.

It should also be clear by now that "paradise" in Buddhism is not an original state, a Garden of Eden at the beginning or end of time. It is indeed a place of bliss and delight. Sometimes, according to the legend, it is to be found as a city; at other times it is in the wilderness. What is central to its description is the presence of a Superhuman Agent, a Buddha, a Universal Ruler, or, in other Buddhist traditions, a Bodhisattva. The most important thing to remember in all this is that the Buddhist paradise, as is the case with all things, is not permanent. It too has a beginning, middle, and end and must be defined by the ontological principle "all things in truth must perish" because "all things are impermanent."

We now return to the fatal episode in the story. As you will recall, after acknowledging the fall from paradise, the beings decide to select the best-looking person, the most capable among them, to become the king who will restore order for a share of their rice. They find such a person and call him Mahasammata. Keeping the legends of the wheel-turning kings in mind, we discover that although he has some of the qualities of such persons, he is not a Universal Monarch of the four quarters because, for one thing, he has agreed to rule by punishing those who have stolen and lied. It is a kingship that is opposite that of a Universal Monarch; it is a kingship well known in human history. Mahasammata rules like an ordinary king. Universal Monarchs are not elected by the people. They are Great Agents by virtue of their karmic legacy and the vows they have taken.

Two points must be highlighted here. The first brings us back once again to the notion of paradise. The cosmology opens with an evolution that entails beings living in a paradise: they do not need to work; they have no property; kinship, kingship, and possessions do not exist. They are content, happy, and free from desire. Stealing, lying, sexual misbehavior, and violence do not exist. As we know, this is a good description of exactly what asceticism means in the Buddhist tradition.

Paradise, in this cosmological setting, is described as an ascetic, homeless life. We might say that the preliminal and postliminal stages of life have become one with the liminal stage in the legend of the cosmology. Looked at in isolation, it is a life in which opposites do not exist; there are no rites of passage there, and thus no classification. The Five Precepts and the ascetic life of the renouncer in Buddhism might be called the "natural mode" of living. We might call it "perpetual liminality." And yet, in Buddhism it is inevitable that things change: "all things are impermanent." Paradise is not forever; it too must pass in the infinite evolutionary process and countless aeons of time.

Nevertheless, the point that needs to be stressed here is that the "natural mode of living," or "life before the fall" is the same kind of life the Great Agent lives as a Universal Monarch. As the text says, "He undertook mighty deeds to good purpose, unwavering in good conduct of body, speech and thought." These words are the formula for the proper livelihood of a monk who has decided to follow the Eightfold Path. It is a life "free from the wilderness, and robbers, it is prosperous and happy." A Universal Monarch may, indeed, have one thousand sons, yet at the moment when he becomes a Wheel-Treasure monarch of the four quarters, he begins a celibate life, as does the Buddha when he renounces the life of the household.

I cannot improve on how Steven Collins makes the point, albeit for different reasons: "Although monastic status is not a necessary condition for liberation, the celibate life is." His insight here needs expansion: although monastic status is not a necessary condition either for liberation or for conquering the four quarters, the celibate life is. The celibate life provides the interlocking relation between the Universal Monarch and the Buddha. To put this in other terms, it is the celibate life that defines the relation between a Universal Monarch and a Buddha. And, as we shall see in the last chapter, this defining relation can be viewed as mediated by gifts.

The second point I want to stress is the nature of the "fall from paradise." What caused it? Laziness! And laziness begets desire. The whole wheel of bad karma starts turning again with the appearance of stealing, lying, censorship and violence, which are the consequences of laziness in getting daily rice that never needed tending of any kind. When I first read this myth of the fall of humanity from paradise, I thought that the early Buddhists might just be the first existentialists; the fall from paradise is due to laziness? Human existence is absurd.

But, then, we know that the cosmology does not end there; in fact, it never does end. That might seem depressing if not for the fact that the problems caused by laziness are solved. Paradise regained is a possibility, at least temporarily, and is regained by the appearance of either a Universal Monarch or an enlightened Buddha, not by the election of a king.

The extinction of paradise is a consequence of an explicit violation of the Five Precepts, the entrance gate into Buddhism. To put this in a positive framework, the Five Precepts emphasize the Buddhist notions of compassion, kindness, generosity, and contentment. The Eightfold Path is the path for the realization of these virtues; it is the Buddhist definition of asceticism. And, if I read the legends correctly, its perfect realization takes place when an Enlightened One and a Universal Monarch appear together in a single aeon. Moreover, this conjunction may well be reflected in the union of both these Great Agents in the figure of the Bodhisattva in Mahayana Buddhism.

Laziness and desire cause paradise to come to an end; rice no longer reproduces itself daily. The fallen beings decide to elect someone king, someone who is the best-looking and most capable among them. The description also fits Universal Monarchs; they are handsome and capable. But there are two major differences here between the about-to-be-elected king and a Universal Monarch, a Turner of the Wheel.

The first glaring difference between the first king and all Universal Monarchs of the four quarters is that the first king will be given a job description by the people. They tell him what they want done. A Universal Monarch's action, however, is founded on his own discovery of the wheel of justice and truth by means of meditation. The Wheel-Treasure, it is made clear, is not negotiated, it is not a contract with the people, and it is certainly not inherited as a divine right of the king. It must be won anew by each king, by means of his own past karmic legacy, as shown by thirty-two physical marks on his body, and through his own meditative efforts that are usually signified by the performance of ascetic rituals on the fifteenth day of the lunar month, and finally consultation with a royal sage.

The second major difference between an appointed king and a Universal Monarch of the four quarters is that what the people want a king to do is the exact opposite of what all Universal Monarchs do upon becoming "wheel turners of what is right." The myth of the cosmos tells us the people want the newly elected king to censor and punish those who do not do what is right. In other words, they want him to do what most "real" kings do! A Universal Monarch, on the contrary, teaches the precepts to the kings of the four quarters. The basic precept that appears over and over again is the principle of nonviolence. Universal Monarchs reign through actions that are nonviolent; they do not punish. To say, "But this is absurd; no king, in India or anywhere else, rules this way," is to miss the point. Of course they don't! And that is the point.

We can put it this way. Just as the Buddha, or the monastic community, is not the ideal model for individuals as householders, just so, the Universal Monarch is not the ideal model for kingship. In brief, myths are not charters or models that we try to imitate. How could we? Myths are about superhuman agents who can do things that we cannot do. Now if this is true, then Malinowski, to mention just one popular scholar of religion, was mistaken not only about explaining the meaning of myth as a function of the satisfaction of needs but also about his influential notion that myths are "charters" for society.

Let us now move to a review of the second text in *The Long Discourses*, entitled "The Lion's Roar on the Turning of the Wheel."

After telling the monks "to be a refuge unto themselves," letting the "true Doctrine regarding what is right be their island, their refuge," and "their raft," he tells them about Dalhanemi, who possessed the seven treasures of a wheel-turning monarch and conquered the four quarters "without stick or sword." After many hundreds of thousands of years the wheel-treasure "slipped from its position," and the king knew he would soon die and appear in heaven. He tells his son that the "wheel treasure" is not an heirloom, but that he must win it for himself by observing the fast day on the fifteenth of the month and then observing and ruling by means of the Doctrine that is true and right. Only then will he be able to control "this ocean-bounded land." After installing his son, the king "shaved off his hair and beard, donned yellow robes, and went forth from the household life into homelessness." All this is quite familiar. It is the usual description of a Universal Monarch. But notice that it is also a major event in the life of the Buddha.

Before the king leaves, the son requests advice about the duties of a wheel-turning monarch. Dalhanemi's response to this important question is worth quoting in full:

Depend on the Truth (Dhamma), honoring it, revering it, cherishing it, doing homage to it and venerating it, having the Norm of Truth as your emblem and banner, acknowledging the Norm as your master, you should establish, guard, and protect your own household, your troops, Brahmins and householders, town and country folk, ascetics and Brahmins, beasts and birds according to the Norm. Let nothing contrary to the Norm prevail in your kingdom, and to those who are in need, give property. And whatever ascetics and Brahmins in your kingdom have renounced the life of sensual infatuation and are devoted to forbearance and gentleness, each one taming himself, each one calming himself and each one striving for the end of craving, if from time to time they should come to you and consult you as to what is right and what is wrong, what is blameworthy and what is blameless, what is to be followed and what is not to be followed, and what action will in the long run lead to harm and sorrow, and what to welfare and happiness, you should listen, and tell them to avoid evil and do what is good. That, my son, is the duty of an Ariyan wheel-turning monarch.

The son did as he was told. And when he performed the proper rituals on the fast day of the fifteenth of the month on the top of the veranda of his palace, the Wheel-Treasure appeared, and he became a "Turner of the Wheel." He marched to the four quarters with his fourfold army, and as we now know is the case of all conquerors of the four quarters, he instructs the kings as follows: (1) do not take life, (2) do not take what is not given, (3) do not commit sexual misconduct, (4) do not drink strong drink, and (5) be moderate in eating. His reign was followed by seven consecutive universal conquerors, who upon their death went on to dwell in the Brahma-world. We must remember that these "episodes" take place within the cosmological framework of aeons of time, that is to say, hundreds of thousands of millions of years!

At this point in the legend a fatal episode repeats itself. The eighth king does not ask his royal sage for instructions about winning the appearance of the wheel. Nor does he observe the fast day on the fifteenth of the month. Instead, he rules according to his own ideas, and his kingdom does not prosper. He then turns to his ministers for help, and they instruct him concerning what they think are the proper duties of a wheel-turning monarch.

To make a long story short, poverty soon appears, and with it theft. The thief is brought before the king, and the king asks him, "Why?" The thief replies, "Your Majesty, I have nothing to live on." At this point something very interesting happens. The king gives the thief some property, saying, "With this, my good man, you can keep yourself, give gifts, keep a wife and children, promote your welfare that leads to a happy rebirth with a pleasant result in heaven." The king repeats this action, and word quickly travels that stealing yields a gift from the king. The king eventually decides to execute a thief on the grounds that giving property to those who steal only increases theft!

With the introduction of punishment, violence becomes widespread; people form vigilante groups and then became robbers themselves. As a consequence, life decreases from eighty, to forty, then twenty thousand years, to one hundred years. Most of the virtues of a good life also disappear.

"A time will come," the Buddha tells the monks, when "people will have a life span of ten years and girls will be marriageable at five years." There will be no word for "moral," and no one will act in a moral way. Violence will reign among the people. In brief, the Norm of Truth is in eclipse.

After a time some of the people will think, "Let us not kill or be killed by anyone! Let us head for the jungle, the inaccessible mountains, and live on the roots and fruits of the forest." After seven days they emerged and recalled that they had become addicted to evil ways and instead should practice doing good. They agree first of all to abstain from taking life, then from taking what is not given, lying, and so on. In other words, they begin to practice an ascetic life, and on account of this, life once again increased to forty and finally to eighty thousand years.

The Buddha then tells the assembled monks that once again a wheel-turning king will appear called King Sankha. During his reign "there will arise in the world a fully enlightened Buddha named Metteyya." When Metteyya appears, King Sankha will give up his kingship, shave his head, and become a monk—an act, you will recall, that is identical to that of King Dalhanemi at the moment when the "wheel-treasure" slips from its position and disappears at the end of his reign.

The legends of Universal Monarchs are quite clear about who these monarchs are. They are beautiful people. Their lives are committed to ruling nonviolently for the sake of righteousness, truth, and happiness. They become Universal Monarchs because of the karmic legacy of their past lives, and by the performance of specific rituals, they become renouncers. As trustees or keepers of the Wheel-treasure they produce a kingdom that is a paradise, a paradise that is always temporary even if it lasts several aeons. At the end of their lives they are usually reborn in heaven.

When we review the legends as a series in a vast cosmological story, we note that something quite interesting takes place. When the eighth king appears in "The Lion's Roar on the Turning of the Wheel," he does not follow the advice of his ancestors but rules according to his own ideas. As a result his rule declines. We are then told that he assembled all his ministers and consulted them, and they in turn explained the duties of a wheel-turning monarch to him. He then goes about establishing protection for his subjects but fails to give property to the needy. As a result poverty becomes severe and a theft appears. When the king finally does give property to the needy, not only do his troubles as a monarch increase, but also human life itself begins a long decline. Why?

If we go back in this legend, to the reign of Dalhanemi, you will recall that he gave his son instructions on the duties of a Universal Monarch. The son, with the appearance of the Wheel-treasure, was to establish, among other things, protection and, "to those who are in need, give property." The eighth king failed here. He does not give property to those in need, but to those who have already become thieves. He then violates a second fundamental rule of all Universal Monarchs by having a thief executed. Let us follow the story one more step as it shifts into the future.

Violence has now been unleashed in the kingdom, and life now lasts no more than ten years. Then, among a small group of people, an amazing thing happens (this is, after all, a myth!). Some of these beings (humans have been reduced to acting like wild beasts) think, "Let us not kill and be killed, let us go into the inaccessible forest and live on roots and fruits." After seven days they emerge from the forest and conclude, since they are still alive, that they should continue to do good. For example: "Let us abstain from taking life and do other good things, thus attaining long life and beauty." Life span increases once again to eighty thousand years, and the wheel-turning monarch, King Sankha, makes his appearance in the story along with Metteyya, the future Buddha.

The episode of the eighth king follows the narrative constraint, the framework, of the "genesis" story. Notice that once again greed, theft, and violence appear during the reign of the eighth king. Before his rule the people lived in a wheel-turning paradise, having long life, beauty, happiness, wealth, and power. But, after his rule there is no wise king or royal sage to go to, and the "beings" themselves get together and decide "not to kill" and to "do good." And what do they do? Unlike the original people, they renounce the life of householders and head for the forest. After seven days (compare Vessantara and Buddha), they return from the forest and agree to live a life of nonviolence according to the Norm. In this legend it is a group who restore and maintain order by means of an ascetic retreat.

After an immense period of time, life is restored to a span of eighty thousand years, and girls become marriageable once again when they become five hundred years old. In other words, paradise has once again returned to the world. And during that time two things happen. First a wheel-turning king, a conqueror of the four quarters named Sankha, will appear. Second, a fully enlightened Buddha named Metteyya will also appear. Sankha will give his palace away to the people and become a homeless monk, in order to follow the Buddha Metteyya.

Once we link these stories together, it becomes clear that they are variations on a theme, versions of a "genesis" myth. At the beginning of the master story a fatal event occurs when, out of laziness, a "being" desiring rice takes what is not given to him. This act marks the origin of "theft, censorship, lying, and punishment" among the people. The people come together, lament the arising of evil, and agree to elect the most handsome among them and give him instructions on how to rule. They instruct him to (1) show anger when anger is due, (2) censor those who deserve it, and (3) punish those who require it. This advice, this rule, will eventually end in complete failure for the king, the people, and the world.

Notice that the instructions they give to the king are the exact opposite of that given by royal sages to their sons for winning the appearance of the Wheel-treasure. Moreover, we discover that the rule of the eighth king following Dalhanemi is also opposite the code of Universal Monarchs. He fails as king because he pays heed to the advice of the people. The eighth king is a duplicate of the first king.

At some point in the long devolution of human history some of the people recognize what is wrong, retreat to the forest, and return with the proper rules for length of life, beauty, happiness, wealth, and power. Once again, renunciation, the ascetic life, is a necessary condition for winning the appearance of the Wheel-treasure.

Some of the legends explicitly tell us that the Universal Monarchs observed Uposatha on the fifteenth of the lunar month. This is a well-known term for what some scholars refer to as "the Buddhist Sabbath," a fast day held weekly on the first, eighth, fifteenth, and twenty-third days of the lunar month when the Doctrine (*dhamma*) is rehearsed. They also traverse the four levels of meditation and view the four quarters of the cosmos, through meditation that the Buddha himself practiced during the night of his awakening. They also know the Four Noble Truths, for, as the Universal Monarch Mahasudassana tells his wife just before his death, "All things that are pleasing and attractive are liable to change, to become otherwise."

The eighth king following Dalhanemi failed to observe the ritual of the renouncers on the fifteenth day of the month. He was a good king, with the best of intentions, but he was not a Universal Monarch of the four quarters. In fact, he was much more like the real kings we know about in history. Universal Monarchs, as we have seen, do not take the advice of ministers and people but teach the Five Precepts. When the Wheel-treasure appears, Universal Monarchs become celibate. We can find this exact same pattern in the legend of Vessantara.

Vessantara has all the characteristics of a wheel-turning king of the four quarters. His story is clearly within the narrative constraints that provide us with the characteristics of a Universal Monarch. Vessantara, we are told, is very handsome, wise, and capable. He gives property to the needy and fulfills the duties that all Universal Monarchs follow. He rejects the advice and verdict of the people, who, in the end, find him guilty for acting like a Universal Monarch. He asks advice from a royal sage, his father, during the evening before setting out for the wilderness. His leaf-hut is the opposite of a palace such as Mahasudassana's, nevertheless, it is built by Vissakamma and is in a setting explicitly described as a paradise.

It is this paradise that the most recent translators of the legend, in a prefatory note, call "this tedious botanical catalogue." You then discover that they have cut out about three pages of the description of paradise in the text; what would they do if they were asked to translate, let's say, the first several books of the Hebrew Bible? The paradise is a world full of blossoms and fragrance, spices of all kinds, fruit the size of a drum, trumpet flowers brilliant as crests of flame, lotus ponds, numerous animals, and birds with their varied songs. It is in this natural paradise that Vessantara lives with his family and meditates, and from which he gives away his children and his wife. I have called it a "natural paradise." It is, in fact, exactly the opposite of the detailed pages of the description of Mahasudassana's "cultural paradise," a city and palace built under orders of Sakka made of gold, silver, and other precious materials, with lakes and ponds. Both live in a paradise that is the opposite of the other; the one is a city and palace, the other is a wilderness and leaf-hut. One might be tempted to say that the first is a "cultural paradise," the second a "natural paradise," built nevertheless by Sakka.

Vessantara lives a celibate life in the forest and gives away his children and wife; for a moment the perfection of giving transforms him into a true renouncer who owns nothing. Mahasudassana does not give away his queen, but we learn that Queen Subhadda at one point lives a separate life from the king. Upon returning for a visit after being absent for thousands of years, she is forbidden to enter his place of meditation. Universal Monarchs are renouncers of a special sort. They become renouncers, possessing and producing nothing because of their giving of extraordinary gifts. In brief, giving when we think about it is a form of asceticism; the more you give, the less you have. Parry has called it "a kind of lay exercise in asceticism." Universal Monarchs, however, never exhaust their wealth. Vessantara is no exception to this rule, since Sakka, we learn at the end of the story, steps in and provides all that he needs as the heavens literally rain down gold and precious gems upon the town and the people. We will delve into this more deeply in the next chapter on gifts.

Finally, Vessantara asks Sakka, not his father or the people, for eight wishes, ones that comply with the code of all Universal Monarchs: a reign of nonviolence, long life, beauty, happiness, wealth, and a rebirth in heaven.

At the end of the story the family is reunited, and the mountains roar and the earth quakes. The people of the kingdom agree to become his subjects, and Vessantara is anointed as ruler of the kingdom, shining "in all his jewelry and adornments with the radiance of the king of the gods." A grand procession leads Vessantara, and his entourage, south from the wilderness back to the city. His wishes granted, Vessantara rules as a universal wheel-turning monarch, and Sakka turns the city into a paradise. After a time Vessantara, "full of wisdom," is reborn in heaven. Once that rebirth takes place, the existing paradise begins to disintegrate until the next appearance of either a wheel-turning monarch or a Buddha.

Most scholars notice a relation between the legends of wheel-turning monarchs and the Buddha but then quickly turn to a comparison of wheel-turning kings with actual kings who rule by the sword and thus find many of the stories farcical, totally unrealistic, or full of irony. What I want to suggest is this: the significance of the legends is their relation not to actual kings but to the life of the Buddhas. It is not accidental or trivial that the Buddha tells the monks that he, in fact, was Vessantara or Mahasudassana in a previous existence. Thus as we attempt to understand the legends of the Buddha, it is a mistake to look for the significance of the legends of wheel-turning kings by comparing them to the actual, "realistic" kingship systems of early Buddhism or Hinduism. The "semantic field" is the mythical language of Buddhism. Wheel-turning monarchs are extraordinary in their appearance; they are opposite ordinary kings. Verisimilitude is illusory here.

In the *Mahavastu* the Buddha's father tells his people at the time of the Buddha's visit home that if the prince had not become a renouncer he would be a Universal Monarch of the four continents, possessing the seven treasures. He would reign without weapons or violence and be a monarch of the Universal Law. Now that he has become a renouncer, however, he has deprived them all of both the powers and the protection that his reign as a Universal Monarch would have provided them.

The Buddha himself compares the monks to Universal Monarchs in the great discourse of "The Lion's Roar on the Turning of the Wheel." He reminds them that Universal Monarchs are known for their power, life span, beauty, happiness, and wealth, and he tells them that a monk's power is to be found in meditation. A long life span is linked to the practice of meditation. Beauty, found in right conduct and happiness, is to be found in the detachment from desire. Wealth is gained by a life of loving-kindness. This is, of course, another way of describing the Eightfold Path of the monk.

Wheel-turning monarchs are superhuman agents; they do things you and I cannot do. What human kings do in comparison to them is quite irrelevant. They govern a universal realm just as Buddhas teach liberation on a universal scale. The Buddha often spoke about the Buddhist community, and the *sangha*, as a community of the four quarters. I do not think he meant India or the geography of a particular kingdom. As we have seen, the "four quarters" are clearly cosmic in significance.

We have already noted that one of the requirements of a successful conqueror of the four quarters is that he rules by teaching rather than by the sword. Another requirement is that he leads a celibate life that entails meditation. When Mahasudassana entered the great gabled chamber and sat cross-legged on the golden couch, he attained the exact same levels of meditation that the Buddha reached under the tree of enlightenment. He not only practiced the four levels of meditation but also traveled to the four quarters in his meditation. In fact, we are told that during his meditation in the great gabled chamber he "pervaded the four quarters spreading the thought of loving-kindness, compassion, and joy everywhere." We may safely assume from his brief conversation with his wife that he and the queen understood that existence is a conditioned chain of becoming, caused by the interdependent origination of all conditioned things.

The proper comparative context should now seem obvious. To fully understand the legends of the Buddha, we must compare his legends with those of the Universal Monarchs. Both are called "Great Agents," but it is obvious that they are not identical. Nevertheless, we must not forget that both are described as "The Great Conqueror" and "The Great Renouncer." The relation between the two is one of opposition, not contradiction. Universal Monarchs give but do not receive; Buddhas receive but do not give. It is in the differences that the similarity, asceticism, is made clear.

Both Vessantara and the Buddha begin their lives as Great Agents. They are born into royal families. Vessantara is born in a merchant section of the city, and the Buddha is born in a grove. Both are bright students living and enjoying palatial surroundings. Buddha, upon traveling through the city to a park, returns to the palace after sighting old, sick, and dead people. The palace becomes a gloomy and depressing place. Vessantara, on the other hand, enjoys the company of the people on his daily routes of giving at the four gates of the city. Accused of a misdeed after giving away the magical rain-making elephant, he is exiled from the city. He meets with his family during the night and discusses life in the wilderness. His wife and children insist upon going with him, and he consents.

The Buddha, on the other hand, decides to leave the palace at night in secret while all are sleeping. He leaves the palace alone by the east gate and heads south with his valet and horse; finally abandoning them, he shaves his head and becomes a renouncer of the household life to practice radical asceticism. Vessantara leaves the palace in the morning, at the break of day after performing a huge gift ceremony. He and his family head north, give away their carriage and horses, are entertained by his uncle, and are escorted by a vast army to the edge of the wilderness, eventually reaching the hermitage built for them by Vissakamma.

Vessantara is tested by an old Brahmin and gives away both children and wife; they are eventually reunited, and the reunion is full of joy and celebration. A great festival is performed, and the family, the crowd, and the army travel south back to the city and home. Vessantara continues to practice giving gifts. His home is a city of vast riches and incomparable beauty. He will live in Tushita after a royal funeral.

As we now know, Buddha is also tested. And after the night of enlightenment he eventually heads north to meet his family. The meeting is tense, the family is angry and embarrassed, and the reunion is a disaster. He leaves the town as he came, an ascetic, along with his monks. He eventually heads north again and settles in a shabby "backwater" town, gains final liberation, and is given a funeral fit for a Universal Monarch.

There exists at least one popular chapter in *The Long Discourses* that comes very close to describing the Buddha as assuming the role of a Universal Monarch. The chapter opens with the Buddha staying near Rajagaha on the mountain called Vulture's Peak. A look at the map (see figure 18.3) tells us that Rajagaha is the first city north of Bodh-Gaya, the most southern city in the Buddha's travels. The context of the opening episode of this famous chapter involves a visit to the Buddha by King Ajatasattu's prime minister. The visit is quite odd. The king tells his prime minister to inform the Buddha that he is about to attack the Vaijjians, a confederacy to the north of the Ganges. "Tell him," the king says, "I intend to cut them off and destroy them, bringing them to ruin and destruction. Listen carefully to his response and report back to me exactly what he says." Note the difference here between this ordinary king's rule and the nonviolent rule of Universal Monarchs.

The prime minister does exactly what he is told. But rather than responding to this violent agenda, the Buddha turns to Ananda, who is fanning him, and asks him whether he has heard about the seven things the Vaijjians practice that allow them to prosper and not decline. The Buddha finally turns to the prime minister and tells him that he, the Buddha, taught the Vaijjians the seven principles for an enduring and prosperous social and political life, and that if they followed these principles they would not decline as a society. The prime minister agrees and says that even if they adhered to just one of the principles, they would endure and prosper, and that he is sure that King Ajatasattu would never conquer them by force of arms but perhaps by means of propaganda that would cause disunity among them. In any case, he had much to do and asked permission to depart. The Buddha tells him to "do as he thinks fit." The prime minister departs, and the Buddha asks Ananda to call a meeting of all the monks. When they are gathered together, he instructs them on the same seven principles that produce enduring prosperity, unity, and longevity of the community.

Steven Collins spends several pages on this episode in his excellent book on Buddhism. He notes, quite rightly, that this particular text has been taken apart paragraph by paragraph in search of the original ascetic community, to the extent that the context is destroyed. He asks us to draw our own conclusions about the historical possibility of a king sending his prime minister "to ask a wandering holy man, publicly, how to set about attacking and conquering a neighboring territory. I find it unlikely." Indeed!

Unfortunately, Collins then refers to history as the basis for his interpretation. He says that "if the course of history outside the text may be used to understand what is in it, [the story is] dripping with dramatic irony." Perhaps, but Collins knows better than to use "the course of history outside the text" as an argument; we simply do not have it here. To use a phrase from E. J. Thomas, it may sound like genuine history, "but it can scarcely be said that with this we reach a firm basis of history."

Collins, however, is on the right track in emphasizing the parallel descriptions of the Vaijjian and the Buddhist ascetic community. The stress in this story, its content, has to do with the unity, harmony, and endurance of a society. What is most fascinating is the juxtaposition of the Vaijjian society with the community of monks. The Buddha gives both the Vaijjians and the monks the rules for living a harmonious, prosperous, and enduring life. The reference here is not history but myth. It seems clear that an appeal to history as the basis for an interpretation of this legend would be a misinterpretation of both its structure and its content. Moreover, it would seem that the content of what both the Buddha and Universal Monarchs teach is one and the same thing.

The structure of the story is built upon a set of oppositions. We can describe them as follows. The Vaijjians are opposite the Magadhan in the sense that the king of Magadha is bent on destroying the Vaijjian. The king lives in a world of violence, disharmony, and greed, which is the opposite of the principles that are in effect in Vaijjian society. Recall that this is the same King Ajatasattu who conspired with Devadatta and killed his own father. The Vaijjians, moreover, live north of the Ganges that separated them from the Magadhans, who lived south of the river. North is the region of Kuru and paradise; south is the region of greed, lust, and violence. North is the domain of life and the dawn; south is the land of death and twilight.

The cosmology at the beginning of part I describes a society that is in harmony, unity, and peace, a paradise. It also describes a cosmological hierarchy divided into four quarters with four guardians. The northern quarter is a paradise; the southern quarter is marked with distrust, greed, and violence. The Buddha mediates between the two. The narrative constraint throughout this section of the *Digha Nikaya* comes to the surface once we make visible the logical framework in which the story unfolds.

The story has nothing to do with utopias, or ideal societies versus actual societies. Given the hypothesis of this book, it would be folly to begin looking for historical evidence that would confirm the harmonious life of the Vaijjians. The story is thoroughly mythical. Anyone who has spent some time reading myths knows that myths, Malinowski notwithstanding, are not charters that we attempt to live by. This does not imply that myths are the product of some subjective or highly imaginative impulse or that they are irrelevant to a culture, but that they are generated from within a coherent logic that can be found throughout the culture, and that they often become the foundation for the development and interpretation of doctrine.

What needs to be emphasized here is that both the Vaijjians and the community of monks are placed in the same domain. Both of these social entities are described from the same cosmological point of view even though as social entities they are opposites—ascetics versus householders. Even though they are opposites, they are in turn both opposite the Magadhans, as north is opposite south, as Kuru is opposite Jambudipa.

Much more could be said about this particular episode in the life of the Buddha. It is, for example, one of the few legends, if not the only one, where the Buddha teaches a society, the Vaijjians, how to live according to rules that are clearly nonviolent, rules that are very close if not identical to those practiced by the community of renouncers. They are rules that the Buddha announces will ensure enduring prosperity, progress and longevity.

The rules are as follows:

1. They are to hold regular and frequent meetings.
2. They are to meet in harmony.
3. They must not authorize what has not been authorized.

4. They are to honor, respect, and listen to their elders.
5. They are to abstain from abducting others' wives and daughters.
6. They are to honor, respect, and support their shrines.
7. They are to provide safety, comfort, and support to renouncers.

In fact the Buddha in this legend acts more like a Universal Monarch in this episode that takes place at Vesali, his favorite city that just happens to be the midpoint between the Buddha's birthplace in the north and the place of his enlightenment in the south. When the legends are read from this perspective, it comes as no surprise that the Buddha and Vessantara are both venerated in the Buddhist tradition. A Great Agent always has to decide between two goods of equal value. Although the paths are opposites, they do not contradict each other; they both live for the welfare of others. It is, indeed, in the differences that opposites resemble each other.

In fact, the more you reflect upon the two Great Agents, Buddhas and Universal Monarchs, the more ambiguous the Universal Monarch becomes. He is, indeed, a most interesting character in the myths. He is a house-holder and a renouncer but then again not quite completely a householder or renouncer; he seems to have the qualities of both. He seems to be a "liminal" figure himself, betwixt and between in his desire for the welfare of the people and a destiny in heaven. Yet he also seems to have achieved the enlightenment of a Buddha. I think this mythical figure, this mediator, deserves to be com-pared with the Bodhisattvas in Mahayana Buddhism who dwell in their celes-tial domains possessed of the Ten Perfections, perfect in their wisdom and in their compassion for all sentient beings.

This, of course, would take us into the development of Buddhism in Nepal, Tibet, and China. The study would take us into what the northern Buddhists call the "broad" or "great" vehicle of Buddhism (Mahayana) in con-trast to Hinayana, the lesser or narrow vehicle of the South. Bodhisattvas are all-powerful and all-knowing, perfect in wisdom and compassion, and because of their compassion do not attain perfect happiness until all sentient beings attain that final goal. Simple recitation of the texts dedicated to them or utter-ance of their names produces merit that guarantees a place in their celestial domain. The texts tell us that hundreds of thousands, if not millions, of devo-tees are seated before them as they teach seated on luxurious thrones in a celestial paradise.

No one has quested for the historical Bodhisattvas known as Avalokiteshvara or Amitabha. Everyone agrees that they are mythical, that is, superhuman beings that do things you and I cannot do. The appearance of "Bodhisattva Buddhism" produces a serious problem in the study of Buddhism. How do you explain it? It is true that many of the texts that describe these great mythical beings are in Sanskrit, thus Indian in origin. But this fact simply prolongs the problem, and the emphasis on the origin of Buddhism as an "otherworldly" ascetic philosophical movement in India around 540 B.C. only deepens the problem, if not turning it into a problem that is not solvable.

It would be folly to think that the two great developments in Buddhism are in fact identical, that they represent an essence in Buddhism that endures and evolves through history. Yet I do think that a holistic theory that posits the inseparability of the Buddha and the Universal Monarch may lead us to an answer that is not arbitrary. If, as we shall see in the final chapter, the Buddha and the Universal Monarch are fundamental opposites in defining Buddhism, then the Bodhisattva may well be the mythical being in Buddhism that attempts to bring the two together into a unity.

There is a great deal of evidence in the texts on Bodhisattvas that allow us to conclude that they certainly resemble a Universal Monarch and his paradise, and a great deal of evidence that they are also Buddhas perfect in their wisdom. The Bodhisattva could be studied and interpreted as a superhuman agent that is both a Buddha and a Universal Monarch. Thus we might say that Theravada Buddhism is the relation between Buddha/renouncer ↔ Universal Monarch/householder, whereas Mahayana Buddhism combines the oppositions into a unity, as the Bodhisattva.

21

The Gift, the Renouncer, and the Householder

What is the first thing you imagine when you hear the word "Buddhism" or "Buddhist"? It is probably an image of a saffron-robed monk with his begging bowl or a rotund meditating Buddha. And from where do we get these first images of Buddhism? We get them from the hundreds of books written about Buddhism as an otherworldly, ascetic religion, a religion of the monk with the Buddha as the central focus. In brief, our view of Buddhism is very ascetic and "Buddhacentric."

Throughout part II, I have emphasized the superhuman, mythical character of the Buddha. I have also argued that the Buddha and the ascetic community cannot be fully understood as if they were isolated, complete in themselves, in other words, a view of the Buddha and his monks as if they are sui generis. They are best understood as complementary yet oppositional and necessary elements of a complex whole that includes the Universal Monarch and the householders that we can simplify into a basic set of oppositions we label as householder ↔ renouncer.

The history of Buddhism can then be viewed as a logical development of this basic set of relations. The Buddhism of myth is not history, however; as is the case with all religions, myth is both a product and a source of doctrine and belief. It is a structure whose narrative constraint and framework are composed of two oppositional elements, the renouncer and the householder. I have argued that this approach to the legends of the Buddha resolves many of the problems created by the single focus on the Buddha as this is presented in the received tradition. Nevertheless, it remains incomplete. There is a third element that must be brought into the framework; it is the element of the gift. It is the gift that defines and unifies the relation between Universal Monarchs, Buddhas, and the community into a coherent religious system.

In this chapter I want to reemphasize a crucial point of the book: Buddhism is not otherworldly asceticism, in spite of Max Weber's famous words. In fact, it is not essentially or even originally a religion of monks, even though one hundred years of Western scholarship have tried to make it so.

Buddhism is a communal system of propositional attitudes and practices that are related to superhuman agents. The three terms that are important in this definition, as you will recall, are communal system, propositional attitudes, and superhuman agents. In this chapter I want to highlight a specific set of relations that define the Buddhist communal system.

There are many paths we could use as an entrance into this complex subject. One such path is an event in the legends of the Buddha that is usually overlooked. The reason it is overlooked or cast aside is, we can be sure, that it is a purely mythical event. Nevertheless, we can identify this event as the origin of Buddhism and its structure as a religion. I am referring here to the legend of the meeting of Buddha and Sujata. In this part of the legend, as you will recall, the Buddha had renounced the life of the householder and was living in the forest. He had renounced his royal status and existence as son, husband, and father. And, since it is seldom if ever mentioned, this entails that he has also rejected the path of becoming a Universal Monarch.

Recall that at this point in the legend Sujata's maid discovers Gotama at the base of a tree and mistakes him for a tree spirit; his radical ascetic life has brought him near to his own death. She informs Sujata of her discovery. Sujata is elated at the news because she had promised she would make an offering to the spirit if she ever got married and gave birth to a son. Now married and with a son, she wanted to make the offering, and it just so happened that it was the full-moon day of April/May, that most auspicious date in the legends of the Buddha. Sujata rushes to bring him a meal of boiled milk and rice cooked with the help of the gods of the four quarters as chefs, Sakka as the fire keeper, Brahma as the attendant of the canopy, and the sentries of the four quarters as guards, a cosmological kitchen if there ever was one.

Upon finding Gotama, Sujata recognizes him as a holy man and gives him the golden dish, and he says, "For this you will receive great merit." As a consequence of her gift, Gotama is able to become the Buddha, and Sujata receives a guaranteed place in heaven. This episode marks the origin of Buddhism in our era. If you study it carefully, the scene contains all the elements I have emphasized as the narrative constraints of Buddhism: cosmology, superhuman agents, karma/merit, householder, and renouncer.

If Sujata's gift marks the beginning of the Buddha's awakening, Cunda's invitation to a meal marks the end of the Buddha's enlightened life. Recall that the meal takes place the day of the Buddha's final liberation. This mysterious meal, eaten only by the "perfected one," makes the Buddha quite ill. Later he reminds Ananda to make certain to tell Cunda that he should in no way feel remorseful or blame himself for the fact that he prepared the Buddha's last meal. "Tell him," the Buddha says, "this is your merit, your good deed, that the Perfect One gained final liberation after taking his last meal from you. For I have heard from the Enlightened One's own lips that there are two almsgiving events that are of very great merit, of very great result, more fruitful than any other. Which two? The one is the almsgiving after which the Perfected One attains supreme enlightenment, the other after which he attains final liberation. Cunda's deed is conducive to long life, to good looks, to happiness and fame, to heaven and lordship." Notice that the merit that Cunda will receive has the explicit qualities of a Universal Monarch, qualities of life, moreover, that Vessantara requested from Sakka before leaving the forest to begin his life as a king. Note also that Vessantara was given a meal, breakfast given by his uncle, just *before* he entered the wilderness.

The point of this focus on Sujata and Cunda is that the "origin" of Buddhism from this point of view stresses two legendary events that involve the giving of a gift, in this instance the gift of a meal, "more fruitful then any other." The first marks the Buddha's awakening; the second marks his final liberation from birth, death, and rebirth. We will return to these episodes once again later in this chapter.

These two major events in the legends of the Buddha mark three important concepts that I believe are necessary for understanding Buddhism. They are significant because they involve relations that define Buddhism. This is a conceptual explanation that follows the legends themselves rather than conjectures about the external/historical context of the texts, of which we know nothing. Moreover, it also highlights the nature of the origin of the Buddhist communal system as a relation between the Buddhas as renouncers and the householders who give gifts and receive merit in return. The concepts of the system can be easily remembered by using the following simple set of terms and relations:

$$A : B :: B : C$$

Renouncer <————————> Gift <————————> Householder

The three concepts highlight the oppositional relation between renouncer and householder mediated by the gift. As opposites they do not contradict each other. Opposites are not contradictions; black does not contradict white. One cannot be both a householder and a renouncer. The renouncer is the inverse of the householder, and the element that binds the renouncer and the householder together is the gift. The schema tells us that A is to B as B is to C, and that A is the inverse of C: the Buddha (renouncer) is to the gift as the gift is to the householder and the Buddha is the inverse of the householder. It is the gift that mediates between the inverse relations. It is this set of elements and relations that is the basic structure, the "atom" of Buddhism and its development. Let us now turn to a closer look at the gift as the mediating element.

Because we have all given and received gifts, this approach to Buddhism should be easy to understand. Gift giving seems to be a universal practice among human beings. When we think about what makes us different from the rest of the animal world, language and gift giving would certainly count as two items on the list. Language and the gift, giving, seem to be ubiquitous traits in all cultures, and both always seem to involve reciprocity; both are inherently social. Although a great deal of progress has been made in explaining these human traits, they also seem to be as elusive as "time," "freedom," or "consciousness."

Marcel Mauss, who thought that gift giving was the origin of culture and society, the foundation of economic exchange, a social practice that prevented violence and war, wrote an essay on the subject in 1924, *Essai sur le don: Forme et raison de l'échange dans les sociétés archaïques*. Mauss's work is not very long, about 180 pages, half of which consist of footnotes. It has been translated into English twice and has been called, "revolutionary," "monumental," "profound," "a classic," "a precious document," "a brilliant example of the comparative method."

Mauss's little book is difficult to read in either French or English. You soon discover that the first English translation was close to a total trashing of both the text and the footnotes as actually written by Mauss. Moreover, when you read the articles and books on Mauss's *The Gift* to help you understand the complex and sometimes opaque passages of the text, you begin to realize that there is no consistent agreement among scholars on just what the argument of the book is about, either in French or in English. When you are finished wrestling with Mauss's text, however, you know you are in the presence of a brilliant scholar who opened up a new area of analysis on a very complex subject that everyone is familiar with. As is often the case, it is the kind of questions we ask that open up new areas of study and reflection. Mauss had the gift of asking such questions in many areas of religion that seemed so obvious and matter-of-fact, or, in some other cases, about problems that remained unsolved.

Without focusing on the long debate that Mauss's essay has caused, we can extract what I think is important to this chapter. Mauss tells us in the very first sentence of the "Programme" in the "Introduction" of his book that although we think gift giving is free, voluntary, a gratuitous act, it is actually "given and reciprocated obligatorily." The giving of gifts involves three elements: the obligation to give, the obligation to receive, and the obligation to reciprocate. Mauss ends his book by pointing out that charity is not a gift. "Charity wounds the person who receives it"; it makes the person who receives it inferior, since the relation of reciprocity has been broken.

Mauss drives home the point. He is interested in a specific characteristic of gift giving. Although it appears that gift giving is voluntary and involves generosity, it is in fact "wrapped in polite fiction, formalism, and social deceit," actually caused by obligation and economic interest. "What rule of legality and interest," he then asks, "in societies of a backward or archaic type, compels the gift that has been received to be obligatorily reciprocated? What power resides in the object given that causes its recipient to pay it back?" The question then comes down to, "What causes the obligation of reciprocity?" Mauss's answer to the question is that the object, the thing given, is endowed with a certain power, a "spiritual mechanism." He says, "Even when it has been abandoned by the giver it [the object given] possesses something of him. Through it the giver has a hold over the beneficiary just as, being its owner, through it he has a hold over the thief." There is, says Mauss, a "spiritual mechanism" operating in the reciprocal obligation of giving.

In brief, Mauss thought that in ancient times "person" and "thing" could not be separated as they have been in the evolution of modern culture. But he thinks that we still have reflections of this inseparability, the existence of "spiritual mechanisms" in the possession of "heirlooms" and ancestral property. Such objects are inalienable because of the "spiritual mechanisms" that bind them to the owner. Mauss went on to speculate that this might also account for the purchase of large sections of land, or the collection of antiques, and expensive collections of art by those whose wealth is newly acquired. It is not the price of the object(s) or the tax write-off but the "heritage" that is gained and can now be passed on as a gift to others, including museums. They have become priceless, as are the worthless necklaces and armbands of the kula ritual among the Trobriands. What Mauss is really looking for here is the "original" gift, the act from which both economics and morality arise, the gift as the "total social fact," the bedrock of culture. As he says, the gift is "the basic principle of action and will always be so: to emerge from self, to give, freely and obligatorily. We run no risk of disappointment." He then quotes a Maori pro-verb: "Give as much as you take, all shall be very well," or, "As much as Maru gives, so much Maru takes, and this is good, good."

Note that in quoting the Maori proverb Mauss also stresses equivalence in the gift; giving and taking are equal, "give as much as you take, and that's good, good!" But is this true? Is the reciprocity in giving, the giving and taking, the same? Moreover, are they the same, synonymously? Obviously not. To give does not mean to take. They are in fact opposites, and the famous examples of the potlatch seem to indicate what happens when equivalence is attempted in this relational opposition of giving and taking. In the story of Vessantara, if not in all cases of giving in Buddhism, there is always excess in the act of giving and taking, which may well explain the obligation of reciprocity that is found in giving—"for this you will receive great merit." Thus it would seem that the reciprocity in giving and taking is asymmetrical.

There are two main objections to Mauss's analysis of the gift. In brief, the first criticism accuses Mauss of using the ideology, the beliefs, of a culture as an explanation of gift giving. Mauss's notion of a "spiritual mechanism," the *hua*, or *orenda* cannot be used as an explanation of why there is an obligation to reciprocate a gift for the simple reason that such a mechanism does not actu-ally exist; in fact, it is a part of ideology, it is part of a superstructure, a projec-tion consisting of beliefs that need to be explained. In other words, Mauss used the ideology, the superstructure of belief systems (spiritual mechanisms), to explain the infrastructure, the actual exchange that is basically economic and political. What he should have done instead, we are told, is use the economic/political system to explain the ideology of gift giving. In brief, what he should have done is demonstrate how gifts function as a variable for the satisfaction of needs in a particular political/economic system.

We can sum up the criticism very neatly by using a quote from Lévi-Strauss in his critique of "totemism," substituting the word "spirituality" for "affectiv-ity": "As spirituality is the most obscure side of man, there has been the con-stant temptation to resort to it, forgetting that what is refractory to explanation is *ipso facto* unsuitable for use in explanation. A datum is not primary because it is incomprehensible: this characteristic indicates solely that an explanation, if it exists, must be sought on another level. Otherwise, we shall be satisfied to attach another label to the problem, thus believing it to have been solved." Unfortunately, attempts to use "other levels" as explanations of gift giving have also failed, and the debate continues. The origin of giving, as is the case with the origin of language, remains an important puzzle or problem that awaits a solution.

The second criticism focuses on Mauss's use of India and seems more dev-astating. According to the critics, both Hinduism and Buddhism clearly violate Mauss's basic principle that reciprocity is obligatory. In a sense this criticism is quite right. In Hinduism the law of religious giving, called *danadharma*, stipulates that Brahmins must receive gifts, but they are prohibited from recip-rocating; Mauss knew these texts and the Hindu tradition very well.

Mauss did not use Buddhism in his essay. It would seem to provide clear and convincing evidence that he is wrong. It is not just that the Buddha and his monks are prohibited from the obligation of returning gifts to a donor; they literally cannot reciprocate, since even if they wanted to, they own and produce nothing that they can give in return. Moreover, the enormous amount of gifts given to the monks in all Theravada Buddhist countries cannot be explained, as some critics have maintained, as an economic/political quid pro quo on the part of the layperson. The principle of obligation and reciprocity as an explana-tion of giving seems to collapse when the religions of India are examined.

In looking at the evidence in Hinduism, Jonathan Parry put it this way: "Where we have the 'spirit' reciprocity is denied; where there is reciprocity there is not much evidence of 'spirit.'" He drives the point home by saying, "The obligation to make a return is *not* therefore encoded in the *danadharma*." But is this true? At first glance it seems to be. Brahmins do not reciprocate in the giving of gifts. The Buddha and his monks do not return gifts because they do not have anything to give in return. Is Mauss wrong? I do not think so. I think that Mauss's appeal to the belief system of a culture, the "spiritual mech-anism," was on the right track. His critics have tried to explain the phenomena of giving gifts by reducing giving to another level, to an economic/political exchange. But, as I read Mauss, he resisted this reduction.

In brief, the argument against Mauss claims that "spiritual mechanisms" do not exist as a part of the real world; they are ideologies, superstructures. The task, therefore, is to reduce the ideology of giving gifts, the beliefs, to economic and political explanations; giving is a symbolic form of economic and politi-cal exchange that functions to provide peace, solidarity, and survival for the individual and the group. To put it crudely, giving gifts fulfills certain social, psychological, and biological needs. But we know that this theory, known as functionalism, has been thoroughly dismantled as logically invalid.

Why then do Hindus and Buddhists give gifts? They give gifts *because* they believe that the Doctrine of karma is true. The Doctrine of karma tells us that all intentional actions involve causal efficacy, "a strict moral retribution according to their moral quality," as Thomas Trautmann calls it, usually in the life to come. This Doctrine, which may be a "quaint theory" to many of us, is a central part of the conceptual system in both Buddhism and Hinduism, and we brush it aside much too easily in our study of both these religions. As the Buddha said, "for this you shall receive great merit." Buddhist householders have accepted this assertion literally, as the truth, for many centuries. What is important to see here is that if we, including many modern Southeast Asian Buddhists, conclude that the belief is false, we then change the subject when we go on to ask, Why do they persist in believing what is false? There are three important issues here that are often confused. The first has to do with the question, What are the legends of the Buddha all about? The second question is, Do people in South East Asia believe that the legends are true? If we conclude that the answer to the second question is yes, and we have good reasons to think that such beliefs are false, we may then want to go on and ask, Why do they persist in believing what is false? The point to be made here is that these three questions are obviously not synonymous.

We may develop a better understanding of giving in Buddhism by comparing the concept in Hinduism. Hindus give gifts to Brahmins, who, according to the creation story, are created first, that is to say, they are at the top of the hierarchical caste system, formed from Brahma's head. They are ritual specialists as well as teachers who remain pure through the performance of rituals and vegetarianism, as well as their isolation from other castes, especially the lowest castes formed from Brahma's feet. It is a defining characteristic of Buddhist householders to also give to the ascetic community of monks who are neither pure nor impure because they have renounced the life of the householder, that is, they have renounced caste. Thus, although we might say that the doctrine of karma is pan-Indian, there are deep differences between the two religions, beginning with the giving of gifts, the demotion of the Brahmin caste in Buddhism from the top of the social hierarchy, according to the Buddhist cosmology, and the Buddhist denial that a soul or an immortal "self" transmigrates through the karmic cycles of time. In brief, although Buddhism in India did not abolish caste or the doctrine of karma, it did radically shift the giving of gifts away from the ritual specialist/teachers, the Brahmins, to the "community of the four quarters" and redefined the meaning of karma and the production of merit.

Although the evidence from Buddhist texts seems to falsify Mauss's basic thesis, that the gift involves giving, receiving, and the obligation to reciprocate, a second look indicates that this is simply not the case. It is only when we drop the doctrine of karma from our study of Indian gift giving that Mauss's definition fails. The Indian doctrine of giving religious gifts remains a mystery when we omit the belief system that is an essential element in any religion. The doctrine is transcendental. It states that anyone who gives to the Buddhist community of monks will automatically receive merit in return, either in this life or in the life to come. You can bet on it; it is a fundamental law of this religion. It is a constraint in all of the legends you have read in part I of this book.

Let us take another look at two episodes that I have stressed as important for our understanding of Buddhism, the stories of Sujata and Cunda. It is very interesting to observe that in both of these cases the giving is due to either a mistake or ignorance that is corrected by the Buddha. In Sujata's story she has mistaken the Buddha for a "tree spirit," and the giving of a gift in this case is clearly reciprocity for the gift of fertility and a child. In Cunda's case the Buddha instructs Ananda to return and assure him that he should not blame himself for preparing the Buddha's last meal. In both cases giving gifts results in "great merit." And, as we learn from the episode between the Buddha and King Pasenadi in chapter 11, give gifts to "whomever it pleases [you] most," but if you want "the most fruit" in return for your gift, give it to the virtuous monk whose virtues have redefined the meaning of purity.

Is the gift really voluntary, disinterested, and spontaneous? Or, as Mauss stresses, is it obligatory and interested, wrapped up in gestures that are a polite fiction, a formalism and social deceit? I think the best evidence is to be found in the many invitations to the Buddha for a meal. Here we seem to have a gesture, a formal, polite fiction, a social deceit if there ever was one. The Buddha, we are told over and over again, remains silent whenever the invitation is made. Why? Remember, gifts obligate both donor and recipient. But by not responding the Buddha literally says neither yes nor no. He is a renouncer and by remaining silent remains true to his departure from the world of the householder; formally, he does not accept the gift, he remains uncommitted, silent. Yet we all know that his silence signifies consent.

The Buddha and his monks cannot accept gifts for the simple reason that they have nothing to give in return. Nevertheless, the householder believes that those who do give gifts "will receive merit in return." The householder takes silence as consent and also believes that the giving of this religious gift will automatically cause great merit in the next rebirth. Thus, although the giving of religious gifts in Buddhism is asymmetrical, such gifts are both for the welfare of the monastic community and reciprocally for the next life of the householder. Although the Buddha does not reciprocate in gift-giving transactions, he and the community of monks are the mediation between the householder who gives gifts and the transcendental merit that is automatically transmitted by means of the causal efficacy of karma. We will return to other examples of this important transaction in a moment. What I want to stress here is that the Doctrine of karma is present in every instance of religious giving in Buddhism. Why do Buddhists give gifts? The simple explanation is because they believe that the Doctrine of karma is true.

I think that this approach is more adequate for three reasons. First, it avoids the theoretical traps and pitfalls that Mauss and a host of scholars in the cultural sciences confront when they attempt to explain social and cultural institutions such as the gift by means of causal/functionalist premises. The second reason is based on empirical evidence from India. Religious giving is always an act that entails automatic transcendental consequences. That is, the recipient of the gift, whether person or group, has nothing to do with this transcendental transaction; he is at best the pure channel through which the transactions take place. Although he is obligated to receive the gift, the monk cannot reciprocate even if he wants to. In fact, not even the gift itself, the object that is given, is essential to the transaction. It can be a simple meal or a large parcel of land that produces merit in return. The third reason is crucial for not only understanding Buddhism but also all other religions as well. Buddhists believe in the doctrine of karma because they believe the doctrine is true. Whether the doctrine is true or false is not the issue here. What is at issue is the importance of the cognitive values, the propositional attitudes of any religious system. The issue of the truth-conditions of any religion are easily by-passed in contemporary studies of religion by simply ignoring the question or by dismissing "religious belief" as nonrational or by what seems to be the more comfortable position of adopting cultural or cognitive relativism; "people live in different worlds." Let us simply admit that to conclude that the Buddhist doctrine of karma is false is not to say that either the doctrine or the believers are nonrational.

One gift episode in part I, mentioned at the beginning of this chapter, remains a puzzle. It involves the episode in chapter 14 of Buddha's illness after eating Cunda's meal. Cunda invites the Buddha "together with his order of monks for a meal." Cunda prepares a dish I have called "pork special" for the banquet. Buddha tells Cunda, "Serve the 'pork special' to me, and serve the remaining soft and solid food to the order of monks." He then tells Cunda that he should take what is left over of the "pork special" and bury it in a pit because he, the Buddha, could not think of anyone else in the whole cosmos who could digest it. Of all the invitations and meals we have read about in part I, this is indeed an extraordinary if not unique episode. It is not just extraordinary because of the mystery of the odd course Cunda prepares. It is also odd that Cunda, a blacksmith, should know about it! What is extraordinary about the whole episode is that the Buddha should request that Cunda not give this special dish to the monks because only he, the Buddha, could digest it. It turns out that after he delivers a "delightful after-dinner talk on the Doctrine," this special course almost kills him! What is going on here?

Speculating on what the words *"sukara-maddava"* mean will get us nowhere. For even if we determined that they mean "special pork chops" or "a species of truffles" this would not help us resolve the enigma that not only are both Cunda and the Buddha familiar with this food but Buddha goes on to claim that only Perfect Ones can digest it so it would be best to bury what he does not eat in order to protect the monks. Moreover, after eating this special food of Perfect Ones, he gets hit with a severe if not deadly case of diarrhea! Should we conclude that he is not a Perfect One?

This episode is often interpreted as an imaginative account reflecting actual history; it records an event in which the Buddha almost, or, really did die from food poisoning and the rest is myth. But, this interpretation is not an option for those of us who are convinced that the meaning of myths is not explained by theories of mythical language as a code or some kind of symbolic system. So, let us return to the mythical event as recorded in part I with the advice to take the legend literally.

After recovering from the diarrhea that produced "sharp pains as if he were about to die," the Buddha tells Ananda that he will achieve final liberation in the last watch of the night that very evening. He lays down "bearing in mind the time of his enlightenment years ago." After his rest he asks Ananda to find Cunda and tell him that he should not feel remorse, thinking, "It is my fault, my misdeed that the Perfected One gained final liberation after taking his last meal from me." Ananda should tell him that the Buddha said, "That is your merit, Cunda, that is your good deed, that the Perfected One gained final liberation after taking his last meal with you. For I have heard from the Enlightened One's own lips that there are two alms-givings that are of very great merit, of very great result, more fruitful then any other. Which two? The one is the almsgiving after which the Perfected One attains supreme enlightenment, the other after which he attains final liberation. Cunda's deed is conducive to long life, to good looks, to happiness and fame, to heaven and to lordship." In other words Cunda's gift will produce conditions in his future life that match the life of a Universal Monarch! (See, Vessantara's list of wishes.) It is the legend itself that gives us the proper contexts and episodes for comparison.

The gifts of Sujata and Cunda are brought together here. These two events, identical in structure are clearly in opposition to each other marking the beginning and end of the Buddha's career in our era. Sujata's, a young mother, gives milk-rice that restores the ascetic Gotama to life once again while seated in a grove at sunrise. Cunda, a mature adult male and black-smith prepares a special meal in a grove at sunrise that marks an end to the Buddha's life that very night. Notice that the Buddha does not raise the issue of "indigestion," or, being "poisoned," but, that Cunda might feel remorseful because he served him the last meal before his final liberation. Thus although there is no connection between Cunda's meal and Buddha's physical distress, the Buddha's request remains a mythical mystery.

One requirement must be satisfied for the system of giving to work. The monks must remain pure; they must observe the rules that define the life of a monk, the regulated observance of confession that also involves the receiving of alms. We should not forget that one of the primary duties of laypersons is to make certain that the monastic community remains pure; it is, after all, the "spiritual mechanism" for gaining merit. If we had the space to look closely at the vast number of monastic rules, we would note that they all conform to what we may call the "master rule" of the gift for monks: following the lead of the Buddha, they, as "sons of the Buddha," do not reciprocate gifts. When on their alms routes, they too remain silent. What they receive is for the community of monks and not for themselves. Any property they have at the time of death is returned to the community of monks. Any reciprocity takes place on a transcendental level, where the giving of a gift is transformed into an exchange. What seems voluntary, free, without formal constraint or reciprocity is in fact a mandate for all Buddhist householders for whom the giving of a gift produces merit in return. It is a religious law. It is not the monk, or the Buddha himself, but the community of the four quarters that receives gifts.

This relation of exchange is made clear in the Buddha's response to Ambapali, "a courtesan of the city." If you return to chapter 14, you will find that Ambapali invited the Buddha for a meal, for which she is offered "a hundred thousand pieces" if she allowed a group of elite men to extend the invitation instead. She told them she would not give up the invitation for such an important meal for all the revenues taken in by the city of Vesali. When the Buddha attended the meal, she announced that she had also given "this park to the order of the monks with the Buddha as its head."

In chapter 8, King Bimbisara, after careful consideration, decides to give the "Bamboo Grove to the order of the monks with the awakened one at its head." He seals the donation by pouring water over the Buddha's hand from a ritual bowl made of gold. The Buddha, we are told, remained silent; the "acceptance of the gift transferred great merit to the king."

This episode is repeated in chapter 11, where we find Anathapindika, a wealthy merchant, buying a piece of property, a pleasure garden, from Prince Jeta, which he wants to transform into a monastery for the Buddha and his monks. After buying the property he builds the monastery with its cells, halls, bathrooms, terraces, and lotus ponds. A clear distinction is being made in this story between buying and giving. Buying is a legal transaction governed by the courts; giving is a transaction that is governed by religious belief.

When the Buddha arrived, Anathapindika asked him how he should transfer this property to the Buddha and the order. The Buddha told him that he should "give it to the Order of Ascetics of the four points of the compass whether now present or hereafter to arrive." Anathapindika then "poured water from a golden bowl over the hands of the Buddha, saying, "I give Jetavana to the Order of Ascetics of the four points of the compass with the Buddha at the head, and to all from every direction now present or hereafter to come." The text makes it explicit that he did not give this gift to the Buddha or to the monks who were with the Buddha. The gift is alienable, given to the ascetic order of the four quarters. Because of the formality involved and its exact repetition on other occasions, we may safely assume that Anathapindika knew that he would receive great merit in return.

Given these examples, it may be more accurate to say that the Buddha and the monks, the sons of the Buddha, are transmitters or mediators of gifts. They are the means by which we may give gifts to the total community of the four quarters, the same four quarters of the cosmos ruled by Universal Monarchs. In brief, and this should come as no surprise even though it is often forgotten in our analysis, karma, the effects of our karmic legacy and the reciprocity giving in return for merit, is a transcendental affair made possible by the Buddha and his "sons." There is a sense in which the Buddha and his "sons" do not receive the gift that is given to the community of the four quarters. This can be seen more clearly in the gift of a meal. The gift is consumed, destroyed, as in a sacrifice. It is the act itself, the exchange, that is important in giving, not the gift itself, for the gift itself is priceless.

What about the Universal Monarch? Does he give in order to receive? The answer seems to be a clear no. Does he receive but not reciprocate? The answer is no once again. This should come as no surprise. Having read the legends, you know that Universal Monarchs are both renouncers and house-holders. But how can this be? It is to this question that use of the rite-of-passage structure becomes helpful for an answer. You cannot, obviously, be a householder and a renouncer at the same time, although I find it interesting that both Vessantara and Mahasudassana come very close to making it happen. Although Vessantara withdraws from his family while living in the wilderness, he remains husband and father, living with his family albeit in a separate cell; Mahasudassana never leaves his palace but lives separated from his wife.

It is at this point that the use of the structure of a rite of passage becomes helpful once again in our interpretation of the concept of giving in Buddhism. When we view Vessantara's life as a rite of passage, we find that all of his gifts, save one, are given in liminality, when he is betwixt and between his lives as prince and king. And, as we have learned from a study of rites of passage, it is precisely in liminality where we may expect ambiguity or episodes that are the opposite of life in pre- or postliminality—just so Vessantara's life while liminal during his stay in the wilderness. And it is precisely in this period of liminality where he gives away his horses and chariot, his children, and his wife. But are they really gifts? In the case of his children he seems to know that they will be returned to him at the right price; in the end it is never paid. As for his wife? The exchange is a trick that is quickly revealed. Nevertheless, they are all freely given away by Vessantara while living in liminality.

There is one gift, however, that brings real trouble to Vessantara: the gift of the rain-making elephant while he is a prince. For this act the people of the kingdom demand his going into exile, and he accepts his punishment even though he does not understand why he is being punished for gift giving. What he apparently does not understand is that the rain-making elephant was not his to give! This elephant was a "people's elephant," owned by the community. As such it is inalienable and thus not an object he can give away. Nevertheless, it is this intentional act of giving that triggers exile, liminality and his wishes before returning as a "Great King."

The legend of Mahasudassana, as I have already mentioned, is opposite both Vessantara and the Buddha's liminal period. Although both his rites of passage take place in a paradise, the paradise is a luxurious palace, not a wilderness. And yet he takes on the characteristics of a renouncer who is alone separated from his wife.

Moreover, the king does not receive because he has more wealth than he can give away. When the Brahmins and householders attempt to give him a gift, he refuses it with the explanation that "he has enough wealth and that they should take it back with more besides." Here is an example of a refused gift that is also asymmetrical with what we find in the gift relation with the Buddha. A gift to the Buddha yields great merit in return, whereas a refused gift to Mahasudassana yields more than what was offered to him. Although the gift relations are in opposition to each other—one is accepted, the other is refused—the consequences are the same. Both of the initial givers receive far more than they give. Both the Buddha and Universal Monarchs as Great Agents exist for the welfare of all beings in both a cosmological and a karmic/merit framework.

The story of Vessantara, nevertheless, is also a problem for Buddhists. The gift of the children to an old, mean Brahmin has been a major topic for centuries in Buddhist countries. It appears as a topic for discussion, for example, in one of the longest sections in *The Questions of King Milinda*. This text (ca. second century A.D.) remains one of the important authoritative representations of what we now call Theravada Buddhism. It is cast as a dialogue between a distinguished monk named Nagasena and a king from a foreign country named Milinda.

King Milinda asks Nagasena several questions regarding Vessantara. He first asks whether Vessantara was unique or whether all future Buddhas give away their children and wives. Nagasena answers that they all give them away. King Milinda then asks a more profound kind of question. He asks whether Vessantara had any kind of pity at all when he watched his children leave, tightly bound together at their wrists. He says, "Why, I ask, would a man who seeks to gain merit cause others to suffer? Should he not rather give himself away?" Nagasena replies that the point is the difficulty and greatness of what he did. This act of giving was so difficult that his fame spread throughout all the world systems and throughout all the ages.

Milinda is not satisfied. He asks whether someone who gives gifts that cause others to suffer produces a good rebirth and happiness. Nagasena replies that indeed it does, and gives Milinda an example. Suppose, he says, that a king raised a just tax from his subjects and then used that tax to bestow a gift to all. Would that king enjoy fame on that account? Would that gift not produce happiness and a good rebirth? King Milinda agrees that it certainly would. However, he remains unsatisfied.

"But isn't it an excessive gift to give away your children and wife? And do not the wise believe that excessive gifts are to be censured and avoided?" the king asks. "After all," he continues, "too much weight breaks an axle and sinks a ship; bankruptcy follows lavish generosity, floods follow a heavy rain, porridge boils over through too hot a fire; just so, Nagasena, excessive giving is held worthy of censure and blame."

Nagasena disagrees. On the contrary, "giving generously is approved by the wise in the world," he responds. "Just as fire with its exceeding heat burns, the earth by its exceeding size supports all, and the ocean by its exceeding greatness can never be quite filled, a monk by his exceeding virtues becomes an object of reverence, and a Buddha because of his exceeding perfections is peerless, just so is exceeding generosity praised, applauded, and approved by the wise. Those who give away anything as a gift just as it may occur to them acquire the fame of being nobly generous. Just so was Vessantara because of his giving praised and exalted throughout the world systems. And let us not forget that it is because of his mighty giving that he, King Vessantara, has now, in our days, become the Buddha, the chief of gods and men."

Nagasena then asks the king, "Is there anything in the world which ought not to be given as a gift to someone who is worthy?"

"No, sir," answers Milinda, "some give food, others give dwellings, money, and some give their lives."

"Well, then," replies Nagasena, "if some give their own lives, why do you rave against Vessantara, the king of givers, for his virtuous gift of children and wife? Isn't it true that there is a custom according to which a father who has fallen into debt or lost his livelihood can use his son as a deposit toward payment of the debt or sell him?"

"Quite so," replies Nagasena. "In accordance with custom, Vessantara, distressed at not having obtained the insight of Omniscient Ones, pledged and sold his wife and children for that treasure. Why then do you attack him for doing what others have done?"

The king says, "I don't blame him for giving but for not entering into a bargain with the beggar, giving himself away instead of his wife and children."

"But that," Nagasena responds, "would be an act of a wrongdoer, to give himself when he was asked for his wife and children. For the thing asked for, is that which ought to be given. Vessantara did just that in his quest for Enlightenment. It was not that he did not care for them, or that he could not support them that he gave his wife and children away. He gave them away for two reasons: first, because he was asked for them, and second because the jewel treasure of omniscience, the insight of enlightenment, was dear to him. Moreover, Vessantara not only knew that the old Brahmin would not be able to hold onto the children but that he would ransom them to their grandfather, and he informed his son about the details of the transaction."

Although the story is not identical to the versions we have, gaining merit is a dominant theme of the gift. Notice the rule here; an act of generosity demands that you give what you are asked for. Giving involves a moral "ought"; "the thing asked for is that which ought to be given." The second reason given King Milinda involved the means to an end, the achievement of enlightenment. Here once again the doctrine that renunciation is the prerequisite for enlightenment is reinforced. What is striking as you reach the end of the story is that Vessantara does not achieve the end he holds so dear, omniscience, perfect enlightenment, liberation from suffering, perfect happiness, an end to the indefinite rounds of birth, death, and rebirth. This fact is almost completely lost sight of in the family reunion, the grand celebration and parade home. The story, not only in its ending, is a celebration of the householder. No wonder it remains the most popular story in Southeast Asia. Let us take a closer look.

First of all, they seem to fit the analysis given by Mauss. It is true that the children are given to the Brahmin with the condition that they are to be ransomed by their grandfather; Vessantara makes this very clear to his son.

Nevertheless, Vessantara performs the ritual of donation, pouring water over his hand before giving them away; the earth quakes as a witness to his deed. It is after they leave, escape, and are bound and physically abused that he reminds himself that he cannot go after them and retrieve them because "a virtuous person cannot request the return of a gift." It is not the gift that causes Vessantara's sadness but the physical abuse and the pain of separation the children endure that causes Vessantara to grieve at their absence.

It is precisely at this moment in the story that Vessantara, full of grief and tears, remembers that "all this suffering comes from the desire of affection, and no other cause; I must quiet this desire and be at peace. And thus by the power of his knowledge he abolished that sorrow and sat still as usual." It is not for nothing that Vessantara disciplined himself in the quest for enlightenment during the seven months living in the wilderness/paradise in a compound built for him by Vissakamma. It is the power of his knowledge that allows him to overcome the paralysis of anguish and grief. What knowledge? The knowledge that desire is the cause of suffering that all things are conditioned, are born, exist, die, and are reborn. It is important to remember at this point in the story that Vessantara is not an ordinary human being; he is a Great Agent about to become a Universal Monarch, and he has yet to perfect the virtue of giving by giving away his wife. However, before that happens something incredible occurs that brings the liminal period to a close. It begins with Maddi's return to the hermitage.

Here is the scene as I so brutally abbreviated it in chapter 2. When Maddi returns, quite late, from gathering food, she notices immediately that the children did not come out to meet her, nor did Vessantara utter a word. The first thing that crosses her mind is, "The children must be dead!" She searches the forest three times during the night, and as the dawn breaks and the sun begins to rise, she returns home. Fatigued by the search and wasted by the pain of loss, she faints in front of Vessantara, who has remained silent.

This is a fantastic scene. For one thing, it extends the pain, sorrow, the anguish and love of both Vessantara and Maddi. But the context here is remarkable; the focus has turned to Maddi. It is the exact reverse, the opposite, of the Buddha's scene of enlightenment as presented in chapters 4 and 5. Buddha's quest, you will recall, begins with leaving the palace and his women at night. His flight from home will leave an enduring alienation between himself and his family. His enlightenment takes place in the three watches of the night. In the Vessantara legend, however, we are told that Maddi, returns home and finds the children missing; her husband remains silent. We are then told that she searches the complete forest three times in three different domains and fails to find her children. She returns home, at sunrise, fatigued and full of sorrow—just the opposite of the Buddha's successful threefold quest for liberation after he leaves his family for the wilderness and before the sun rises in the east.

It is in the midst of this failure and suffering, similar to the pain of the family's exile at sun rise, that another stunning event takes place. When Maddi returns, she passes out from fatigue and stress. What happens next? Vessantara thinks she has died and immediately wonders what he should do with her here in the middle of the forest. Without thinking, he gets some water, sits down, and places Maddi's head in his lap and caresses her. As the text reminds us, "Although for seven months he had not touched her body, in his distress he could no longer keep his ascetic vow and with tears in his eyes he raised her head and laid it upon his lap, sprinkling it with water, he stroked her face and bosom." She recovers and praises his gift of the children: "I do rejoice, a greater gift than children cannot be." At this point, Sakka appears disguised as a Brahmin and asks for Maddi. Vessantara, "without question, indifferent, unattached, with no clinging of mind," pours water over his right hand perfoming the ritual of donation. Maddi fully consents. The earth quakes as a witness. Sakka, returning to his true form, expresses his approval and immediately gives Maddi back to Vessantara and asks him to make eight wishes. Although Sakka violates the rule of gift giving by returning Maddi to Vessantara, just as Vessantara violates giving by negotiating a ransom for the children, Vessantara has passed the test and accomplished the ten perfections. In doing so, however, he has also given up, rejected, the life of the renouncer.

The story of Vessantara is a stunning description of giving, the gift, as a form of renunciation. Vessantara's rite of passage finds him "betwixt and between" prince and king. Sakka had no real choice in the matter; he had to give Maddi back else Vessantara would indeed have entered the life of the renouncer who possesses and produces nothing. Instead of receiving the eight wishes, he would enter on a life defined in the Eightfold Path of the ascetic. Given what we now know about the legends of the Buddha, Vessantara as a Great Agent at one time chose to become a Universal Monarch. In doing so, he became a giver of gifts. The story of Vessantara teaches us that the perfection of giving presupposes knowledge as the power to achieve the perfection but also that in achieving it the householder transforms himself into a renouncer, a taker of gifts.

Imagine Buddhism as both sides of a sheet of paper. On the one side is a description of the perfect giver of gifts; on the other side is a description of the perfect receiver of gifts, one the opposite of the other. The point is, when you cut the paper, you cut both sides at once. To say that Buddhism is otherworldly asceticism, that the Buddha as the perfect monk is the essence of Buddhism, is to say that you can cut one side of the paper without cutting the other side. Both sides constitute the whole. What mediates that set of relations is, once again, the gift, which entails the twin transcendental doctrines of karma and merit. The Buddha and the Universal Monarch, the prince and the king, householder and renouncer are inseparable; the one defines the other mediated by the gift.

Notes

Note on the citation of Pali Buddhist texts: There is no single set of volumes that contain the complete canonical texts in English translation. The Pali texts are usually cited by their Pali titles. This is unfortunate for those who may not be familiar with the language or the texts. This situation can often lead to further difficulties in locating the exact book, chapter, and verse. I have tried to sidestep these problems by using the English translations of the texts published by the Pali Text Society, citing title, volume, and page number, as well as other translations with the hope that this will allow easier access to the sources. Buddhist texts will have a separate entry at the beginning of the bibliography.

The following is a list of the Pali Text Society English translations of the *Tipitaka*, together with the Pali titles of the texts used in part I:

The Pali Text Society	The *Tipitaka*
I. *The Book of Discipline*	*Vinaya Pitaka*
The Analysis of Rules	*Sutta Vibhang*
Groupings of Rules	*Khandhaka*
Summaries	*Parivara*
II. *The Discourses* (Sayings)	*Sutta Pitaka*
The Long Discourses of the Buddha	*Digha Nikaya*
The Middle-Length Discourses of the Buddha	*Majjhima Nikaya*
The Book of the Kindred Sayings	*Samjutta Nikaya*
The Book of Gradual Sayings	*Anguttara Nikaya*
The Minor Anthologies	*Khuddaka Nikaya*

PREFACE

viii. "Among the founders of religions." Rahula 1. For an excellent example of a short book on Buddhism, see Carrithers 2001, 2–8, 81.

PART I

2. "Among the known biographies." See Reynolds; Reynolds and Hallisey.

3. Lamotte. See Lamotte.

CHAPTER 1

5. Why is there something rather than nothing? *Book of Kindred Sayings,* 2:101ff.

5. How long is an aeon? *Book of Kindred Sayings,* 2:121ff.

6. After many aeons this world contracts: *Long Discourses,* 409–415.

8. "Delighted others in his use of the law." "Law" → *dhamma* (Sanskrit: *dharma*). *Dhamma* is one of the words in Pali that is often said to be untranslatable. It is indeed a complicated and complex term to translate. Pali and Sanskrit dictionaries give it several columns of definitions. Here I have used "law" as a proper term in English in the context of a king's rule. The word *dhamma* can also mean (1) that which supports, a foundation, structure, or constitution, as for example, "the structure of the cosmos," "the foundation of society," and so on; (2) rationality; (3) morality, righteousness; (4) the Doctrine or truth of the Buddha's teaching. In most cases I will translate *dhamma* as "Doctrine," truth discovered and taught by the Buddha, summarized in many places as "He teaches the Doctrine true at the beginning, in the middle, and at the end, complete, perfect and pure (*Middle Length Discourses,* 272).

Dhamma can also mean the elements that make up the "interdependent origination of all conditioned things" that some scholars believe to be the heart of the Buddha's teaching. The context is always a useful guide in translating the term. It has been suggested that a good label for identifying this religion should be "dhamma-ism" or "dharma-ism."

8. In accordance with the universal Doctrine. Universal Doctrine → *dhamma.*

9. He knew the Sacred Words (the Vedas). The Vedas are the words spoken by the mythical ancestors at the beginning of each creation and form the foundation of Hindu life, especially as this is practiced in Hindu rites of passage where verses from the Veda are chanted as mantras. According to tradition there are four Vedas. The Upanishads are classified as "the end of the Veda," and the Bhagavadgita is often cited as a "First Veda." There are many passages in the *Tipitaka* where the Buddha declares the Vedas to be irrelevant, if not a hindrance, for gaining perfect happiness.

9. "I could realize perfect happiness here and now." "Perfect happiness" → *nibbana* (Sanskrit: *nirvana*).

10. "The ten perfections" The Ten Perfections that are satisfied by all Buddhas are as follows: (1) giving, (2) moral discipline, (3) renouncing the world, (4) wisdom,

(5) exertion, (6) patience, (7) truthfulness, (8) resolution, (9) love, (10) even-mindedness.

10. A Conqueror's memorial. "Memorial" → *thupa* (Pali), *stupa* (Sanskrit).

CHAPTER 2

11. "After several world evolutions." The story of Vessantara is told in *Jataka 547, Jataka Stories,* vol. 3. The most recent translation can be found in Cone and Gombrich 1977.

16. "Omniscience is a hundred." Omniscience refers to the knowledge gained at enlightenment, the knowledge of former births, that is, the Doctrine of karma. Here the perfection of giving leads to that knowledge and perfect happiness (*nibbana*).

CHAPTER 3

21. Queen Maya. *Buddhacarita or Acts of the Buddha,* trans. E. H. Johnston, 23. Also *Long Discourses,* 201.

22. The antigods. Antigods (*asuras*) are a class of superhuman agents who dwell in the West opposite the gods and are in perpetual conflict with them. They are often mistakenly identified as demons.

23. The child had the characteristic thirty-two marks of a "superhuman agent." See chapter 20, and note 00.

23. Asita. *The Minor Anthologie,* 2:78–79. Thomas gives another version of the story of Asita from the *Lalita-vistara,* in Thomas 1956, 39–43.

23. Superhuman agent. A *Mahapurisa,* usually translated as "great person," used as a title for a Buddha or a Universal Monarch of the four quarters. See also chapter 20.

23. Mother's death and name giving. *Buddhist Birth-Stories,* 149–161; also *Acts of the Buddha,* 1–23; *Long Discourses,* 203–204.

23. Righteousness and virtue were practiced. "Righteousness and virtue" → *dhamma.*

23. Marriage, birth of son, and marriage. *Acts of the Buddha,* 1–56; *Middle-Length Dicourses,* 609; *Book of Gradual Sayings,* 1:128.

24. "Who is this man with the white hair…?" *Acts of the Buddha,* 1–65; *Buddhist Birth-Stories,* 166–168.

CHAPTER 4

27. Flight from the palace. *Acts of the Buddha,* canto V, pp. 61–80; *Middle Length Discourses,* chap. 26, "The Noble Search," 253–268. Compare the story of Vipassi, a former Buddha, at *Long Discourses,* 207–210.

30. The story of Sujata, also known as Nandabala. *Acts of the Buddha,* 185–187; *Buddhist Birth-Stories,* 184–188.

CHAPTER 5

33. The story of the enlightenment. *Buddhist Birth-Stories*, 187–205; *Middle Length Discourses*, 340–342; compare *Acts of the Buddha*, 186–217. The most succinct account of the enlightenment is given in the discourse called "The Noble Search," *Middle-Length Discourses*, 253–268.

37. The third watch and the four forces. I have translated the technical term *asava* as "force." It literally means "outflow" or an "extract," a secretion from a sore or the sap of a tree or flower. But it also entails force, influence, and causal efficacy. The "four forces" are very important for understanding the Doctrine of karma, since these secretions or forces befuddle the mind. It is precisely the technique and practice of the fourfold meditation that roots out these forces and destroys the source and cause of the secretion. The many medical metaphors used in the texts are directly related to this notion of force. Perhaps "virus" would be a more apt metaphor. *Asava* has been translated as "sin" or "depravity"; this, I believe, is a serious misunderstanding of the term.

37. The twelvefold links of the dependent origination of all conditioned things, *paticca-samuppada*. This term covers a fundamental axiom in Buddhist teaching: we might call it the "ontological axiom" of Buddhism. The Buddha's last words, "Subject to decay are all conditioned things," provide a brief definition of this law, and the first three noble truths presuppose it. Descriptions of the principle can be found in most of the texts, including the *Book of Discipline* (the *Vinaya-Pitaka*), pt. 4, vol. 14, pp. 1–2; *Middle Length Discourses*, 353; *Book of Kindred Sayings*, pt. 2, pp. 1–5. It is also described in one of the most important commentaries on the Buddha's teaching by Buddhagosa (4 C.E.), who devotes a complete chapter to the principle. See Buddhaghosa, *The Path of Purification*, trans. by Bhikkhu Nanamoli, chap. 17, pp. 525–604. All introductory books on Buddhism provide at least a brief interpretation of the axiom. Collins 1998, 139, follows what he calls "the standard" interpretation of the twelvefold causal links in terms of the three consecutive lifetimes:

I. **Past Life**
  1. With ignorance as condition there arise Conditioning Factors, that is, the constituent elements of personality.
  2. With Conditioning Factors as condition there arises consciousness (at the moment of conception).

II. **Present Life**
  3. With consciousness as condition there arises mind-body.
  4. With mind-body as condition arise the six senses.
  5. With the six senses as condition arises sense-contact.
  6. With sense-contact as condition arises feeling.
  7. With feeling as condition arises craving.
  8. With craving as condition arises grasping.
  9. With grasping as condition arises becoming.
  10. With becoming as condition arises birth.

III. **Future Life**
1. With birth (as rebirth) as condition there arises distress, grief, suffering, sorrow, and unrest.
2. With this mass of unhappiness as condition there arises old age and death.

One of the best philologists of the day puts the twelvefold chain this way: The Buddha started from where he was that night. Putting the formula in reverse, as it is often described, "He knew that he would grow old and die. Why was he going to grow old and die? Because he had been born. Why had he been born? Because of existence. Why was there existence? Because of clinging. Why was there clinging? Because of craving. Why was there craving? Because of feeling. Why was there feeling? Because of contact. Why was there contact? Because of the six senses. Why were there six senses? Because of name and form. Why were there name and form? Because of consciousness. Why was there consciousness? Because of the compounded formations. Why were there compounded formations? Because of ignorance. That is to say: the beginning of all this existence, which we know is suffering, is ignorance" (Norman 1997, 33).

Thus we can easily see that given this fundamental Buddhist principle, if we think of ignorance as "lack of knowledge," then the Buddha's "awakening" entails its destruction, and with it the causal chain of the interdependent origination of all conditioned things. The awakening puts an end to karma, for to break one link in the chain is to break all of the causal links. As the Buddha says, "Now I have attained it, rebirth is destroyed, ignorance is dispelled."

37. "I have run through a course of many births" is also quoted in the *Dhammapada:* "I have run through a course of many births looking for the maker of this dwelling and finding him not; painful is birth again and again. Now you are seen, O builder of the house, you will not build this house again. All your rafters are broken, your ridgepole is destroyed, the mind, set on the attainment of liberation, has attained extinction of desire" (vv. 153–154). According to tradition, these are the first words the Buddha spoke after his awakening.

CHAPTER 6

39. The seven days and the four weeks. *Book of Discipline,* The Great Division, pt. 4, vol. 14, pp. 1–10.

40. The merchants. *Book of Discipline,* vol. 4 (Mahavagga), pp. 5–6.

40. The Doctrine. Doctrine → *dhamma* (Sanskrit: *dharma*).

40. Brahma persuades Buddha to teach. *Book of Discipline,* 4:6–9. Also *Middle-Length Discourses,* 261.

40. The Perfected One → *Tathagata,* a title for an enlightened one.

41. Upaka. *Book of Discipline,* vol. 14, 4:11–12.

41. The five mendicants. *Book of Discipline,* 4:13–21; *Middle Length Discourses,* 264–268.

42. "Happiness," "liberation," "the end of suffering," → *nibbana* (Sanskrit: *nirvana*).

I do not think that *nibbana* is a mysterious word, ineffable, thus beyond translation. Collins (1998) at times translates it as "happiness," and I think he is quite right—happiness not in the sense of "slaphappy" but complete contentment in both a cognitive and an emotional sense. Happiness in the Buddhist sense is always in the context of understanding, knowing, the truth of the Doctrine, to have the right views, to know the Doctrine that existence is impermanent, that the hope for immortality is an illusion born in ignorance. It is the destruction of the forces of karma. In brief, "happiness," "liberation," is the end of suffering. *Nibbana*, liberation, happiness, is not a state'; it is not a thing we can possess. The Buddha tells his disciples that "the untrained, undisciplined ordinary householder perceives the earth as the earth. He then thinks of earth, he thinks in earth, he thinks out of earth, he thinks earth is mine and he delights in earth [he also perceives and thinks similarly of water, fire, air, and so on] and finally thinks of liberation in the same way. Why is that? Because he has not fully understood it, I say." The Buddha ends this discourse by telling the monks that a Perfected One, "free from obsessions, who has lived the life, done what was to be done, laid down the burden, attained the true goal, destroyed the fetters of becoming, completely liberated by means of the highest knowledge...he knows liberation as liberation; because he knows, he does not think of liberation; he does not think of himself in liberation; he does not think of himself as liberation, he does not think 'liberation is mine,' nor does he delight in liberation. Why is that? I say it because it is thoroughly understood by him" (*Middle Length Discourses*, "The Root of All Things," 83–89).

42. The Middle Way and the Four Noble Truths. *Book of the Discipline*, vol. 4, pp. 15–18; also *Long Discourses*, 344–350.

43. Doctrine is similar to a raft. *Middle-Length Discourses*, 228–229.

44. "Accepted as a renouncer." Renouncer → *pabbajja* (going into homelessness).

44. "May I receive ordination?" Ordination → *upasampada*.

44. "Come, monks." Monks → *bhikkhu* = a beggar.

44. Second discourse. *Book of the Discipline*, vol. 4 (Mahavagga), pp. 20–21.

44. The five aggregates → *khandhas* (Sanskrit: *skandhas*). (1) Corporeality (the four elements earth, water, fire, and wind and matter derived from them); (2) feeling; (3) perception; (4) volition; and(5) consciousness. The five aggregates are inseparable. Also translated as "forces," "habitual tendencies," "conditioning thing," or "event," they are a mental formation and can also signify active causal or volitional forces, as well as the results of such actions and forces as factors in our karmic legacy.

45. Yasa. *Book of Discipline*, 4:21–28.

46. The Buddha, the Doctrine, and the community. This triple formula is found in most Buddhist rituals and is a vow taken by most Buddhists, both householders and renouncers, at the beginning of each day. It states: "I go to the Buddha for refuge, I go to the Doctrine for refuge, I go to the community for refuge" (Doctrine → *dhamma;* community → *samgha*). The "community" covers both the

restricted monastic life and the all-encompassing community that includes both monks and householders.

    47. "Ordain others." *Book of Discipline*, 4:29–30.

CHAPTER 7

    49. The miracles and the matted-hair ascetics. *Book of Discipline*, 4:32–46.

    53. "The Fire Sermon." *Book of Discipline*, 4:45–46.

CHAPTER 8

    55. Bimbisara. *Book of Discipline*, 4:47–52.

    57. Sariputta and Moggallana. *Book of Discipline*, 4:52–57.

    57. "Of all existent elements." This has obvious reference to the law of "interdependent origination of all conditioned things" that the Buddha discovered during his awakening. This statement became close to a creedal formula for various Buddhist traditions.

    58. Kaludayin. *Buddhist Birth-Stories*, "The Story of the Lineage," 215–219.

CHAPTER 9

    59. Complaints and new rules. *Book of Discipline*, 4:56ff.

    60. Warriors ordained. *Book of Discipline*, 4:91–92.

    60. Upali. *Book of Discipline*, 4:96–98.

    61. The serpent. *Book of Discipline*, 4:110–111.

    62. The monk and his wife. *Book of Discipline*, 4:124–125.

    64. The "ritual of liberation" → *Patimokkha*. The *Patimokkha* is a code of conduct that contains 227 rules for monks (more were added for nuns) recited twice a month, in the period of the full and new moon, in a ritual called the *uposattha*. As each rule is recited, the monks either remain silent or confess a violation of the rule. "If there is no offence you should remain silent. By your silence I shall know that you are quite pure" (p. 132). Violation of any of the first four rules is cause for expulsion; violation of the others entail suspension for a period of time or other penalties. This bimonthly ritual is clearly a ritual of purification, necessary for both the monks and the householders who support them and gain merit in return for their support by means of gifts to the monks; the mechanism of merit demands that the ascetic community remains pure; a corrupt monk also defiles the community and ruptures the dynamic reciprocity of receiving merit in return for gifts. The story of the origin of this ritual and a description of the rules is found in *Book of Discipline*, 4:130ff. A translation and reconstruction of the *Patimokkha* rules are also available in Oldenberg's translation, *The Vinaya Texts*, pt. 1 (Sacred Books of the East 0), 13:1–69. (*Vinaya Pitaka*. Ed. By H. Oldenberg, London, 1879–1883.)

CHAPTER 10

66. The visit home and the twin acts of magic. *The Mahavastu*, 3:93–122; *Buddhist Birth-Stories*, 220–221; *Acts of the Buddha*, 85–92.

67. "Not so, replied the king…" → *Maha Sammata*, apparently referring back to the creation of society and the caste system in chapter 1.

68. Ordination of Rahula and Nanda. *Buddhist Birth-Stories*, 227; *Book of Discipline*, 4:103.

CHAPTER 11

69. The young men from Anupiya. *Book of Discipline*, 5:253–259.

71. Anathapindika. *Book of Discipline*, 5:229–230; *Buddhist Birth-Stories*, 228–230.

73. King Pasenadi. *Book of Kindred Sayings*, pt. 1, pp. 93–126.

75. The ten undecided questions. *Middle-Length Discourses*, 117–122.

CHAPTER 12

77. The Buddha needed a break. *Book of Kindred Sayings*, pt. 1, p. 11. See also page 12, where the Buddha takes a three-month leave of absence.

77. Angulimala story. *Middle-Length Discourses*, 710–717.

80. "Bear it, Brahmin! Bear it!" The commentary explains: any volitional act, that produces bad karma has consequences of three kinds taking place either in this lifetime, in the next lifetime, or in any future lifetime. By becoming a monk, Angulimala has escaped the last two but not the first, since he is subject to the consequences of actions in the present life before becoming a renouncer.

80. Famine and drought in Vesali. The story can be found in *The Minor Anthologies*, book 1, "The Jewel Discourse," 175–178. The verse itself, called "Ratana," or "The Jewel," can be found in *Group of Discourses*, 2:25–26. It is a magical, protective verse chanted by monks to this day for protection against disease, natural disasters, and the like. See Spiro (1982), chap. 6.

82. The visit and conversation with Mahapajapati and Ananda. *Book of Discipline*, 5:352–356.

82. The Eight Major Rules for nuns. *Book of Discipline*, 5:354–355. The eight additional rules are as follows: (1) A nun must greet and do homage to all monks regardless of when they were ordained. (2) A nun must not spend the rainy season in a residence in which there is no monk. (3) Every half month a nun should request the observance rituals by monks. (4) At the end of every rainy season a nun must request a retelling of what was seen, heard, and concluded. (5) A nun who commits an offense must undergo discipline for half a month before both orders. (6) A nun must seek ordination from both orders. (7) A monk must never be abused or reviled by nuns. (8) Reproof against faults by nuns of monks is forbidden, but reproof of nuns by monks is allowed.

83. The trip to the heavenly abode of his mother. *Acts of the Buddha*, 99.

84. Anathapindika's death. *Middle Length Discourses*, 1112–1113.

CHAPTER 13

85. The story of Devadatta. *Book of Discipline*, 259–284.

CHAPTER 14

91. The legends in this chapter and in chapter 15 can be found in *The Long Discourses*, "The Great Passing, The Buddha's Last Days" (*Mahahparinibbana Sutta*), pp. 231–277.

93. Sariputta's illness and death. *Book of Kindred Sayings*, pt. 5, pp. 140–143.

94. Moggallana's death and the eulogy. *Book of Kindred Sayings*, pt. 5, pp. 144. My description is also based on Thomas 1956, 141–142.

95. The visit to Patalagama. *Long Discourses*, 236–239.

97. The four roads of power are described in *The Long Discourses*, 404–405.

98. The "pork special." The story of Cunda's meal *Long Discourses*, 256–257, remains unknown. Just what *sukara-maddava* (pig-soft, or pig-withered) means remains a mystery; not even the commentaries seem to know. It could mean something that pigs like, mushrooms, for example, or a tender part of the pig. But this is only part of the mystery and not, I think, its most tantalizing part. The Buddha tells Cunda to bury any leftovers of the pork special in a pit because "I can see none in this world...[that] could thoroughly digest it except the Perfect One." Did the "pork special" cause his illness as many scholars think is the case and if so is he a Perfect One? The Buddha does not make this causal connection in his instructions to Ananda and I do not think we should either. This leaves us with the mystery concerning the "pork special." One question we might ask is, How did Cunda, a blacksmith, not only know about the dish but also how to prepare it?

As far as I know, there is only one other instance of this kind of event in the life of the Buddha. It takes place at a river where a Brahmin has just performed a Vedic fire ritual and wondered to whom he could give the leftover food from the ritual offering. Spotting the Buddha seated at the root of a tree with his head covered, he offered it to him. The Buddha replied, "I see no one in this whole world of gods, men and Maras, who if he ate this food, could thoroughly digest it, save only a Perfect One or one of his disciples. Therefore, Brahmin, it would be best to either pour it out on bare ground or throw it in water that has no living creatures." The Brahmin did so, and the water hissed and steamed and smoked (*Book of Kindred Sayings*, pt. 1, pp. 209–213).

CHAPTER 15

101. Once upon a time, Ananda. *Long Discourses*, 147, 279–290. A part of the legend can also be found in Jataka 95, *Jataka Stories*, 1:230–231.

101. A wheel-turning monarch → *cakkavatti* (Sanskrit: *cakratvartin*), a great agent who rules over the four quarters of the cosmos.

CHAPTER 16

107. Settled down in Kusinara. Continuation of the last days; *Long Discourses,* 262–277.

108. "There are four persons worthy of a memorial." "Memorial" → *stupa,* a great mound of earth usually covered in plaster and precious metals such as gold. All *stupas* are royal memorials and became special monuments for the Buddha's relics in South and Southeast Asia.

108. Nonteaching Buddha → *pacceka-Buddha.*

PART II

113. As Davidson once described it. Davidson 1984, 24.

120. Functionalism. Penner, in Frankenberry and Penner 1999.

120. Why do people persist in believing them to be true? There are answers to this question throughout the history of the study of religion. For an analysis of the question and some answers, see Penner in Frankenberry and Penner 1999; Godlove 1989; Lawson and McCauley 1990; Pals 1996; Penner 1989; Preuss 1987, Smith 1982.

CHAPTER 17

125. Collins 1990, 89.

126. Reginald Ray. Ray 1994, 62.

126. One of the best philologists. K. R. Norman, in Bechert 1991, pt. 1, pp. 302–303; see Bechert's reaction on p. 336.

126. "Such an extremity of skepticism now seems absurd." Gombrich 1990, 1:5.

127. E. J. Thomas concluded. Thomas 1956, 211.

127. Two different questions. Thomas 1956, 225.

127. David Strauss's *Life of Jesus.* Thomas 1927, 225–226.

128. The fundamental question. Thomas 1927, 235–236.

129. Lamotte. Lamotte 1988, 15, 639–640.

130. Warder's account. Warder 1970, 332–335.

131. LaFleur tells us. LaFleur 1988, 13.

131. Peter Harvey also leaves little room for doubt. Harvey 1990, 15.

131. Carrithers begins his account. Carrithers 2001, 3, 81.

132. Rupert Gethin tells us. Gethin 1998, 15–16.

132. Gethin then says. Gethin 1998, 15–16.

134. There are always exceptions. Robinson, et al., 20055.

134. Heinz Bechert, thirty years later. Bechert 1991, 1, 8, 20.

135. Warder and Schumann. Warder 1970, 44; Schumann 1989, xii, 10–13.

135. Carrithers. Carrithers 2001, 8.

135. LaFleur. LaFleur 1988, 11.

135. Harvey. Harvey 1990, 9.

135. The first World Buddhist Congress. Quoted from Bechert 1991, pt. 1, p. 4.

136. Schopen calls "doctrinal specialists." Schopen 1997, 32–33, and chaps. 9 and 11.

136. As Collins puts it. Collins 1998, 351.

136. Thus Warder is quite right. Warder 1970, 334–335.

140. Lamotte. Lamotte 1988, 652.

CHAPTER 18

143. Some scholars say. See Collins 1998, 448–451.

143. Norman on joking. Norman 1997, 159.

144. Max Weber. Weber 1963, 145. Read "rational" for "formal."

146. The Formless Sphere. See Collins 1998, 298–299.

150. The Brick house at Nadika. *Long Discourses*, chap. 18.

152. The setting is Rajagaha. Protective verses. *Long Discourses*, chap. 32.

153. Cosmology/geography and Jambudipa. See Collins 1998, chap. 4.

156. The Buddha at Kuru. *Middle Length Discourses*, chap. 10, and notes 133, 134. Great caution should be used when told that a page, paragraph, or chapter is "one of the most important." A longer, virtually identical text can be found in *Long Discourses*, chap. 22.

CHAPTER 19

161. Arnold van Gennep proposed a theory. Van Gennep 1960.

163. Victor Turner. Turner 1967, 93–111.

CHAPTER 20

178. The fact that some scholars.... I have not found a book or a substantial essay on the actual life of a Universal Monarch, let alone a study that compares Buddhas with Universal Monarchs in Buddhism. Two essays come to mind that provide helpful ideas for understanding the Universal Monarch. Both, however, anchor the significance of the Monarch to kingship in India in a mistaken attempt at realistic verisimilitude (see Tambiah 1987; Collins 1998, 470–496). Collins tells us that "much has been written on the CV [i.e., the Universal Monarch] who has already been introduced (5.2.b); I can be brief." The footnote cites three encyclopedia entries, a dictionary of proper names, and two books that are of little relevance for understanding this important mythical figure in Buddhism. Collins does give us a fine translation of a myth about the joint appearance in the future of the Buddha Metteyya and the Universal Monarch Sankha that deserves to be studied together with the stories you have read in part I and the interpretation in this chapter. Universal Monarchs are

the central focus in an interesting debate between Collins (1993, 1996) and Huxley (1996) from the point of view of social contract theory. The subject and interpretation of the myths remain an obvious problem.

178. Collins 1998, 490; Tambiah (1987), 3,5.

179. Maurice Walshe. *Long Discourses*, 610n.939.

181. Davidson put it this way. Davidson 1984, 194.

182. Taking modern linguistics as our guide. See Saussure 1983; Lévi-Strauss 1963.

182. As Lévi-Strauss taught us. Lévi-Strauss 1963.

183. "These, monks, are the thirty-two marks." *Long Discourses*, chap. 30. The thirty-two marks are as follows: (1) flat feet, (2) wheels of a thousand spokes on both feet, (3) projecting heels, (4) long fingers, (5) soft and tender hands, (6) weblike or netlike feet and hands, (7) high ankles, (8) legs like an antelope, (9) he can touch his knees while standing, (10) genitals in a sheath, (11) light complexion like gold, (12) smooth skin that does not collect dust, (13) one hair to a pore, (14) hair that grows upright and curls in rings to the right, (15) a straight body, (16) seven convex surfaces, (17) a body like a lion, (18) no hollow between his shoulders, (19) proportioned like a banyan tree, (20) a rounded bust, (21) perfect sense of taste, (22) jaws like a lion, (23) forty teeth, (24) even teeth, (25) no spaces between his teeth, (26) his canine teeth are very bright, (27) a long tongue, (28) a voice like Brahma, (29) deep blue eyes, (30) eyelashes like a cow, (31) white and soft hair between his eyes, (32) a head like a royal turban. *Long Discourses*, chap. 30, pp. 441–442.

184. Steven Collins has argued. Collins 1998, 448–450.

185. Bodhisattva (Sanskrit). A Buddha-to-be with infinite compassion and wisdom in Mahayana Buddhism. See p. 199 and note for p. 199.

188. Malinowski was mistaken. Malinowski 1954, 96–111.

188. *Long Discourses*, chap. 26.

193. Parry, "a kind of lay exercise in asceticism." Parry 1986, 468.

194. In the *Mahavastu*. *Mahavastu*, 3:105–106.

194. The Buddha compares monks to Universal Monarchs. *Long Discourses*, chap. 26, pp. 404–405.

196. The Buddha and the Universal Monarch. *Long Discourses*, chap. 16, pp. 231–234.

199. The Bodhisattva and Mahayana Buddhism. The Bodhisattva (either male or female) in Mahayana Buddhism is the Achilles' heel of Buddhist studies. No one denies that the great Bodhisattvas are mythical beings; thus a historical quest is out of the question. The texts (sutras) provide full descriptions of them and also proclaim that they are "protective"; to just hear them read provides great merit, safety, benefits to health, and eventual arrival at the Bodhisattvas's paradise at death! Now that you have read a good deal of the Pali scripture, you know that that is nothing new. But if myth is a sign of irrationality, or the nonrational, or a degeneration from the rational, we can well imagine why a sign saying "no trespassing" is posted around such texts. How else do you explain the fact that you will not find a full description or analysis of who or what Bodhisattvas are in any book that claims to be an introduction to

Buddhism? You will not find a description of the myth in any article on Buddhism or the Bodhisattva in *The Encyclopedia of Religion,* ed. Mircea Eliade (New York: Macmillan, 1987). We are fortunate to have an English translation of one of the texts, entitled Saddharmapundarmika Sutra (The Lotus of the True Law), trans. H Kern, in *The Sacred Books of the East,* vol. 21. See also vol. 49, *Buddhist Mahayana Texts.* The best introductory overview of this development can be found in E. J. H. Thomas, *The History of Buddhist Thought,* chaps. 14, 15, and 16. (London: Routledge & Kegan Paul Ltd., 1933).

199. Bodhisattva and Ten Perfections., See note 21.

CHAPTER 21

202. In spite of Max Weber's famous words. The words are *weltablehnende Askese* (world-rejecting asceticism). Weber 1963, 166, 169, 171, 266.

204. When you are finished wrestling with Mauss's text. For the wrestle, see, among many books, Godelier 1999; Weiner 1992; Parry 1986; Derrida 1992; Lévi-Strauss (1987).

205. Mauss tells us. Mauss 1990, 3.

205. He is interested in a specific characteristic. Mauss 1990, 3.

205. As he [Mauss] says, the gift encompasses "the basic principle of action." Mauss 1990, 71, and p. 155n14.

205. The first criticism. See Parry 1986; Sahlins 1972, 149–183; Godelier 1999.

206. We can sum up the criticism. Lévi-Strauss 1963, p. 69.

207. Jonathan Parry. Parry 1986, 461.

207. Thomas Trautmann. Trautmann 1981, 279, 227. *The Questions of King Milinda,* in Sacred Books of the East, 36:114ff.

214. *Questions of King Milinda,* 36:114ff.

Bibliography

BUDDHIST SCRIPTURES IN TRANSLATION

The Book of Discipline (Vinaya-Pitaka). Translated by I. B. Horner. 6 vols. London: Pali Text Society, 1982–1992.

The Book of the Gradual Sayings (Anguttara-Nikaya). Translated by F. L. Woodward and E. M. Hare. 5 vols. London: Pali Text Society, 1986–1990.

The Book of the Kindred Sayings (Sanyutta-Nikaya). Translated by F. H. Woodward. 5 vols. Oxford: Pali Text Society, 1980–1992.

Buddhist Birth-Stories (Jataka Tales. Nidana-Katha of the Khuddaka Nikaya). Translated and revised by Mrs. Rhys Davids T. W. Rhys Davids. New Delhi: Asian Education Services, 1999.

The Dhammapada (Khuddaka-Nikaya). Translated by S. Radhakrishnan. Madras: Oxford University Press, 1950.

The Group of Discourses (Sutta-Nipata of the Khuddaka Nikaya). Translated by K. R. Norman. Oxford: Pali Text Society, 1995.

The Jataka or Stories of the Buddha's Former Births. Translated by W. H. D. Rouse, Robert Chalmers, and H. T. Francis. Edited by E. B. Cowell. 3 vols. London: Luzac, 1957.

The Long Discourses of the Buddha (Digha Nikaya). Translated by Maurice Walshe. Boston: Wisdom Publications, 1995.

The Mahavastu. Translated by J. J. Jones. 3 vols. Sacred Books of the Buddhists. London: Luzac, 1949–1956.

The Middle Length Discourses of the Buddha (Majjhima Nikaya). Translated by Bhikkhu Nalamoli and Bhikkhu Bodhi. Boston: Wisdom Publications, 1995.

The Minor Anthologies of the Pali Canon (Khuddaka-Nikaya). Translated by I. B.
    Horner, H. S. Gehman, Bhikkhu Nalamoli, K. R. Norman, and F. L. Woodward.
    5 vols. Oxford: Pali Text Society, 1974–1995.
Psalms of the Early Buddhists: The Brethren (Theragatha of the Khuddaka-Nikaya).
    Translated by Mrs. Rhys Davids. London: Pali Text Society, 1937.
Psalms of the Early Buddhists: The Sisters (Theragatha of the Khuddaka-Nikaya).
    Translated by Mrs. Rhys Davids. London: Pali Text Society, 1932.
The Story of Gotama Buddha (Nidana-Katha of the Khuddaka Nikaya). Translated by
    N. A. Jayawickrama. Oxford: Pali Text Society, 1990.

GENERAL BIBLIOGRAPHY OF BOOKS AND ARTICLES

Ashvaghosha. *Buddhacarita or Acts of the Buddha*. Cantos i to xiv. Translated by E. H.
    Johnston. Delhi: Motilal Banarsidass, 1972.
———. "Buddhacarita: The Buddha's Mission and Last Journey (Cantos xv–xxviii)."
    Translated by E. H. Johnston. *Acta Orientalia* 15 (1937): 26–292.
Bechert, Heinz. ed. *The Dating of the Historical Buddha* 2 vols. Göttingen:
    Vandenhoeck and Ruprecht, 1991.
Buddhaghosa. *The Path of Purification (Visuddhimagga)*. Translated by Bhikkhu
    Nanamoli.   Kandy: Buddhist Publication Society, 1991.
Carrithers, Michael. *Buddha: A Very Short Introduction*. Oxford: Oxford University
    Press, 2001.
Collins, Steven. "On the Very Idea of the Pali Canon." *Journal of the Pali Society* 15
    (1990): 89–126.
———. "The Discourse on What Is Primary: An Annotated Translation." *Journal of
    Indian Philosophy* 21 (1993): 301–393.
———. "The Lion's Roar on the Wheel-Turning King: A Response to Andrew
    Huxley's 'The Buddha and the Social Contract.'" *Journal of Indian Philosophy* 24
    (1996): 421–446.
———. *Nirvana and Other Buddhist Felicities*. Cambridge: Cambridge University
    Press, 1998.
Cone, Margaret, and Richard F. Gombrich, trans. *The Perfect Generosity of Prince
    Vessantara: A Buddhist Epic*. Oxford: Oxford University Press, 1977.
Davidson, Donald. *Inquiries into Truth and Interpretation*. Oxford: Oxford University
    Press, 1984.
Derrida, Jacques. *Given Time: I. Counterfeit Money*. Chicago: University of Chicago
    Press, 1992.
Fontenrose, Joseph. *The Ritual Theory of Myth*: Berkeley: University of California
    Press, 1966.
Frankenberry, Nancy K., ed. *Radical Interpretation in Religion*. Cambridge:
    Cambridge   University Press, 2002.
Frankenberry, Nancy K., and Hans H. Penner. *Language, Truth, and Religious Belief*.
    Atlanta: Scholars Press, 1999.
Gethin, Rupert. *The Foundations of Buddhism*. Oxford: Oxford University Press, 1998.

Godelier, Maurice. *The Enigma of the Gift*. Translated by Nora Scott. Chicago: University of Chicago Press, 1999.

Godlove, Terry F., Jr. *Religion, Interpretation, and Diversity of Belief*. Cambridge: Cambridge University Press, 1989.

Gombrich, Richard F. "Recovering the Buddha's Message." In *The Buddhist Forum*, ed. Tadeusz Skorupski, 1:5–20. London: University of London School of Oriental and African Studies, 1990.

Harvey, Peter. *An Introduction to Buddhism*. Cambridge: Cambridge University Press, 1990.

Huxley, Andrew. "The Buddha and the Social Contract." *Journal of Indian Philosophy* 24 (1996): 407–429.

LaFleur, William R. *Buddhism: A Cultural Perspective*. Englewood Cliffs, N.J.: Prentice Hall, 1988.

Lamotte, Étienne. *History of Indian Buddhism*. Translated by Sara Webb-Boin. Louvain-La Neuve: Catholic University of Louvain, 1988.

Lawson, E. Thomas, and Robert N. McCauley. *Rethinking Religion*. Cambridge: Cambridge University Press, 1990.

Levi-Strauss, Claude. *Totemism*. Translated by Rodney Needham. Boston: Beacon Press, 1963.

———. *Introduction to the Work of Marcel Mauss*. Boston: Routledge, 1987.

Malinowski, Bronislaw. *Magic, Science and Religion* Garden City, N.Y.: Doubleday Anchor, 1954.

Masuzawa, Tomoko. *In Search of Dreamtime: The Quest for the Origin of Religion*. Chicago: University of Chicago Press, 1993.

Mauss, Maurice. *The Gift: The Form and Reason for Exchange in Archaic Societies*. Translated by W. D. Halls. New York: Norton, 1990.

Norman, K. R. "Observations on the Dates of Jina and the Buddha." In *The Dating of the Historical Buddha*, pt. 1, edited by Heinz Bechert, 300–312. Göttingen: Vandenhoeck and Ruprecht, 1991.

———. *A Philological Approach to Buddhism*. London: University of London Press, 1997.

Pals, Daniel L. *Seven Theories of Religion*. New York: Oxford University Press, 1996.

Parry, Jonathan. "The Gift, the Indian Gift and the 'Indian Gift.'" *Man* 21 (1986): 453–473.

Penner, Hans H. *Impasse and Resolution: A Critique of the Study of Religion*. New York: Peter Lang, 1989.

Preuss, J. Samuel. *Explaining Religion*. New Haven, Conn.: Yale University Press, 1987.

Rahula, Walpola. *What the Buddha Taught*. New York: Grove Press, 1974.

Ray, Reginald A. *Buddhist Saints in India*. New York: Oxford University Press, 1994.

Reynolds, Frank E., and Donald Capps, eds. *The Biographical Process: Studies in the History and Psychology of Religion*. The Hague: Mouton, 1976.

Robinson, Richard H., Willard L. Johnson, and Thanissaro Bhikkhu. *Buddhist Religions: A Historical Introduction*. 5th ed. Belmont, Calif.: Wadsworth, 2005.

Sahlins, Marshall. *Stone Age Economics*. Chicago: Aldine-Atherton, 1972.

Saussure, Ferdinand de. *Course in General Linguistics*. Translated by Roy Harris. LaSalle, Ill.: Open Court, 1983.

Schopen, Gregory. *Bones, Stones, and Buddhist Monks: Studies in the Buddhist Traditions*, ed. Luis O. Gomez. Honolulu: University of Hawaii Press, 1997.

Schumann, H. W. *The Historical Buddha*. Translated by M. O'C. Walshe. London: Penguin Books Arkana, 1989.

Smith, Jonathan Z. *Imagining Religion*. Chicago: University of Chicago Press, 1982.

Spiro, Melford. Buddhism and Society. Berkeley:University of California Press, 1982.

Tambiah, Stanley Jeyaraja. *The Buddhist Conception of Universal King and Its Manifestation in South and Southeast Asia*. Fifth Sri Lanka Endowment Fund Lecture. Kuala Lampur: University of Malaya, 1987.

Thomas, Edward J. *The Life of Buddha as Legend and History*. London: Routledge and Kegan Paul, 1956.

Trautmann, Thomas R. *Dravidian Kinship*. Edited by Jack Goody. Cambridge: Cambridge University Press, 1981.

Turner, Victor. *The Forest of Symbols*. Ithaca, N.Y.: Cornell University Press, 1967.

van Gennep, Arnold. *The Rites of Passage*. Translated by Monika B. Vizedom and Gabrielle L. Caffee. London: Routledge and Kegan Paul, 1960.

Warder, A. K. *Indian Buddhism*. Delhi: Motilal Banarsidass, 1970.

Weber, Max. *The Sociology of Religion*. Translated by Ephraim Fischoff. Boston: Beacon Press, 1963.

Weiner, Annette B. *Inalienable Possessions: The Paradox of Keeping-While-Giving*. Berkeley: University of California Press, 1992.

Index

Italicized page numbers refer to figures.

aeon, incalculability of, 5, 222nn2, 3
Agama, 129
Ajatasattu, Prince/King, 85–87,
    196–98
Akamanda, 101
Alara Kalama, 28, 35, 41
Allahabad, 151
alms round/almsgiving
    of Angulimala, 79–80
    of Assai/Assaji, 57
    of the Buddha, 77–78, 80–81, 83,
        88, 97–99
    the Buddha's rules for, 44, 59,
        61, 77
    and the Buddha's visit home, 65, 67
    Devadatta's rules for, 89
    and gift giving, 203, 211–12
    of Gotama, 28, 30, 65, 67
    in quest for historical Buddha, 138
    at Rajagaha, 59, 61, 158
    in rites of passage, 165
    and Sakka, 83
    Suddhodana troubled by, 65, 67
Amara, 9

Ambapali, 96, 212
Amitabha, 199
Ananda
    becoming ascetic, 70
    and the Buddha as Great Agent,
        196–97
    and the Buddha as teacher,
        138–39
    and the Buddha's last days,
        95–99, 101, 105, 169, 172,
        203, 209, 211–12
    and the Buddha's rules, 61, 63
    concerning liberation for devotees
        from Magadha, 150
    and Jewel Protection Utterance,
        81, 228n80–81
    and last watch, 107–10, 169
    and Mahapajapati, 82–83
    in quest for historical Buddha,
        138–39
    at Rajagaha, 61, 63, 85, 91
    and Sariputta and Moggallana,
        93–95
    visit to Anathapindika, 83–84

Anathapindika (wealthy merchant)
    conversion of, 71
    death of, 83–84
    gift giving of, 72–73, 158, 212–13
    park of, 1, 93, 138, 158, 181, 212–13
        (see also Jeta Grove)
Anga, 50
Angulimala, 77–80, 145, 228n77
annihilation, 42, 53, 144
antigods (asuras), 6, 22, 148, 149–51,
        223n22
Anupiya, 69, 71
Anuruddha, 69–70, 85, 110, 156
Aparagoyana, 150, 151. See also West
archetypes, 116, 133
Asala (Asalhi), month of (June/July), 21
ascetics, 8. See also community;
        homelessness; renouncers
    Asita as, 22
    and the Buddha as teacher, 41–44, 46,
        52–53
    and the Buddha's funeral, 154
    and the Buddha's miraculous power,
        49–51
    the Buddha's rules for, 59–64, 227n64
    in cosmological framework, 3, 151,
        153–54, 157–58, 184–85
    and Eightfold Path (see Eightfold Path)
    Five Precepts of, 184, 186–87, 192–93
    Gotama as, 27–31, 154, 172, 196, 202
    and Great Agents, 183–93, 195–98, 200
    Kassapa of Uruvela as, 49–56
    and Kumbha Mela (Hindu ritual), 151
    Malunkyaputta as, 75–76
    observance days of, 64
    as part of communal system, 118, 197
    at Rajagaha, 55–64
    and rites of passage, 167, 169, 171–73
    ritual of liberation of, 64, 227n64
    and Sanci memorial shrine, 136
    and sexual activity, 62, 184
    Suddhodana's fear that Gotama will
        become, 23–24

Sumedha as, 9
Upaka as, 41
Vessantara as, 14–16, 18, 154, 157,
        170–72, 217
Ashoka (ca. 250 B.C.), 125, 135–36
Ashvaghosha, 2
Asita, 22–23, 223n23
Assai/Assaji, 41, 44, 57
attachments, 37, 40, 42, 54
Avalokiteshvara, 199
Avici hell, 33
Awakened One. See the Buddha
Ayodhya, 125

Bamboo Grove, 55, 57–64, 89, 212
Banyan Park, 97
banyan tree, 30–31, 39, 232
Banyon Grove, 66
Bechert, Heinz, 134–35
begging. See alms round/almsgiving
Beluva, 95
Benedict XVI, Pope, 120
Bhaddiya. See Bhatia/Bhaddiya
Bhagu, 70
Bhagus hermitage, 28
Bhallika, 40
Bhandagama, 98
Bhatia/Bhaddiya, 41, 44, 70
Bimbisara, King
    Ajatasattu as son of, 85–87, 196–98
    and the Buddha's rules, 59–60, 64
    and the Buddha's visit to Rajagaha,
        55–57, 59–60, 64
    death of, 87
    gift giving of, 56–57, 74, 212
    power of, 73
    rebirth in heaven of thirty-three gods, 150
    and Vesala drought, 80
Bodh-Gaya, 39, 53, 55, 89, 110, 153,
        156–57, 196. See also tree of
        enlightenment
Bodhisattvas, 185, 187, 199–200,
        232–33n185

Bodhi tree, 35. *See also* tree of
    enlightenment
Borobudur (memorial at Java), 2, 149
Brahma
    and the Buddha as teacher, 40, 139–40
    and the Buddha's miraculous power, 50
    in cosmological framework, 149, 159
    and Gotama's quest for
        enlightenment, 202
    and Great Agents, 183, 232n183
    at Great Sudhamma Hall meeting, 159
    in Hinduism, 208
    and Mahasudassana, 105–6
Brahma-heaven/world, 105, 171, 189
Brahmins
    Angulimala as, 77, 80, 145, 228n77
    with Bimbisara, 55
    and the Buddha's funeral, 111
    Dona as, 111
    and gift giving, 74, 207–8, 214, 216
    and Great Agents, 183, 188–89, 196
    in Hinduism, 208
    and Mahasudassana, 103–4, 106
    origin of caste of, 8
    Pasenadi's knowledge of, 73
    and prophecy at the Buddha's birth,
        22, 25, 139
    in quest for historical Buddha, 139
    and rituals, 23, 98, 164, 169–71,
    Sakka disguised as, 17, 56, 153–54, 171,
        217–18
    in Sariputta's conversation with the
        Buddha, 91, 93
    Sumedha as, 9
    Vessantara's gifts to, 12–18, 169–71, 196
    views on annihiliationism, 53
Brick House at Nadika, 150
the Buddha. *See also* Gotama; *names of
    the Buddhas*
    allowing monks to ordain, 47
    awakening of, 3, 35–37, 39, 43, 131,
        140, 154, 168, 172–73, 192, 203,
        224–25nn33, 37, 227n57

    backaches of, 2, 91
    biographies of
        in *Buddhacarita (Acts of the Buddha)*
            (Ashvaghosha), 2
        cosmological framework for, 121–22,
            135–36, 140–59, 223n11
        and historical Buddha (*see* historical
            Buddha, quest for)
        in *Jataka*, 2, 135, 223n11
        in *Long Discourses, The (Digha
            Nikaya)*, 138–40
        narrative constraint in, 121–22,
            140–42, 149, 153, 156, 158–59,
            177, 191, 193, 198, 201, 203
        problem for scholars, 2, 121–22, 134
        and rites of passage, 174
        in *Tipitaka (The Three Baskets)*, 1–3,
            124, 129–30, 221,
    chronology of, 125–26, 134–35, 200
    Devadatta's attempt to kill, 85–89
    father of (*see* Suddhodana, King)
    food for, 2, 40, 44, 46, 50, 56–57,
        67, 71–72, 96–99, 158, 202–3,
        209–13
    funeral of, 1, 110–11, 154, 156, 172,
        175, 196
    and gift giving, 202–3, 207, 212, 214
    as Great Agent, 35, 121–22, 139, 177–88,
        190–92, 194–200, 214
    in heaven, 11–12, 19, 21–22, 83, 147
    illness of, 95–96, 98, 210–11, 229n98
    karma of, 24, 145, 169, 174, 214
    last days of, 91–99, 101, 210–11
    last rebirth of, 21–22, 43, 156, 172, 203
    last watch for, 107–10
    last words of, 110, 156
    lay disciples of, 40, 46, 56, 64, 73, 83,
        87–88, 95, 136, 152, 165
    on length of "aeon," 4, 5
    meditation of, 92, 110, 146–47, 150,
        156, 170, 172, 195
    memorials for, 108, 111, 136, 158,
        230n108

the Buddha (*continued*)

  miraculous power of, 45–46, 49–50, 66, 78, 95, 141

  mother of (*see* Maya, Queen)

  in opposition to Universal Monarch, 101–6, 121–22, 153, 169, 171–75, 184, 195, 199–202, 211

  prophecy at birth of, 22–23, 25, 66, 122, 139

  questions rejected by, 75–76

  relics of, 111, 230n108

  as renouncer, 3, 28, 122, 153, 157, 169, 178, 194, 196, 202, 204

  and rites of passage, 167–75

  under rose-apple tree, 29, 66

  rules of, 59–64, 68, 77, 197–99, 209, 227n64

  and Sariputta and Moggallana, 91–95, 138

  son of (Rahula), 24, 26–27, 67–68, 172

  stepmother of (Mahapajapati), 3, 23, 81–82, 169, 172, 174

  as superhuman agent, 23, 30, 66, 115, 121, 128, 130, 141, 155, 175, 180, 200, 223n22

  as teacher, 39–47, 52–53, 74, 76–77, 92, 109, 138, 140, 157–58, 168, 172, 196–98, 226n40

  ten months as term of birth for, 12, 22

  and Vesala drought, 80

  visit to home of, 58, 65–68, 154, 171, 194

  during watches of night, 36–37, 146–47, 155, 224–25n37

  and women as ascetics/lay disciples, 46, 81–83, 172, 174

Buddha: A Very Short Introduction (Carrithers), 131

Buddhacarita (Acts of the Buddha) (Ashvaghosha), 2

Buddhacentric focus, 173, 177, 182, 185, 201–2

Buddhagosa, 224n37

Buddhism, 3–4. *See also* Doctrine; interdependent origination; karma

  and belief in superhuman agents, 118

  "Buddhist era," 135

  "Buddhist Lent," 164, 166

  as communal system, 202–3

  cosmogony and creator god absent in, 143–44, 148

  and fatalism, 145

  and gift giving, 203–7 (*see also* gift giving)

  and historical Buddha (*see* historical Buddha, quest for)

  immortal soul or self, denial of, 2, 44–45, 144

  narrative constraint of, 202–3

  origin theories of, 203

  as philosophy, 130–31, 135–37, 149

  rites of passage in, 164

  and Sanci memorial shrine, 2, 135–36

  "son of the Buddha" initiation rite, 164, 174, 212–13

  as system of propositional attitudes, 202

Buddhist Religion, The, 134

Capala Shrine, 97

Carrithers, Michael, 131–32, 135, 140

Ceta, 14

Chandaka (Gotama's groom), 27–28, 154, 196

Chinese language, 129

Christianity, 143–44, 162, 164, 177

Chundaka, 98

Collins, Steven, 125, 136, 178, 184–86, 197, 224n37, 226n42, 231–32n178

community

  and the Buddha as Great Agent, 188, 195, 197–98

  and the Buddha as teacher, 44, 46–47, 52–53

  the Buddha's rules for, 52, 59–64, 77, 227n64

as communal system, 4, 117–18,
   161–63, 167, 202–3
in cosmological framework, 136, 154, 158
Devadatta's desire to lead, 85–89
and gift giving, 201–2, 208–9, 212–14
and Great Agents, 188, 195, 197–98
lay disciples in, 40, 46, 56, 64, 73, 83,
   87–88, 95, 136, 152, 165
and Mahapajapati, 3, 81–83, 169, 174
in quest for historical Buddha, 128, 131
reincorporation back into, 162, *162*, 172
in rites of passage, 161–62, 165, 172–74
separation from, 162, *162*
threefold formula for entrance into,
   46–47, 56, 71, 73, 109, 226–27n46
women ascetics/lay disciples in, 46,
   81–83, 172, 174
cosmogony, 143–44, 148
cosmological framework for life of the
   Buddha, 140–59, *146, 148*
cosmic evolution in, 6–8, 184–87
   and "fall" from paradise, 7–8, 184–87
   mind-born beings in, 6–7, 153, 184
cosmic space in, 5–6, 9, 146–48, *146*
   highest sphere of (Formless Sphere),
      5, 146–47, *146*
   lowest sphere of (Sphere of Sense-
      Desire), 5–6, 146–47, *146*
   middle sphere of (Sphere of Form
      Only), 5–6, 146–47, *146*
evidence for, 2, 135–36
and gift giving, 202–3
and Great Agents, 184–87, 189–90,
   195, 198
maps of, 142, 151, 156–57, 159, 196
oppositional syntax in, 121–22,
   149–59, *151*
and rites of passage, 166–67
"Cosmology and the Great Declaration," 147
creationism, 120
creepers, 6–7, 16
Cunda, 93, 98–99, 144, 159, 203,
   209–12, 229n98

Dalhanemi, 188, 190–92
danadharma, 207
Dartmouth College, 166–67
Davids, Rhys, 179
Davidson, Donald, 113, 181
Deer Park, 41, 44–45, 57, 140
Depankara (the Conqueror), 9–10, 67
Devadatta, 70, 85–89, 197–98
Dhammaka, Mount, 9
Dhammapada, 124, 225n37
Dhamma Palace, 104–5, 168–69,
   172–73, 193, 214
Dhatarattha, King (ruler of the East),
   6, 150, 152
Digha Nikaya. See *Long Discourses, The*
Dipankara, 9–10, 67
"Discourse on the Marks of No-Self,
   The," 44–45
Doctrine. *See also* Eightfold Path;
      interdependent origination; karma
   Anathapindika's knowledge of, 72,
      83–84
   Angulimala's knowledge of, 78–79
   and the Buddha as teacher, 40–46,
      52–53, 226n42–44
   and the Buddha's last days, 91–96, 98
   and the Buddha's miraculous power,
      50, 52, 56
   and the Buddha's rules, 60–64
   in cosmological framework, 136, 145, 152
   Dalhanemi's knowledge of, 188
   and Devadatta, 86–89
   "Discourse on the Marks of No-Self,
      The," 44–45
   "Fire Sermon, The," 53–54
   Four Noble Truths, 45, 77, 89, 109,
      130, 170
   of impermanence, 42, 44–45, 52–53,
      105, 147, 168, 173, 185–86, 226n42
   and lay disciples, 40, 46, 56, 64, 73,
      83, 87–88, 95, 136, 152, 165
   and Mahapajapati, 81–83
   as Middle Way, 42, 44, 53

Doctrine (*continued*)

"Mirror of the Doctrine, The," 95

in quest for historical Buddha, 124, 130, 139–41

Sariputta's knowledge of, 89, 91–94

and Subhadda (ascetic), 109

"Turning of the Wheel of Doctrine, The," 41–44

wrong views of, 8, 36–37, 52, 77, 86–89, 94, 175

Dona, 111

drought, 80–81, 228n80

Durkheim, Émile, 116, 117, 180

dvi-ja (ritual of being twice-born), 163–64

East

and the Buddha in Patalagama, 95

and the Buddha's funeral, 110, 156, 169

and the Buddha's miraculous power, 66

in cosmological framework, 146, 148, 149–52, 154–56, 159

and Dhamma Palace, 104

Dhatarattha rules over, 6, 150

gate of Kapilavatthu, 27

in Gotama's quest for enlightenment, 28, 30, 33–35, 154–55, 172, 196

in Queen Maya's dream, 21

in rites of passage, 164, 169, 172

of tree of enlightenment, 34–35, 172

and wheel-turning monarchs, 102

Eightfold Path

and the Buddha as teacher, 42–43, 52, 77, 109

in cosmological framework, 144–45

Devadatta's search for, 85

and Great Agents, 186–87, 195

in quest for historical Buddha, 127, 130

and rites of passage, 170, 218

Sariputta's knowledge of, 89

Sumedha's search for, 9

Eight Major Rules for nuns, 82–83, 228n82

elephants

in Amara, 9

Elephant-Treasure, 102

glorious white rain-making, 12–14, 169, 195, 214

Kaludayin's description of, 65

of Mara, 34–35

Nalagiri (man-slaying elephant), 88

in Queen Maya's dream, 21

of Sanjaya, 18

Eliade, Mircea, 116

Enlightened One. *See* the Buddha

enlightenment

and the Buddha as Great Agent, 182–84, 187, 190–91, 196, 199

and the Buddha as teacher, 39, 41–45, 76–77

and the Buddha's last days, 97–99, 211

and the Buddha's visit home, 66–68

in cosmological framework, 145, 154–57

of Devadatta, 85

fourfold meditation as prelude to, 35–36, 43, 168, 224n33

and gift giving, 203, 211, 217

Gotama's quest for, 28–31, 33–34, 129, 145, 155–56, 169, 173

and last watch, 107–9

of Mahasudassana, 168–69, 173

omniscience as knowledge gained at, 16, 216, 223n16

of Pasenadi, 73

and prophecy at birth of the Buddha, 23, 139

in quest for historical Buddha, 137–38

as rite of passage, 167–75

of Sankha, 184

and Sariputta and Moggallana, 91–93, 95

of Suddhodana, 81

Sumedha's search for, 9

tree of (*see* tree of enlightenment)

of Vessantara, 15–16, 170–71, 173, 216–17

Vipassi's quest for, 139

Enlightenment, era of, 119, 123
Essai sur le don (Mauss), 205
evil
    and the Buddha as teacher, 42–43
    Devadatta as, 85–87, 89
    and "fall" from paradise, 7–8, 184,
        189, 192
    and Gotama's quest for
        enlightenment, 25
    and Great Agents, 184, 189–90, 192
    and karma, 144–45
    Sumedha's meditation on, 9
    and warrior caste, 59–60
evolution versus creationism, 120

"Fire Sermon, The," 53–54
five aggregates, 44–45, 226n44
Five Precepts of asceticism, 184, 186–87,
    192–93
forest. *See* wilderness
Foundations of Buddhism, The (Gethin),
    132–33
Founder, 128–30, 132, 137, 177. *See also*
    the Buddha
fourfold meditation, 35–36, 43, 168,
    224n37
four forces, 37, 224n37
Four Great Kings
    and bowls for the Buddha's food, 40
    and the Buddha as teacher, 44
    and the Buddha's miraculous power, 50
    in cosmological framework, 147, 150,
        152, 158–59
    dwelling place of, 147
    and Great Agents, 188–89
    at Great Sudhamma Hall meeting,
        150, 159
    in Queen Maya's dream, 21–22
    in quest for historical Buddha, 139
    and rites of passage, 169
    and Vipassi, 139
Four Noble Truths, 45, 77, 89, 109,
    130, 170

Freud, Sigmund, 116, 174, 180
functionalist theories of myth/religion,
    116–17, 120–21, 230n120

Gabled Hall of the Great Grove, 81, 98
Ganges River, 80, 85, 95, 103, 151, 159,
    196, 198
Gethin, Rupert, 132–33
Gift, The (Mauss), 205
gift giving, 201–19
    of Ambapali, 96, 212
    of Anathapindika, 72–73, 158, 212–13
    of Bimbisara, 56–57, 74, 212
    the Buddha's rules for, 61, 63, 207,
        209, 212, 216, 227n64
    in cosmological framework, 136,
        153–54, 157–59
    of Cunda, 93, 98–99, 144, 159, 203,
        209–12, 229n98
    and Great Agents, 186, 189, 193–94,
        196 (*see also under names of Great
        Agents*)
    of householders, 61, 68, 73, 207–9,
        212–14, 216
    and karma, 145, 203, 207–10, 212–16,
        218–19
    of Mahasudassana, 104, 168–69
    and Mara, 35
    Mauss on, 204–10, 216, 233nn204–205
    and origin theories, 206
    Pasenadi's knowledge of, 74
    perfection of, 15–19, 153–54, 170–71,
        193, 218, 223n16
    and reciprocity, 204–10, 212–13
    to renouncers, 203–4, 207–10, 213
    in rites of passage, 164, 168–71, 213–14
    ritual of, 16–17, 57, 73, 171, 212–13,
        217–18
    at Sanci memorial shrine, 136
    of seven hundred, 13–14, 169
    "spiritual mechanisms" of, 205–7
    of Sujata, 30–31, 144, 154, 202–3, 209,
        211, 223n30

gift giving (*continued*)
  of Universal Monarchs, 201–3, 211,
      213–14, 217–19 (*see also under*
      names of Universal Monarchs)
  of Upali, 70
  of Vessantara, 12–19, 35, 153–54,
      157, 169–72, 193, 195–96, 206,
      216–18
Gombrich, Richard F., 178, 230n126
Gotama (name of the Buddha before his
    awakening), 3
  as Alara Kalama's student, 28, 35, 41
  as ascetic, 27–31, 154, 172, 196, 202
  under banyan tree, 30–31, 39
  in cosmological framework, 153–57
  desire for liberation from rebirth,
      27–29, 34–37, 224–25nn33, 37
  father's fear of his becoming ascetic,
      24–26
  food for, 29, 30–31, 211
  as householder, 23–27, 202
  meditation of, 28–29, 33–37, 155–57,
      224–25n37
  quest for enlightenment of, 28–31,
      33–35, 129, 153–57, 168–69, 172,
      196, 202, 211, 217
  in quest for historical Buddha, 125–29,
      133–34, 137, 140–41
  and rites of passage, 23, 168, 171–72, 175
  under rose-apple tree, 29, 66
  and sensuous pleasure, 24–25, 35, 37
  students of, 29, 31
  Sumedha's future as, 9–10
  and Ten Perfections, 34–35
  tours of parks outside city, 24–26,
      168, 195
  as Uddaka Ramaputta's student, 28, 41
  views of sickness, old age, and death,
      24–26, 35, 195
  during watches of night, 36–37, 146–47,
      155–56, 172, 217, 224–25n37
Great Agents, 177–200
  and ascetics, 183–93, 195–98, 200

the Buddha as, 35, 121–22, 139, 177–88,
      190–92, 194–200, 214
  celibate life of, 186, 192–93, 195
  karma of, 180, 182–83, 185–87
  and paradise, 184–86
  in quest for historical Buddha, 139
  rebirths of, 183–84, 189–90, 194
  as renouncers, 181–86, 190, 192–96,
      198–200
  and rites of passage, 172–74
  as teachers, 195, 197 (*see also* the
      Buddha, as teacher)
  thirty-two marks of, 23, 139, 179,
      181–83, 187, 223n23, 232n183
  Universal Monarchs as, 121–22,
      177–80, 184–97, 199–200, 214,
      231n178, 232n183
  Vessantara as, 15–16, 171, 179, 191–96,
      199, 214, 217–18
  wheel-turning monarchs as, 181,
      183–84, 194–95, 230n101
Great Sudhamma Hall, 150, 159

Harris, Roy, 137
Harvey, Peter, 131, 135
heavens, 6, 146, 147. *See also* Tushita
    (fourth heaven)
  and rebirths of Great Agents, 184
  Tavatimsa (second heaven), 6, 146,
      147–48
    home of thirty-three gods, 11–12, 22,
      94, 104, 146, 147, 150, 159
  Yama (third heaven), 147
hells, 6, 8, 33, 89, 94, 146, 147, 154
Himavant, Mount, 9
Hinayana Buddhism, 199
Hinduism
  caste system in, 208
  and cosmological framework, 145,
      149, 151
  creation story of, 208
  gift giving in, 207–8
  and karma, 2, 207–8

and quest for historical Buddha,
124–26
rites of passage in, 163–64
and transmigration, 2, 208
and Vedas, 9–10, 148–49, 222n9
historical Buddha, quest for, 121,
123–42
"absurd" to deny existence of,
125–26, 129
and authentic sayings of the Buddha,
121, 124, 127–29
"bare outline" of, 125, 134, 137–40
and chronology of the Buddha,
125–26, 134–35
concept of teacher in, 124, 130
and cosmological framework, 155,
158–59
"demythologization" of documents
for, 124
Doctrine in, 124, 130
Eightfold Path in, 127, 130
Great Agents in, 177–80, 185–86,
197–98
importance of Founder in, 128–30,
132, 137, 177–78
and "interlocking" of legends, 178, 186
lack of evidence for, 125–26, 128–29,
131–37
lack of records on social conditions for,
125–26, 180
lost text as source for, 129, 131–33, 137
and myths, 125–26, 131–35, 137
and origin theories, 123–25, 127–29,
134–35, 159, 179–80, 185
and "popular Buddhism," 130–32,
136–37, 149
received tradition for, 126–36, 141,
178–79, 201–2
and rites of passage, 167
superhuman agents in, 128, 130, 141,
177–79
symbolic/transcendent meaning in,
132–33, 179–81

texts for, 124–40, 179 (see also Agama;
Pali Buddhist scriptures; names
of texts)
Historical Buddha, The (Schumann), 135
historical Jesus, quest for, 124, 127
History of Indian Buddhism (Lamotte), 129
homelessness. See also ascetics;
renouncers
and Angulimala, 79–80
and the Buddha as teacher, 41, 45
the Buddha's rules for, 61
and Great Agents, 182–83, 186, 188, 191
and Mahapajapati, 81–83
and Vipassi, 139
and Yasa, 45
householders
Anathapindika as, 71, 73, 83, 158
becoming ascetic, 8, 59
Bhaddiya as, 70
with Bimbisara, 55
and Brahmin's prediction concerning
the Buddha, 22, 139
the Buddha as teacher of, 39–42,
45–46
and the Buddha's rules, 59, 61, 64,
227n59
and the Buddha's visit home, 68
in cosmological framework, 136, 153,
157–58
gift giving of, 61, 68, 73, 203–4,
208–9, 212–14, 216
Gotama as, 23–27
Great Agents as, 181–83, 188, 191,
198–200 (see also under names of
Great Agents)
Mahanama as, 69–70
Mahasudassana as, 103–5, 172
Malunkyaputta as, 75
Nobleman-Treasure as, 103
in opposition to renouncers, 3–4, 121,
136, 153, 173, 178, 182–83, 185,
188, 198–201, 203–4, 213, 218
as part of communal system, 118, 203

householders (*continued*)
  in quest for historical Buddha, 130–32, 139, 141
  rites of passage of, 162, *162*, 165–66, 172–73
  vow taken by at beginning of day, 226–27n46
  Yasa's father as, 45–46
Huxley, Andrew, 231–32n178

ignorance
  the Buddha as remover of, 22, 182–83, 209
  and the Buddha as teacher, 39–40, 45, 53, 226n42–44
  and the Buddha's awakening, 36–37, 39, 224–25n33
  and Gotama's quest for enlightenment, 25
immortality, drink of, 150–51
immortal soul, denial of, 2, 44–45, 144, 146–47, 208
impermanence
  and the Buddha as teacher, 42, 44–45, 52–53, 226n42
  and cosmological framework, 147
  and Great Agents, 185–86
  and Mahasudassana, 105, 168
  and rites of passage, 168, 173
Indra. *See* Sakka
instincts, 115–16
interdependent origination
  and cosmological framework, 148
  and karma, 145
  Mahasudassana's knowledge of, 195
  in quest for historical Buddha, 124, 138–39
  Sariputta's knowledge of, 89
  and twelvefold links of dependent origination, 37, 39, 56–58, 71, 76, 224n37, 227n57
irony, 137, 143, 179–80, 194, 197
Isipatana, 45
Islam, 143–44, 162, 177

Jali, Prince (Vessantara's son), 12, 14, 16, 18, 169–71, 196, 214–17
Jambudipa (India and Kapilavatthu), 21, 150, *151*, 159, 198. *See also* Kapilavatthu; South
Jataka (legends of Buddha's former births), 2, 135, 223n11
Jesus, 118, 124, 127
Jeta, Prince, 72, 158, 212
Jeta Grove, 1, 4–5, 72–73, 75, 79, 83–84, 93, 138, 181, 212–13
Jetavana. *See* Jeta Grove
Jetuttara, 11–12, 14, 18–19
Jewel Protection Utterance, 81, 228n80
jokes/joking, 113, 143, 179–80, 184
Judaism, 143–44, 164
Jujaka, 15, 18

Kakusandha, Lord Buddha, 138
Kakuttha river, 98
Kalinga, 12, 15
Kaludayin, 58, 65–66
Kanhajina (Vessantara's daughter), 12, 14–16, 18, 169–71, 196, 214–17
Kanthaka (Gotama's horse), 27–28, 196
Kapilavatthu
  the Buddha's visit to, 58, 65–70
  in cosmological framework, 157, 159
  Gotama's birth/early life in, 21–28, 122
  and Suddhodana's death, 81
Kappa/Vappa, 41, 44
karma (doctrine of life as births, deaths, and rebirths), 2. *See also* merit
  of Angulimala, 145
  of the Buddha, 24, 145, 169, 174
  in cosmological framework, 136, 141, 144–45
  of Devadatta, 88
  and fatalism, 145
  and gift giving, 145, 203, 207–10, 212–16, 218–19
  Gotama's knowledge of, 21, 36–37, 224–25n37
  of Great Agents, 180, 182–83, 185–87, 190

in Hinduism, 2, 207–8
of Mahasudassana, 169, 173
of Moggallana, 94, 145, 174
of Nobleman-Treasure, 103
and omniscience, 16, 216, 223n16
Pasenadi's knowledge of, 74
responsibility for our actions, 80,
    144–45, 228n80
and rites of passage, 164, 167, 169,
    173–75
of Sariputta, 174
of Vipassi, 139
as wheel, 23, 39, 41, 44, 108, 144 (see
    also wheel-turning monarchs)
Kassapa, Lord Buddha, 138
Kassapa of Gaya, 52–54
Kassapa of Uruvela, 49–56, 67, 85, 110–11
Kattika, month of (October/November), 93
Khanda, Prince (Vipassi's half
    brother), 140
Kimbila, 70
Koliyas, 28
Konagamana, Lord Buddha, 138
Konkani/Kondanna, 41, 44
Kosala, 73–74
Kosambi, 86
Kotigama, 95
Krishna, 118, 124–26
kula rituals, 205
Kumbha Mela (Hindu ritual), 151
Kuru. See Uttarakuru (Kuru)
Kusavati, 101–5, 159, 167–68, 170. See
    also Kusinara
Kusinara, 98, 101, 107, 109–10, 151,
    159, 172

LaFleur, William, 131, 135, 137
Lamotte, Étienne, 3, 129–30, 132, 134,
    140–41
laziness, 7, 74, 184, 186–87, 192
legends. See myths
Lévi-Strauss, Claude, 181–82, 206
liberation from rebirth
    Anathapindika's knowledge of, 71

Angulimala's knowledge of, 79–80
and the Buddha as teacher, 39–43, 47,
    52–53
and the Buddha's last days, 95–99,
    203, 211–12
for citizens of Nadika, 150
in cosmological framework, 136,
    140–41, 150, 151, 154, 157
and gift giving, 203, 211–12, 216, 218
Gotama's quest for, 27–29, 34–37, 172,
    224–25n33–37
and Great Agents, 186, 195–96
and Kassapa of Uruvela, 51
and last watch, 107–10
of Mahapajapati, 174
Malunkyaputta's knowledge of, 75–76
Pasenadi's knowledge of, 74
in quest for historical Buddha, 131–32,
    136, 140–41
and rites of passage, 170, 172, 174
and ritual of liberation, 64, 227n64
and Sariputta and Moggallana, 57,
    91–93, 174
Sumedha's meditation on, 9
and "the fruit of the nonreturner," 68
Licchavi, 80–81, 96
Life of Jesus (Strauss), 127
liminality, 161–63, 162, 166–72, 186,
    199, 213–14, 217
"Lion's Roar on the Turning of the
    Wheel, The," 188, 190, 194
Long Discourses, The (Digha Nikaya),
    138–40, 150, 178, 196, 198, 221
    "Great Discourse on Origination,
        The," 138
    "Great Discourse on the Lineage, The,"
        138, 141
    "Great Passing the the Buddha's Last
        Day, The," 138
    "Lion's Roar on the Turning of the
        Wheel, The," 188, 190, 194
    "Marks of a Great Agent, The," 179,
        181–88
Lumbina, 22–23

Madda, King, 11–12

Maddi (Vessantara's wife), 12–18, 169–71, 196, 214–18

Magadha, 28, 50, 55, 59, 73, 150, 197–98

Mahanama (Anuruddha's brother), 69–70

Mahapajapati (the Buddha's stepmother), 3, 23, 81–83, 169, 172, 174

Mahapurisa ("great person"), 223n23

Maharaja/Mahanama, 41, 44

Mahasammata, King, 8, 185

Mahasudassana, King, 101–6
   in cosmological framework, 157, 159
   and Dhamma Palace, 104–5, 168–69, 172–73, 193
   enlightenment of, 168–69, 173
   gift giving of, 104, 168–69, 213–14
   lotus ponds of, 103, 168
   meditation of, 104, 157, 168–69, 172–73, 195
   rebirth of, 105, 168
   as renouncer, 157, 169, 172–73, 214
   and rites of passage, 167–70, 172–73, 214
   tours of parks outside city, 103, 168–69
   as Universal Monarch, 101–6, 159, 168–69, 179, 192–95

Mahavadanasutra, 141

Mahavastu, 194

Mahayana Buddhism, 187, 199–200, 232–33n199

Malinowski, Bronislaw, 188, 198

Mallas, 28, 109–11, 156

Mallika (Pasenadi's wife), 74

Malunkyaputta, 75–76

Manu, 23

Maori proverb, 206

Mara (the tempter)
   abode in Yama (third heaven), 147
   and the Buddha's last days, 97–99, 106, 229n91
   and Gotama's quest for enlightenment, 34–35, 153, 157, 172–73
   and Great Agents, 183

Mardi Gras, 162

"Marks of a Great Agent, The," 179, 181–88

Marx, Karl, 180–81

Mauss, Maurice, 204–10, 216, 233n205

Maya, Queen, 10, 21–23
   conversion of, 83, 147

meditation
   of Alara Kalama, 28, 35
   of Bimbisara, 64
   and Brahmins in cosmic evolution, 8
   of the Buddha, 92, 110, 146–47, 150, 156, 170, 172, 195
   in cosmological framework, 146–47
   fourfold, 35–36, 43, 168, 224n37
   of Gotama, 28–29, 33–37, 155–57, 224–25n33–37
   of Mahasudassana, 104, 157, 168–69, 172–73, 195
   of Malunkyaputta, 75
   of Queen Maya, 22
   Sariputta's knowledge of, 89, 92
   of Sumedha, 9
   of Uddaka Ramaputta, 35
   of Universal Monarchs, 146, 156, 187, 194
   of Vessantara, 173

mendicants, 28–29, 31, 41–44, 46, 51

merchants
   Anathapindika as, 71–74, 158, 212
   becoming ascetic, 8, 59
   caste of (Vaishyas), 8
   Tapussa and Bhallika as, 40
   Vessantara as son of, 12, 169, 195
   Yasa as son of, 45–46

merit. *See also* karma
   and Ananda, 109
   and Anathapindika, 158, 213
   and Bimbisara, 57
   and Bodhisattvas, 199, 232n185
   and the Buddha, 12
   and Cunda, 99, 203, 211
   for gift giving, 15, 17, 31, 40, 57, 68, 136, 145, 208–16, 219

and Gotama, 24, 31, 202
and Hinduism, 151
and Kaludayin, 65
for memorials, 108, 136, 158
and Phusati, 11
and rites of passage, 164–66
rules for, 61
and Sujata, 31, 202
and Sumedha, 9
and Vessantara, 15, 17, 171, 206, 215
Meru, Mount (Mount Sineru), 6, 21, 146,
    147–49, *148*, 155
metaphor, 113, 127, 132–33, 170, 179–80,
    224n37
Metteyya (the future Buddha), 184,
    190–91, 231–32n178
Middle Way, 42, 44, 53
Milinda, King, 215–16
"Mirror of the Doctrine, The," 95
Moggallana
    and the Buddha as teacher, 138
    and the Buddha's funeral, 110
    and the Buddha's visit home, 65, 67
    and the Buddha's visit to Tushita, 83
    death of, 94–95, 145, 174
    and Devadatta, 86, 89
    karma of, 94, 145, 174
    at Rajagaha, 57–58, 85–86, 89, 91
    Tavatimsa as home of, 147
"Mohammadanism," 177
monastic rules, 128, 184, 212. *See also* the
    Buddha, rules of
monotheistic religions, 143–44, 162, 164
Moses, 118
Mucalinda, 39–40
Mucalinda, Lake, 18
Muhammad, 118
myths. *See also* religion; rituals
    communal system of, 118, 163
    and "demythologization" of
        documents, 124, 177–78
    functionalist theories of, 116–17,
        120–21, 207, 210, 230n120

"genesis" myths, 191–92
and Great Agents, 179–81, 188,
    198–200
and historical Buddha, quest for,
    125–26, 131–35, 137, 141–42
as language, 114–15, 155, 179–80
as libretto of rituals, 167
literal sense of, 4, 113–16, 119–21, 155,
    180–81, 211
meaning of, 115–20, 123, 155, 163, 173,
    180, 188
narrative constraint in, 121–22, 140–42,
    149, 153, 156, 158–59, 177, 191, 193,
    198, 201–3, 209
as narrative of superhuman agents,
    117–19, 121, 155, 163, 188
oppositional syntax in, 118, 121–22,
    140–42, 145, 149–59, *151*
as oral traditions, 2, 118
as primary, original expressions, 123
"rational but false" theory of, 119–21
relativist view of, 116, 119, 210
and rites of passage, 163, 167
symbolic/transcendent meaning of,
    4, 115–16, 119–20, 132–33, 155,
    179–81, 211
as system of propositional attitudes,
    117–20, 163, 202, 210
truth content of (*see* truth conditions of
    language)
in "underdeveloped" cultures, 116,
    120–21

Nadika, 95, 150
Naga (venemous snake with
    superhuman power), 49–50
Nagasena, 215–16
Nalagiri (man-slaying elephant), 88
Nalanda, 91, 93
Nanda (the Buddha's half-brother),
    67–68
Nandabala, 223n30. *See also* Sujata
Nanda memorial for Dipankara, 10

Nandana (pleasure garden), 11
Neranjara, 28
Nigrodha Grove, 65, 81
Nikaya, 129. See also *Long Discourses,
    The (Digha Nikaya)*
Niraya hell, 89
nobles, caste of. *See* warrior caste
Non-Returners, 92
nonviolence, principle of, 178, 188,
    190–91, 194, 196, 198
Norman, K. R., 126, 143
Norm of Truth, 188–91
North. *See also* Uttarakuru (Kuru)
    and the Buddha's funeral, 110, 156
    and the Buddha's last days, 96, 101, 158
    and the Buddha's miraculous power,
        50, 66
    and the Buddha's visit home, 196
    in cosmological framework, *146, 148,*
        149–50, 152–54, 156–59
    and Dhamma Palace, 104
    gate of Jetuttara, 13
    in Gotama's quest for enlightenment,
        33–34, 154
    and Great Agents, 196–99
    Kuvera rules over, 6
    and last watch, 107
    Mara's army coming from, 34
    in Queen Maya's dream, 21
    in quest for historical Buddha, 139
    in rites of passage, 164, 168–70, 172–73
    and Vaijjians, 197
    and Vessantara, 14, 153–54, 157,
        169–70, 172, 196
    and Vipassi's birth, 139
    and wheel-turning monarchs, 102
nothingness, 28, 83
nuns
    rules for, 82–83, 227n64, 228n82
    and Sanci memorial shrine, 136

observance days, 64
omniscience (knowledge gained at
    enlightenment), 16, 216, 223n16

Once-Returners, 92, 95, 150
oral traditions, 2, 118
Otto, Rudolf, 181

Pali Buddhist scriptures
    and cosmological framework, 143, 145,
        150, 153
    Long Discourses, The (Digha Nikaya),
        138–40, 150, 178–79, 188, 198, 221
    Nikaya, 129
    and quest for historical Buddha, 124–25,
        130, 135–36, 138, 141–42
    and Sanci memorial shrine, 136
    Tipitaka (The Three Baskets), 1–3, 124,
        129–30, 159, 165, 221,
    and Universal Monarch, 178–79
Pali language, 1, 115, 129,
Pali Text Society, 3, 179
parables, 5, 179, 184
paradise
    Dhamma Palace as, 214
    "fall" from, 7–8, 184–87
    and Gotama's quest for
        enlightenment, 28
    and Great Agents, 169, 184–87,
        190–91, 198, 200
    Jetuttara as, 194
    Kapilavatthu as, 23–24
    in Sakka's heavenly sphere, 22
    Uttarakuru (Kuru) as, 50, 153–54, 157,
        159, 168
    wilderness (forest) as, 14–15, 157, 163,
        170, 185, 193, 217
Parry, Jonathan, 193, 207
Pasenadi, King, 73–75, 77, 79, 209
    problem with weight, 74–75
Patalagama, 95
Pava, 98, 110, 151, 159
Perfected Ones. *See* the Buddha;
        Universal Monarchs
perfect happiness *(nibbana),* 4, 9, 28, 71,
        144, 199, 216, 222n9, 223n16
phonemes, 163, 182
Phusati, 11–12, 18

pilgrimages, 156, 162

"popular Buddhism," 130–32, 136–37, 149

"pork special," 98–99, 210–11, 229n98

potlatch, 206

Problem of the Determination of the Date of the Historical Buddha, The" (1988 conference), 134

propositional attitudes, 117–20, 163, 202, 210

protection

  for the Buddha by king of serpents, 39, 172

  for the Buddha's mother, 22, 139

  and Great Agents, 188, 190–91, 194

  protective verses (paritta)

    in cosmological framework, 151–53

    Jewel Protection Utterance, 81, 228n80

    for pregnant women, 79

    in rites of passage, 165

    unnecessary for the Buddha, 88

Pubbavadeha, 150, 151. See also East

punishment, 7–8, 13, 167, 185, 187, 190–92

Punna (Sujata's maid), 30, 202

Pure Abode, gods of, 140

Questions of King Milinda, The, 214–15

Rahula (the Buddha's son), 24, 26–27, 67–68, 172

rainy season

  and the Buddha as teacher, 47

  the Buddha in Tushita for, 83

  the Buddha's rules for, 63–64, 108

  and Devadatta's rules, 89

  Great Sudhamma Hall meeting held in, 150, 159

  and Kaludayin, 58

  and Mahanama and Anuruddha, 69

  at Rajagaha, 58, 63–64, 71

  rules for nuns in, 228n82

  at Savatthi, 72, 93

  and Yasa, 45

Rajagaha

  and Anathapindika, 71

  Bamboo Grove in, 55, 57–64, 89, 212

  Bimbisara as king of, 55–57

  and the Buddha's last days, 101

  in cosmological framework, 151, 152, 158–59, 231n153

  Devadatta at, 85–88

  protective verses used in, 152

  and Sariputta and Moggallana, 57, 69, 93–94

  Vultures Peak near, 64, 88, 91, 97, 152, 196

Rajayatana tree, 40

Rama, 124–26

Ray, Reginald, 126

rebirth. See also liberation from rebirth

  and Alara's teachings, 28

  of the Buddha, 21–22, 139–41

  and doctrine of karma (see karma)

  and gift giving, 215

  of Great Agents, 183–84, 189–90, 194

  of Mahasudassana, 105, 168

  of Phusati, 11

  of Sujata, 202

  of Vessantara, 18–19, 169, 171, 194, 196, 215

reciprocity, 204–10, 212–13

reincorporation rites, 162, 162, 164, 167, 171–73

religion. See also myths; rituals

  and bloodshed, 120, 125

  communal system of, 117, 163, 167, 202–3

  comparisons of Buddhism to monotheistic religions, 143–44

  functionalist theories of, 116–17, 120–21, 230n120

  meaning of, 115–18, 155, 163, 202

  as nonrational, 119–20, 163

  origin theories of, 123–24

  as prescientific stage of knowledge, 123

  quest for origin of, 121, 123, 128

religion (*continued*)
  "rational but false" theory of, 119–20, 123
  relationship to superhuman agents, 117–19, 163
  relativist view of, 116, 119, 210
  symbolic/transcendent meaning of, 119–20, 123, 132–33, 155
  as system of propositional attitudes, 117–20, 163, 202, 210
  truth content of (*see* truth conditions of language)
renouncers, 3. *See also* ascetics; homelessness
  Angulimala as, 228n77
  Anuruddha as, 70
  the Buddha as, 3, 28, 122, 153, 157, 169, 178, 194, 196, 202, 204
  and the Buddha as teacher, 42, 46
  and the Buddha's visit home, 65, 67–70
  in cosmological framework, 136, 141, 157
  gift giving to, 203–4, 207–10, 213, 218
  Gotama as, 28, 157, 202
  Great Agents as, 181–86, 188, 190–96, 198–200 (*see also under names of Great Agents*)
  at Jetavana, 72–73, 75–76
  Kaludayin as, 58
  Kondanna as, 44
  Mahapajapati as, 3, 81–82, 169, 174
  Mahasudassana as, 157, 169, 172–73, 214
  Malunkyaputta as, 75–76
  in opposition to householders, 3–4, 121, 136, 153, 173, 178, 182–83, 185, 188, 198–201, 203–4, 213, 218
  Pasenadi's knowledge of, 73–74
  and prophecy at the Buddha's birth, 22, 25, 66, 122, 139
  in quest for historical Buddha, 136, 141
  at Rajagaha, 56–59, 61
  rites of passage of, 162, 165–66, 169, 173
  role of in the Buddha's teachings, 42, 44–46
  and Vessantara, 15, 157, 173, 193, 218

  vow taken by at beginning of day, 226–27n46
  Yasa as, 46
Rites de Passage (van Gennep), 161
rites of passage, 157, 161–75, 162. *See also* rituals
  of the Buddha, 167–75
  gift giving in, 164, 168–71, 213–14
  of Gotama, 23, 168, 171
  of Great Agents, 172–74
  in Hinduism, 163–64
  at liberal arts colleges, 166–67
  of Mahasudassana, 167–70, 172–73
  as oppositional sets, 118, 163, 168–75
  received tradition for, 174
  and "son of the Buddha" initiation rite, 164–66, 173, 212–13
  superhuman agents in, 161, 163, 167, 171, 174
  in Thailand, 164–66
  three parts of, 161–63, 162, 166–72, 174, 186, 213–14
    liminal, 161–63, 162, 166–72, 186, 199, 213–14, 217
    postliminal, 161–63, 162, 170, 186, 214
    preliminal, 161–63, 162, 169–70, 172, 186, 214
  of Vessantara, 163, 167, 169–73, 218
rituals. *See also* myths; religion
  and ascetics, 49–51, 56–57
  and Brahmins, 22–23, 229n98
  in the Buddha's funeral, 156
  and the Buddha's rules, 63–64
  communal system of, 118, 161
  in cosmological framework, 142, 151, 154, 156
  and Devadatta's rules, 88–89
  functionalist theories of, 165
  of gift giving, 16–17, 57, 73, 171, 205, 208, 212–13, 217–18
  of Great Agents, 102, 168, 187–90, 192
  in Hinduism, 208

of initiation, 23, 164–66, 173
involving superhuman agents, 118–19,
    161, 167, 171, 174
kula rituals, 205
Kumbha Mela (Hindu), 151
meaning of, 115–18, 123, 161, 173
for naming, 23, 164
as nonrational, 163
for nuns, 228n82
as oppositional sets, 118, 163
and origin theories, 124
of plowing, 29
Protection Ritual, 81, 228n80
and Queen Maya, 21–22
reincorporation rite as, 162, *162*, 164,
    167, 171–73
rites of passage as, 157, 161–68,
    171–74, 186, 213–14
ritual of liberation, 64, 227n64
and Sanci memorial shrine, 136
separation rite as, 162, *162*, 164, 166,
    168–69, 172
and Subhadda (ascetic), 109
and Sumedha, 9
syntax of, 167
and threefold formula for entrance into
    community, 46–47, 226–27n46
Uposatha ritual, 102, 168, 192
use of language in, 165
ritual specialists, 8, 23, 138, 164, 208
Robbers Cliff, 97
Romanticism, 119, 123
rose-apple tree, shadow of, 29, 66

Sakka (Indra) (king of all deities)
    aid to Mahasudassana, 104, 157
    aid to Vessantara, 14, 17, 19, 153–54,
        169–70, 193–94, 203, 218
    army overrun by Mara, 34
    and the Buddha's miraculous power, 50
    causing animals to flee from Vesala, 81
    as chief of the thirty-three gods, 2–3,
        12, 169
in cosmological framework, 153–54,
    157–59
disguised as Brahmin, 17, 56, 171,
    217–18
as follower of the Doctrine, 154
and Gotama's birth, 12
and Gotama's quest for
    enlightenment, 202
at Great Sudhamma Hall meeting,
    150, 159
Mahasammata as ancestor of, 8
orders to Vissakamma from, 9, 14,
    104, 170
Phusati as chief queen of, 11–12
Tavatimsa as home of, 6, 12, *146*, 147
Sakyamuni (name of the Buddha), 3,
    129, 141. *See also* Gotama
Sakyans, 8, 21, 23, 28, 122
    and the Buddha's visit home, 65–66,
        70–71
    women with Mahapajapati, 82
sal-trees, 98, 107
Sanci memorial shrine, 2, 135–36
Sanjaya (ascetic), 57–58
Sanjaya, King (Vessantara's father),
    11–13, 18–19, 171
Sankha, King, 184, 190–91, 231–32n178
Sanskrit, 1, 129, 147, 200
Sariputta
    and the Buddha as teacher, 138
    and the Buddha's funeral, 110
    and the Buddha's visit home, 67–68
    and the Buddha's visit to Tushita, 83
    conversation of with the Buddha,
        91–93
    death of, 93–95, 174
    and Devadatta, 86–87, 89
    karma of, 174
    Nalanda as home of, 91, 93
    at Rajagaha, 57–58, 85–87, 89
    visit to Anathapindika, 83–84
Satapanni Cave, 97
Saussure, Ferdinand de, 182

Savatthi, 1, 5, 71–75, 77, 79–80, 83, 93, 101, 138

Schopen, Gregory, 136

Schumann, H. W., 135

self, denial of, 2, 44–45, 144, 146–47, 174–75, 208

sensuous pleasure/sensual desire. *See also* sexual activity/misconduct
  and the Buddha as teacher, 40, 42–43, 45–46, 74
  in cosmological framework, 7, 146–47, 146, 153, 156, 184, 187, 189
  and Gotama as householder, 24–25, 35, 37
  and Great Agents, 184, 187, 189, 195
  and Vessantara, 15, 170–71, 173

sentence meaning, 113–15, 119, 180–81

separation rites, 162, 162, 164, 166, 168–69, 172

serpents
  the Buddha's rules for, 61–62
  Mucalinda, 39, 172
  Naga, 49–50

Seventh World Sanskrit Conference (Leiden 1987), 126

sexual activity/misconduct. *See also* sensuous pleasure/sensual desire
  the Buddha's rules for, 42, 62
  in cosmological framework, 184, 186
  and rites of passage, 161, 170
  Universal Monarch's rules for, 102–3, 189

Sidhattha (name of the Buddha), 3

Sikhi, Lord Buddha, 138

silence
  of the Buddha, 56, 57, 71, 83, 95, 96, 209, 212
  of Maddi, 17
  of Mahasudassana, 104
  of monks, 59, 64, 94, 109–10, 212, 227n64
  in ritual of liberation, 64, 227n64
  of Sariputta, 93
  of Vessantara, 16–17, 171, 217

Sineru, Mount (Mount Meru), 6, 21, 146, 147–48, 148, 155

Sivi, 11–13

social contract theory, 231–32n178

Sotthiya (grass cutter), 33

South
  and the Buddha's funeral, 110, 156
  and the Buddha's miraculous power, 66
  in cosmological framework, 146, 148, 149–50, 152–54, 156–57, 159
  in Gotama's quest for enlightenment, 28, 33, 35, 154, 157, 172–73, 196
  and Great Agents, 194, 196, 198–99
  and Kusavati, 101
  and Magadhans, 197
  and Mahasudassana, 102, 104
  and rites of passage, 164, 169–70, 172–73
  and Vessantara, 12, 169–70, 194
  Viruha rules over, 6, 150

South/Southeast Asian Buddhism. *See also* Pali Buddhist scriptures; Theravada Buddhism
  and the Buddha's relics, 230n108
  "Buddhist era" in, 135
  and cosmological framework, 143, 148, 148, 151
  and gift giving, 208, 216
  and quest for historical Buddha, 121, 125, 135
  rites of passage in, 164, 173
  and Universal Monarch, 177
  and Vessantara's popularity, 2, 173, 179, 199, 216

Squirrels Feeding-Ground, 97

Sri Lanka, 135

stealing. *See* theft

Sthaviravadins (Buddhist school), 130

Strauss, David, 127

Stream-Winners, 92, 95, 110, 150

Subhadda (ascetic), 109

Subhadda, Queen (Mahasudassana's wife), 105, 168–69, 172, 193

Sudassana (King Pasenadi's nephew), 74–75

Sudatta, 71. *See also* Anathapindika

Suddhodana, King (Gotama's father), 10, 21, 23–25, 28, 175
  and annual ritual of plowing, 29
  and the Buddha's visit home, 58, 65–68, 171, 194
  death of, 81
  status of "the fruit of the nonreturner," 68

suffering
  and birth, 22
  and the Buddha as teacher, 39–40, 42, 44–46, 52–53
  in cosmological framework, 136
  and gift giving, 216–18
  immortality as basic cause of, 144
  and karma, 145, 215, 217
  Malunkyaputta's knowledge of, 76
  and quest for historical Buddha, 129
  in rites of passage, 170, 172, 174
  Sariputta's knowledge of, 92
  and sickness, old age, and death, 9, 24–26, 35, 37, 42, 44, 63, 139, 153, 195, 224–25n33–37
  and twelvefold links of dependent origination, 37, 39, 56–58, 71, 76, 224–25n37

Sujata, 30–31, 144, 154, 202–3, 209, 211, 223n30

Sumedha (the Buddha in former life), 9–10

superhuman agents. *See also* Great Agents
  antigods as, 150, 223n22
  Bodhisattvas as, 200
  the Buddha as, 23, 30, 66, 115, 121, 128, 130, 141, 155, 175, 180, 200, 223n23
  in Buddhism, 130, 174, 202–3
  in cosmological framework, 150, 152, 155–56
  in Great Sudhamma Hall, 150

  in myth/religion, 117–19, 121, 155, 163, 188
  in paradise, 184–85
  in quest for historical Buddha, 128, 130, 141
  removal of obstacles for Yasa by, 45
  in rites of passage, 161, 163, 167, 171–72, 174
  Universal Monarchs as, 118, 156, 175, 180, 188, 195, 200, 223n23
  Vessantara as, 16, 171
  yakkhas as, 152
  Yasa aided by, 45

Tambiah, Stanley, 178

Tapoda Park, 97

Tapussa, 40

Tavatimsa (second heaven), 6, 146, 147–48. *See also* thirty-three gods, home of

teacher
  and Anathapindika, 83–84
  Brahmin as, 8, 208
  the Buddha as, 39–47, 52–53, 74, 76–77, 92, 108–10, 138, 140, 157–58, 168, 172, 196–98, 226n40–44
  in cosmological framework, 157–58
  Great Agents as, 195–98
  in Hinduism, 208
  and last watch, 108–10
  in quest for historical Buddha, 127, 130, 140
  and rites of passage, 162, 165
  Sumedha's thoughts on, 9
  Vipassi as, 140

Ten Perfections, 10, 34, 199, 218, 222–23n10

Thai rites of passage, 164–66

theft, 7–8, 47, 62–63, 184–86, 189–92

Theravada Buddhism, 1, 116, 118, 143, 200, 207, 215. *See also* Pali Buddhist scriptures; South/ Southeast Asian Buddhism

Third World Conference (1954), 135

thirty-three gods
    in battle with antigods, 22, 150–51
    and the Buddha as teacher, 44
    celebrating at the Buddha's last
        rebirth, 22–23
    compared to the troop of Licchavis, 96
    at Great Sudhamma Hall meeting,
        150, 159
    heaven of, 11–12, 22, 94, 104, 146, 147,
        150, 159
    and Moggallana, 94
    Sakka as chief of, 2–3, 12, 169
    and Vessantara, 17
thirty-two marks. See under Great Agents
Thomas, E. J., 127–30, 133, 137, 197
threefold formula for entrance into
        community
    and Anathapindika, 71
    and Bimbisara, 56
    and the Buddha as teacher, 46–47,
        226–27n40–44
    Pasenadi's knowledge of, 73
    and Subhadda (ascetic), 109
Tipitaka (The Three Baskets), 1–3, 124,
        129–30, 159, 165, 221
Tissa, 140
totems, 182, 206
Trautmann, Thomas, 207
tree of enlightenment, 33–37, 39, 55, 68,
        89, 108, 138, 154, 157, 172, 195
Trobriands, 205
truth conditions of language, 113–15,
        119–20, 155, 165, 210
Turner, Victor, 163
"Turning of the Wheel of Doctrine, The,"
        41–44
Tushita (fourth heaven)
    Anathapindika ascended to, 84
    the Buddha reborn in, 19, 21–22, 147
    the Buddha's visit to, 83, 147
    celebration in at the Buddha's last
        rebirth, 22
    in cosmological framework, 6, 146, 147

Queen Maya ascended to, 23, 83, 147
    Vessantara reborn in, 171, 196
    Vipassi descended into, 139

Uddaka Ramaputta, 28, 41
Universal Monarchs. See also Great
        Agents; wheel-turning monarchs
    and the Buddha's funeral, 154, 156
    in cosmological framework, 146–47,
        152–54, 156–57, 159
    Cunda as, 203
    duties of, 188–92
    and gift giving, 201–3, 211, 213–14,
        217–19 (see also under names of
        Universal Monarchs)
    as Great Agents, 121–22, 177–80,
        184–97, 199–200, 214, 231n178,
        232n198
    and karma, 145, 214
    Mahasudassana as, 102–6, 159,
        168–69, 179
    meditation of, 146, 156, 187, 194
    in opposition to appointed kings, 180,
        185–92, 196–98
    in opposition to the Buddha, 101–6,
        121–22, 153, 169, 171–75, 184, 195,
        199–202, 211
    and prophecy at the Buddha's birth,
        22, 122, 139
    protective verses used by, 152
    and rites of passage, 168–69,
        171–75
    Sankha as, 184
    as superhuman agents, 118, 156, 175,
        180, 195, 200, 223n23
    Vessantara as, 153–54, 157, 171,
        193–94, 203, 216–18
university/college rites of passage,
        166–67
Upaka, 41
Upali, 60–61, 70–71, 85
Upava, 107
Uposatha month, 102, 168, 192

Uruvela, 28, 30, 39, 46–47, 49–51, 53, 55, *151*
utopias, 198
Uttarakuru (Kuru), 50, 101, 150, *151*, 152–53, 159, 168, 170, 197–98. *See also* North

Vaijjians, 196–98
Vaishyas, 8
Vamka, Mount, 15, 18–19
van Gennep, Arnold, 161, 163
Varanasi, 5, 41, 44–45, 47, 159
Vedas, 9–10, 148–49, 222n9
vegetarianism, 208
Vesala drought, 80–82
Vesali, 96–98, 172, 199, 212
Vessabhu, Lord Buddha, 138
Vessantara (the Buddha in former life)
  celibate life of, 193, 217
  in cosmological framework, 144, 153–54, 157
  eight favors (wishes) from Sakka, 17, 171, 194, 211, 214, 218
  enlightenment of, 15–16, 170–73, 216–17
  gift giving of, 12–19, 35, 153–54, 157, 169–72, 193, 195–96, 206, 213–18
  as Great Agent, 15–16, 171, 179, 191–96, 199, 214, 217–18
  Milinda's questions concerning, 215–16
  Nagasena's knowledge of, 215–16
  perfection of, 144, 170–71, 193, 218
  Phusati as mother of, 11–12, 19
  popularity of, 2, 173, 179, 199, 216
  rebirths of, 18–19, 169, 171, 194, 196, 215
  and rites of passage, 163, 167, 169–73, 218
  and Sakka, 14, 17, 19, 153–54, 169–70
  Sanjaya, King, as father of, 11–13, 18–19, 171
  in Tushita heaven, 171, 196

as Universal Monarch, 153–54, 157, 171, 193–94, 203, 216–18
and wilderness (forest), 14–17, 153, 157, 163, 169–73, 193–94, 196, 213–14
Vessavana (Kuvera), King (ruler of the North), 6, 150, 152
Vinaya, 124, 184–85, 221
Vipassi (former Buddha), 138–41
Virulhaka (Viruha), King (ruler of the South), 6, 150
Virupakkha, King (ruler of the West), 6, 150
Visakha, month of (April/May), 22, 30, 33, 154, 202
Vissakamma (master architect), 9, 14, 104, 168, 170, 172, 193, 196, 217
Vultures Peak, Mount, 64, 88, 91, 97, 152, 196

Walshe, Maurice, 159, 179
Warder, A. K., 130–31, 135–36
warrior caste, 8, 14, 21, 23, 59–60, 67, 138
Weber, Max, 116, 144, 202, 233n202
West
  and the Buddha in Patalagama, 95
  and the Buddha's miraculous power, 66
  in cosmological framework, 146, 148–52, *148*, 154–55, 159
  and Dhamma Palace, 104
  domain of antigods, 6, 223n22
  in Gotama's quest for enlightenment, 33, 154–55
  in rites of passage, 164
  Virupaka rules over, 6
  and wheel-turning monarchs, 102
Western scholarship. *See also names of Western scholars*
  Buddhacentric focus of, 173, 177, 182, 185, 201–2
  and Great Agents, 177–82, 185

Western scholarship (*continued*)
  and historical Buddha, 3, 121, 125,
    134–35, 141, 202 (*see also* historical
    Buddha, quest for)
  narrative constraint of, 177
  and "underdeveloped" cultures and
    myth, 116, 120–21
wheel, karma as, 23, 39, 41, 44, 108, 144.
    See also wheel-turning monarchs
wheel-turning monarchs. *See also*
    Universal Monarchs; *names of*
    wheel-turning monarchs
  Dalhanemi as, 188, 190–92
  duties of, 188–92
  four properties of, 102, 103, 168
  as Great Agents, 181, 183–87, 194–95,
    230n101
  Mahasudassana as, 101–2, 106, 168
  remains of, 108–10
  Sankha as, 184, 190–91
  seven treasures of, 102–3, 168, 181, 183
    Counselor-Treasure, 103, 105
    Elephant-Treasure, 102
    Horse-Treasure, 102–3
    Nobleman-Treasure, 103
    Wheel-Treasure, 102, 168, 186–92
    Woman-Treasure, 103
wilderness (forest)
  and Angulimala, 78
  in cosmological framework, 8,
    153–54, 157

and Devadatta, 89
and gift giving, 203, 213–14,
  217–18
in Gotama's quest for enlightenment,
  24, 27–28, 153–54, 157,
  168–69, 172
and Gotama's quest for
  enlightenment, 202
and Great Agents, 183, 185–86,
  190–94, 196
and Moggallana, 94
as paradise, 14–15, 157, 163, 170, 185,
  193, 217
and Queen Maya, 22
and rites of passage, 163, 168–73
and Sumedha, 10
Vessantara banished to, 14–17, 153,
  157, 163, 169–73, 193–94, 196,
  213–14, 217
Woman-Treasure, 103
World Buddhist Congress (Colombo,
  1950), 135
wrong views, 8, 36–37, 52, 77, 86–89,
  94, 175

yakkhas, 152
Yama (third heaven), 146, 147
Yasa, 45–46
Yashodhara (Gotama's wife), 23–24,
  26–27, 67–68
yoga, 29